The Book of Shaker Furniture   JOHN KASSAY

The University of Massachusetts Press   Amherst, 1980

This book is affectionately dedicated
to my wife, Mary, and to our children:
June Culbertson, Robert W. Kassay,
Cynthia Lewis, and Catherine Abad, and
to their spouses and children.

Copyright © 1980 by

The University of Massachusetts Press

All rights reserved

Library of Congress Catalog Card Number 79-4017

ISBN 0-87023-275-4

Printed in the United States of America

Designed by Mary Mendell

Library of Congress Cataloging in Publication Data

Kassay, John, 1919–

The book of Shaker furniture.

1. Furniture, Shaker. I. Title.

NK2406.K36   749.214.   79-4017

ISBN 0-87023-275-4

Contents

Foreword

Interest in the United Society of Believers in Christ's Second Appearing, the "Shakers," has steadily increased during the past forty years. It began primarily with the books of Edward Deming Andrews, whose scholarly commentary and illustrations of the exquisitely simple and functional Shaker furniture introduced the American people to a design concept very different from the contemporary idiom. The photographs by William Winter displayed outstanding examples in their normal, stark room setttings. Both rooms and furniture were a refreshing change from the fussy and overstuffed homes many of us grew up in and were familiar with.

There have been several attempts over the years to rebel against the pretentious and overcrowded interiors of Victorian homes—the mission furniture styles of Gustav Stickley, and Elbert Hubbard's Roycrofters for example—but the Shaker tradition was so startlingly different that for many years it was of interest to only a knowledgeable few.

With other books and articles by Dr. Andrews and the building of collections and exhibitions by museums, the American public began to be seriously interested. More books and articles appeared and more collections were put together and opened to the public. As interest grew, so also did the desire to own original pieces of Shaker-made furniture. Antique dealers found themselves besieged with a demand for pieces; auctions were haunted; attics and barns were rummaged—"and still the wonder grew." As prices mounted (astronomically, as time went on), and as previously easily obtained originals became more scarce, increasing numbers of the public turned to cabinetmakers for reproductions and more and more home craftsmen made their own.

But where to find originals to study, compare, and measure? For the most part, desirable pieces were in musuems, albeit some permitted physical examination and photography. The demand, however, far exceeded the supply of published examples. Articles began to appear in popular publications giving procedures and measured drawings—or what were said to be such. A few books have been published with poor photographs and drawings, and most are amateurish, inaccurate, and sketchy at best. These failed very properly to satisfy the home craftsmen or, for that matter, the professional cabinetmakers, especially when they found that when they followed (or tried to follow) the plans given, the results ended in outright failure, or frustration, or worlds apart from what they initially expected.

John Kassay, a professor of wood technology in, of all places, California—a continent removed from Shakerism and its works—caught fire with what could only have been divine inspiration. Skilled in furniture design and construction, in the professional art of drafting, and also in the fine art of photography, he set for himself the goal of providing exquisitely drawn and meticulously detailed construction plans of all the various major forms of Shaker furniture. That he has succeeded in realizing this goal is amply proved in the following pages. To reinforce the drawings, he has supplied splendid photographs of the finished products of each of the pieces shown, and to give depth to the study, has included additional photographs of similar pieces for comparison. Various books of furniture drawings have appeared in the past few years, but none treats its subjects with the exactness and detail of this volume.

While working on his book, Dr. Kassay kept several objectives in mind: to provide inquirers with details of construction revealing the complexities of cabinetmaking and to convey the meticulous care with which the Shaker craftsmen worked; to increase the readers' understanding and appreciation of the pieces that they may own, or wish to own, or that they may see; to give students and scholars both inspiration and the opportunity to learn more about this plain but beautiful furniture; and to give to those interested accurate, well-researched, and easy-to-follow plans of authentic examples of some of the finest Shaker furniture pieces, so that they may restore, or create their own masterpieces. This was no easy task, and Dr.

Kassay has fulfilled it brilliantly. His book has long been needed and eagerly awaited, and will supersede all other volumes on the subject.

However, lest the readers feel that this volume, replete as it is with detailed plans, is intended only as a "how-to" book, they will discover that its scope is much wider in its intended appeal. Interior designers, decorators, antiquarians, antique collectors, historians, restorers, furniture designers and manufacturers, and even architects will find much inspiration, knowledge, and help within its covers. It is indeed a book of many uses. And for the craftsmen, be they amateurs or professionals, its value will prove inestimable. They will find that careful workmanship, an unhurried attention to detail, and a humble approach to the problem at hand will yield results that will prove amply rewarding. The author's own dedication to perfection infectiously transfers itself to his students, and will also to you, his readers.

Robert F. W. Meader

Acknowledgments

More than a decade was spent collecting and preparing material for this book. It required traveling thousands of miles visiting museums, Shaker restorations, former Shaker sites, the two remaining Shaker communities, and many collectors.

Hundreds of sheets of four-by-five film were exposed photographing approximately five hundred pieces of furniture. Over one hundred and sixty pieces were carefully measured on the site, of which eighty-five were later drawn in anatomical detail. Sixty-six representative pieces were selected for inclusion in the work.

Obviously the study has been an ambitious enterprise and its completion would not have been possible without the help of many, many people from all over the country. Their contributions, whether small or large, are greatly appreciated.

A number of people contributed so generously of their time and knowledge to the project that special recognition is warranted.

Shaker scholars A. Hayward Benning, Research Editor, Department of Transportation, Albany, New York; Dr. Robert Bishop, Director of the Museum of American Folk Art, New York; and Charles Muller, Associate Editor of the *Ohio Antique Review,* Worthington, Ohio, read all or portions of the manuscript and made invaluable corrections and helpful suggestions.

Mrs. Faith Andrews, author, and Robert F. W. Meader, author and Director Emeritus of the Shaker Museum at Old Chatham, New York, shared much of their knowledge of the Shakers and gave encouragement from the beginning and throughout the work.

Ejner Handberg, author and furniture-maker, David Lamb, student in the Program in Artisanry, Boston University, Boston, Massachusetts, and Gus and Alice Schwerdtfeger, makers of fine miniature Shaker furniture, supplied me with answers to questions regarding certain pieces of furniture.

Lester Margon, author, furniture designer, and delineator, has critiqued many of the drawings and has given suggestions of inestimable value. His beautiful furniture drawings have been my inspiration through the years.

University colleagues Dr. Richard W. Shackelford and Dr. David W. Wentura helped throughout the study with drafting problems and gave appreciated encouragement along the way.

Also I wish to express my deepest appreciation to the following collectors for their hospitality and generosity in allowing me to come into their homes and examine, measure, and photograph furniture pieces in their collections: David V. Andrews, Tim J. Bookout, Mr. and Mrs. David Castleman, Suzanne Courcier and Robert W. Wilkins, Mr. and Mrs. William Hollinger, Dr. Clifford Josephson, Dr. and Mrs. Thomas R. Kane, Steven S. Kistler, Mr. and Mrs. Peter Marks, Dr. J. J. G. McCue, Dr. Clara Nigg, Mr. and Mrs. Martin Popelka, the late John S. Roberts, Mrs. Joanne Blois Russell, Mr. and Mrs. James Stokes, Dr. Donald Weeks, the late Mrs. Julius Zieget, and several collectors who prefer to remain anonymous.

Special thanks are certainly due the many museum directors, curators, and staff members for their cooperation and assistance in affording me the privilege of making a close and detailed examination of furniture in their care, for providing answers to my numerous questions, and for supplying photographs of selected pieces in their collection: Shaker sisters R. Mildred Barker, Curator of Manuscripts, and Frances A. Carr, Archivist, also Theodore E. Johnson, Museum Director, and David W. Serette, staff photographer, of the United Society of Shakers at Sabbathday Lake, Maine; James L. Cogar, President Emeritus, James C. Thomas, President, and Edward E. Nickels, Assistant Curator, of Shakertown at Pleasant Hill, Inc., Harrodsburg, Kentucky; Meredith B. Colket, Jr., Executive Director, and Jairus B. Barnes, Director, of The Western Reserve Historical Society, Cleveland, Ohio; Mary Glaze, Associate Curator, and Nadi Saporite, Librarian, of The Metropolitan Museum of Art, New York, New York;

Mrs. E. M. Gonin, Associate Curator, retired, of The American Museum in Britain, Bath, England; Deedy Hall, Director, and Julia Neal, Curator, of Shakertown at South Union, South Union, Kentucky; William Henry Harrison, Director of Fruitlands Museums, Harvard, Massachusetts; R. Wistar Harvey, Curator of Decorative Arts, and Beatrice Gowan, Associate Curator, of the Philadelphia Museum of Art; John F. Joline, III, former Headmaster, and David L. Miller, Headmaster, of Darrow School, New Lebanon, New York; Myrtle Lane, staff member of the Glendower Museum, Lebanon, Ohio; Shaker Eldresses Bertha Lindsay and Gertrude M. Soule, and also Charles F. Thomson, Museum Director, and Jack Auchmoody, Business Manager, of the Canterbury Shaker Village, Inc., East Canterbury, New Hampshire; Bruce MacLeish, Curator, Kentucky Museum, Western Kentucky University, Bowling Green, Kentucky; Amy Bess Miller, President, and John H. Ott, Director, of the Hancock Shaker Community, Inc., Pittsfield, Massachusetts; E. Ray

Pearson, Associate Professor at the Illinois Institute of Technology, Chicago, Illinois; the late Hazel S. Phillips, former Director, and Elva Adams, Director, of the Warren County Historical Society, Lebanon, Ohio; Daniel R. Porter, Director, and Joseph E. Lee, District Manager, of the Ohio Historical Society, Columbus, Ohio; Mary Lyn Ray, Assistant to the Director, New Hampshire Historical Society, Concord, New Hampshire; Jerry Reese, Registrar, and C. R. Jones, Conservator, of the New York State Historical Association, Cooperstown, New York; Jackson B. Reynolds, Vice President of The Golden Lamb Inn, Lebanon, Ohio; Nancy E. Richards, Associate Curator, and Karol A. Schmiegel, Assistant Registrar, of the Henry Francis du Pont Winterthur Museum, Winterthur, Delaware; C. Malcolm Watkins, Chairman, Department of Cultural History, and Anne M. Seria, Museum Specialist, at the Smithsonian Institution, Washington, D. C.; Robert G. Wheeler, Vice President of Collection and Presentations, William H. Distin, Curator, and Katharine

B. Hagler, Associate Curator, of Greenfield Village and Henry Ford Museum, Dearborn, Michigan; John S. Williams, Chairman, Warden McL. Williams, President, and R. Peter Laskovski, Director, of The Shaker Museum, Old Chatham, New York.

One of the extra pleasures derived from working on this project was the meeting of so many wonderful people who share the same interest in the subject. Several of these associations have developed into cherished lasting friendships.

During my numerous trips to the east coast, my brother and sister-in-law Robert and Irene Kassay were always good-natured hosts. Living near former Shaker communities made it convenient for me to commute from California to their home and accept their warm hospitality.

My daughter Catherine deserves special recognition for the many hours she spent typing letters, photograph captions, and material lists. My wife, Mary, was caught up in the project very early and maintained a constant dedication to see it through to completion. She has read hundreds of pages of penciled manuscript and typed numerous drafts, all the while maintaining her good humor and patience. Her encouragement, assistance, and advice helped in a very large measure to make this volume what it is.

Introduction

Brief History

Of the more than one hundred experiments in communitarian living that proliferated in America during the nineteenth century, the United Society of Believers in Christ's Second Appearing, whose adherents are best known as "Shakers," is certainly one of the most interesting, successful, and enduring. This book is a collection of furniture made by members of this remarkable American religious sect.

The ancestors of this religious order were the Camisards—French Protestants living in the Cevennes mountains who preached repentance and prophesied the Second Coming of Christ. The revocation of the Edict of Nantes in 1665 withdrew from French Protestants the right to worship publicly and resulted in the emigration of more than 200,000 of their numbers, many of them to England. During the 1740s, descendants of these emigrés united with a small party of dissident Quakers led by James and Jane Wardley.

Ann Lees (Lee), a twenty-two-year-old illiterate mill hand from Manchester, joined this group in 1758. In 1762 she married Abraham Standerin (Stanley) who, like her father, was a blacksmith. During the next four years Ann bore four children, all of whom died in infancy or early childhood. These tragedies may have fostered her belief that only through celibacy could mankind be saved from misfortune.

Through the years 1770–1773 members of the Wardley group were arrested, fined, and imprisoned for disturbing the peace; Ann Lee was one of those jailed during this period. After her release she became very active in the Wardley society and eventually replaced Mother Jane as its spiritual head.

In 1774 Ann and members of her group received revelations which convinced them that their works would take root and flourish if they emigrated to America. They therefore settled their affairs and on May 19, 1774, set sail from Liverpool on the ship *Mariah* for New York. Seven members of the group and her husband (who shortly abandoned her) accompanied Ann. After a long and stormy voyage, the *Mariah* docked safely on August 6, 1774. Upon disembarking, the members of the group separated to find employment.

Hearing of a piece of property that might meet their needs, three of the group traveled up the Hudson River to a place eight miles north of Albany, known by the Indian name "Niskeyuna," which meant when translated "extended corn flats." Here they purchased 200 acres of swampy forest. After felling trees, they built a crude log cabin and prepared the soil for crops. It was two years before the little band was completely reunited and able to begin communal life.

At Niskeyuna, later called Watervliet, the Shakers worked and worshiped in their wilderness home, and waited for converts who eventually came from various parts of eastern New York, Connecticut, and western Massachusetts. In May 1781 Ann and her brother William embarked upon a missionary trip into New England which was to last two years and four months. They traveled to numerous towns, making converts on the way. Though they suffered hardship and abuse, their journey was a success, for it laid the foundations for future Shaker colonies.

Mother Ann died in 1784, at the age of forty-eight, a year after her return to Niskeyuna. Her brother had died a month earlier. Leadership passed to James Whittaker who, although only thirty-three, proved to be a tireless and inspiring leader until his untimely death, three years later.

Joseph Meacham was then selected as leader. He appointed Lucy Wright to head the female line, thus forming a dual order based on sexual equality. Father Joseph and Mother Lucy were both American-born converts to the faith. Meacham staunchly supported the basic principles of Shakerism: confession of sin, separation from the world, common ownership of property, celibacy, sexual equality, pacifism, and universal brotherhood. He formulated and put into operation principles of church law and government, which later became the so-called Millenial Laws of the United Society. He devised the family system whereby potential members were placed in the novitiate or Gathering family and, as they progressed in their dedication to God and the Society, were promoted to the Second or junior family. After signing the covenant, they became members of the Church family. Spiritual matters were in the hands of two elders and two eldresses, while the several branches of agriculture and industry were supervised by deacons and deaconesses. Business transactions with the world were handled by family trustees.

Separation from the world was considered necessary in order to achieve the Shaker principles of celibacy and communal property. Therefore, the ministry at New Lebanon, New York, which had replaced Watervliet as the physical and spiritual center of Shakerdom, sent word to converts in the countryside to gather together at New Lebanon to worship and work communally.

During the years 1788–1792, converts came from rural New England and the upper Hudson River Valley. They were relatively poor farmers, merchants, small tradesmen, and laborers. Women and children, young and old, individuals and entire families flocked to New Lebanon, Watervliet, and other newly established Shaker communities. Eleven communities with approximately one thousand Believers had been established by 1800. By 1826 there were three communities in New York, one in Connecticut, two in Maine, two in New Hampshire, four in Ohio, two in Kentucky, and one in Indiana (there were also several short-lived communities). Growth was rapid and the movement reached its peak in membership, wealth, and accomplishments around 1850, when there were over six thousand adherents living in eighteen communities. Eventually they owned more than fifty thousand acres of prime agricultural land, much of which was under cultivation, and over one thousand well-built dwellings, shops, and farm buildings, all adequately furnished and well equipped.

A Shaker community is best described as one whose inhabitants engaged in domestic-religious activities and worked at a variety of cottage industries and agricultural occupations, manufacturing products for their own use and also for sale to the world's people. The economic security this agro-industrial base offered was recognized and promoted from the Society's earlier years.

A list of their labor-saving devices would seem almost endless. They have been credited with well over one hundred patents, although most cannot be confirmed, particularly those claimed in the early nineteenth century when patent records were scanty and patent numbers often lacking. In addition, for years the Shakers had refrained from taking patents out on their inventions, believing them to be monopolistic, selfish expressions, and therefore unchristian. Later they relaxed this position and from 1837 to 1877 applied for and were granted thirty-one numbered patents.

A list of the agricultural and industrial products the Society engaged in would also seem inexhaustible. But mention of a few of the economically more successful will indi-cate the extent and variety of their production. The garden seed industry started on a small scale around 1795, as an expansion of the family gardens. It grew steadily, and became one of the long-lasting economic mainstays of the Society. Their herbal and medicinal extract industries were a natural development of their seed business. They raised and used herbs in their kitchens, and it was a short step to making them available for sale. The medicinal value of certain tree and plant parts had been known long before the founding of the United Society, but the Shakers were quick to recognize the monetary profits that could be realized by processing and marketing herbal plants as medicines and tonics.

In 1798 a Watervliet Shaker brother was credited with inventing the so-called flat broom. This invention necessitated the extensive raising of broom corn, and both activities engaged nearly every community in the manufacture of variously shaped brooms and brushes. Probably the most familiar Shaker product, one quickly identified with the Society, is the oval wooden box. Thousands upon thousands of these boxes, in many sizes, were made over a 163-year period and were another profitable business venture. But of all the products the Shakers made, the best known are the slatback chairs, probably because chairs were the only furniture they mass-produced and marketed. At an early stage New Lebanon became the center of this very profitable, long-lasting industry, although at one time or another all the communities made chairs.

Social and economic changes brought about by the industrialization of the nation created interrelated conditions that directly affected the United Society and ultimately caused its decline. The order, with its economy based on agriculture and handicraft, had been perfectly suited to rural America but found itself out of step with the new industrial age that gave birth to cities, factories, and machine mass-production. Demand for Shaker-made products continued and quality remained high, but handwork was no match for the machine .

During the Civil War marauding bands from both the North and the South occupied the Ohio and Kentucky properties. Many thousands of dollars in buildings, livestock, and equipment were lost. The lucrative seed trade with the South was permanently ruined. In the North, Shaker men were pressed into military service (later, granted indefinite furloughs by President Lincoln). The lack of strong spiritual leadership and a lessening of religious fervor served to further weaken the sect's vitality.

The doctrine of celibacy, while not a dominant reason for the Society's decline, certainly contributed to it by limiting the Society's appeal to only those willing to embrace that tenet. The cities, with their promise of a materially better life and personal independence, attracted many and caused them to leave the Society. The earlier success with agriculture-related industries encouraged those who remained to purchase additional land, which made it necessary to hire outside workers, a practice that ultimately undermined communal separation

and security. Increasing economic costs of maintaining the Society, innumerable financial losses resulting from carelessness, incompetence, or plain bad luck, and misfortune caused by fires and floods also helped to deplete the financial assets of the order. Lawsuits, property settlements with those who left, and sizable donations to public and private charities were other reasons for economic decline. The enactment of state laws governing adoptions, and the establishment of orphanages by other religious groups and government agencies, reduced the number of children available to replenish the order.

From a peak population at mid-century, membership declined to one thousand by 1900; between the years 1875 and 1960 seventeen communities were closed. The few remaining elderly members were transfered to larger communities, and the properties were sold. At this writing there are nine sisters living in two active Shaker communities; three are at Canterbury, New Hampshire, and six are at Sabbathday Lake, Maine.

The Shakers are almost gone; their adventure is nearly over. But their legacy of lessons good for all humanity is great.

The Furniture and Its Artisans

The beginnings of what has become known as the Shaker style of furniture lay in the craft of woodworking, as practiced in the cottage industries of rural New York and New England. It evolved from the simple colonial forms common to those areas. The Shakers further developed these designs by rejecting unnecessary ornament and applying the essentials of pure function and form; in so doing they developed a distinctive furniture, one in harmony with their dress, architecture, and mode of living.

During the early years of the movement, when converts first gathered to live communally they donated the few pieces of furniture they owned and, because the order was growing at such a rapid rate, every piece, regardless of its style, was willingly accepted.

Pieces that reflected worldly taste were later discarded. The Shakers began making furniture for their own use in the late 1770s and as communities grew, they continued to produce furniture. It is likely that all the communities made furniture during the early years; they had little money, and it was economical for them to make their own. Besides, it engaged them in a vital occupation from which they could derive satisfaction, and it also allowed the ministry to regulate style.

Shaker furniture was the work of artisans who lived within a religious community, inspired by the belief that love of God was expressed in the integrity of one's work. To make a piece of furniture was an act of worship, the fulfillment of a religious obligation. It expressed the Believer's understanding of the Creator of the materials and the personal goal of oneness with Him, while its purpose was to be communal. Living, working, and worshiping in large communal families necessitated furniture designed for group rather than individual use. Long work counters, benches, dining tables, and large cupboards were some of the more common forms of communal furniture produced in the Society.

Believers' furniture can be divided into two groups—shop furniture and dwelling furniture. Shop furniture was made to serve the domestic activities and industrial occupations carried on in the kitchens, laundries, and shops. The pieces were usually made of pine, often simply nail-assembled and painted; while many examples lacked complicated joinery, they were adequately constructed for their purpose. Dwelling furniture (an arbitrary designation) was made for dining, gathering, and retiring-rooms. Usually made of hard woods and representing a higher order of craftsmanship, such pieces included chairs, beds, candle stands, and tables.

Shaker furniture passed through three rather distinct stylistic periods. The first is marked by furniture that is visually and physically heavy, plain in form, crudely made, but strong and functional. The pieces suggest the work of mechanics with limited time, tools, and experience. Pine and maple (usually painted) were commonly used. The time of this furniture is approximately 1790 to 1820, and is referred to as the primitive period.

What has become known as the classic period of Shaker furniture started in the 1820s and ended around 1860. The pieces produced during this time were not the result of a studied approach to design or a conscious effort to create masterpieces, but were rather expressions of utility, simplicity, and perfection attributable to spiritual inspiration, moral responsiveness, dedication to a craft, and skill. This golden age of furniture-making was the period of greatest creativity and production, and the pieces reflect a degree of uniformity giving them the characteristic Shaker lines.

Distrusting "worldly ornament," the Shakers found the simplicity of eighteenth-century country furniture an inspiring source for their designs, compatible with the prohibition by the central ministry against "showiness." The result was furniture whose value is inherent in its form. Extravagant turning, carving, fancy veneers, inlay, applied moldings, decorative hardware, and glossy finishes are not found on furniture of this period. What are found instead are subtly tapered, turned pedestals and legs, drawer pulls of simple but elegant form, sensibly used chamfers, tapers, and bevels to protect edges and lighten components, and an effect of delicacy achieved through diminution of parts.

The religious dedication that went into producing creative works during the first half of the nineteenth century went into an irreversible decline around 1860. Decreasing membership and community closings made additional furniture unnecessary and, with the exception of chairs, only a small amount of furniture was produced after the Civil War. There is, however, a furniture style referred to as Victorian Shaker, made after the war and during the last quarter of the century, principally in the New Hampshire and Maine communities, which remained populous and active longer than the others. An inherited New England conservatism and the traditions established by Mother Ann and the Millennial Laws, which governed every detail of their lives, fortunately prevented complete acceptance of Victorianism. But we do see during this period remodeled buildings, pictures on display, secular books, magazines, and newspapers, and other expressions of the Shakers' attempt to keep up with a changing world—while still adhering to their gospel principles.

Much of this later furniture is made of walnut, often finished with dark stains. It seems to have been limited to beds, writing and sewing desks, and small tables. Liberal use of applied moldings and molded edges, complex turnings, applied decorative pieces of contrasting woods, and commercially made ornate drawer pulls are features found on Victorian Shaker. Many of these pieces are signed and dated, and are the work of master craftsmen. To most, pieces of Victorian Shaker are less pleasing than those from the classic era, but the style merits recognition because it is another part of the total story.

In the earliest years the people who joined the order were mainly of farming stock—modest, ambitious, God-fearing Yankees. With limited woodworking experience and often with only crude tools, they dedicated themselves to building an earthly heaven. Later, woodworkers attracted to this heaven probably served an apprenticeship of sorts, making simple country-style pieces whose forms remained constant and familiar. The most skilled and dedicated workers directed the work and set standards for the rest.

While practices varied from time to time and from community to community, in the eastern communities during the 1820s the Shaker cabinetmakers' days would follow, somewhat, this pattern: they rose between four and four-thirty in the summer, and five or five-thirty in the winter, and knelt briefly for a moment of prayer before attending to morning chores. The shop was opened and, if necessary, fires started in the small cast-iron stoves. Working with one or two apprentices, the work for the day was planned. Summoned by a bell to the morning meal, they took assigned places at tables which were segregated by sex. They knelt for prayers before and after meals, and ate in silence. Returning to the shop, they worked steadily and unhurriedly, constructing counters, chests of drawers, cupboards, and any number of other pieces requested by elders or deacons. The purpose of a piece of furniture, and where it would be placed, had been decided in advance, and working with this already in mind tended to increase the functionalism and individuality of the piece. The artisan usually made each piece of furniture one at a time or in very short-run numbers. Having already made similar pieces, design was mostly a mental process, with possibly a few notes and sketches made at the time for

temporary reference. The Shakers believed talents were God-given and that the fruits of these talents were for the good of the order rather than personal recognition; therefore the Millennial Laws forbade cabinetmakers to sign their names on any furniture of their manufacture. Nevertheless, complete control was not possible, and many craftsmen naturally (but humbly) proud of an especially fine piece of work signed and dated pieces, usually in an inconspicuous place.

Only when a dwelling was near completion did the work in the shops take on a sense of urgency suggesting a factory atmosphere. Then a kind of assembly-line operation was begun, that being the most expedient way to produce the required number of pieces in the shortest possible time. The nature of the work in the chair factories was somewhat different from that carried on in the one-person smaller shops. Division of labor prevailed, but jobs were rotated to prevent fatigue and relieve boredom. The brothers made the components

and assembled them and the sisters stained the frames and applied the tape.

The most experienced workers were often called upon to lend a hand in solving a production problem in another shop, to repair a machine, to design a special piece of shop furniture or equipment, or to aid in any number of other tasks normal in an independent, complex, communal society. Believers were encouraged to become skilled in more than one occupation; in so doing they would be able to make a greater contribution to the Society.

A midday bell summoned all to a noon meal and the afternoon's work followed much the same pattern as the morning's. After the evening meal was served, the cabinetmakers and apprentices returned to the shop to secure tools, see that the stove fire was out, and possibly do a bit of planning for the next day's activities. Then a bell summoned the brethren and sisters to their respective retiring-rooms for a half-hour of "laboring," praying for Godlike purity and perfection.

Each evening of the week was devoted to some activity of a wholesome, usually religious, nature. For example, selected newspaper articles were read to the family members on one evening, new marches were learned and rehearsed on another, and "union meetings" for conversation and singing were held on still another night. Thursdays and Saturdays were given over to religious services, and on Friday new songs and hymns were sung. Sunday service for all the families was held at the Church family meetinghouse. Bedtime was at nine or nine-thirty and no doubt eagerly welcomed.

Communities were divided into families containing fifty or more members who lived and worked within a cluster of well-constructed buildings surrounded by neatly trimmed lawns and well-tended gardens. Shaker buildings evolved from the plain architectural styles typical of rural New England and, like the country furniture of the area, the Shakers reduced them to their simplest forms to better serve the needs of communal living. From their exteriors it would be difficult to tell what industrial occupations were being carried on inside, for their painted siding and clean grounds gave them the appearance of residences rather than shops or factories. The woodworking shops were no exception, for the same order and cleanliness prevailed inside as well as out.

Those Shaker cabinetmakers who learned their trade before joining the sect were familiar with all the woodworking joints typically used in making country-style furniture. Although they did not develop any new ones, in some few cases they used conventional joints in an unorthdox manner. Possibly these pieces were the work of apprentices or inexperienced workers. All levels of cabinetmaking ability are represented in Shaker furniture; most pieces are superior, some are excellent, and a few suggest the work of an amateur.

The importance with which tools were viewed by the Society can be seen in the Millennial Laws. Specific rules controlled the borrowing, and prohibited the giving or swapping, of tools. During the precarious formative years, converts brought their personal possessions to the communities, including their livestock, farm implements, and tools. By 1789 Shakers were making tools and machines, and also purchasing machinery from the world for their budding industries. Shortly thereafter, inventories show that their carpenters and joiners used tools similar to those used by non-Shakers. They also purchased professional quality tools such as augers, chisels, planes, saws, and squares from England. An increasing number of tool manufacturers in New England, Pennsylvania, and Ohio provided other sources. Of course, special unavailable or nonexistent tools were readily made by the inventive and innovative Shakers. The tools, machines, and furnishings in the woodworking shops were as carefully made as the furniture in the dwellings, offices, and meetinghouses. Large, heavy workbenches had generous, overhanging, thick maple tops, with cupboards and rows of drawers along both sides at the base; they were splendid examples of utility.

Water-powered sawmills were one of the first industrial facilities erected in a new Shaker community. They provided the lumber needed immediately to build dwellings, laundries, barns, shops, and the meetinghouse. Believers very early made chairs, tables, stools, spinning wheels, tool handles, pegs, pulls, and other required turnings on their homemade wood-turning lathes. By 1813 a water-powered circular saw was operating in New Lebanon, and four years later another at Watervliet was cutting boards for siding, window sash, and tongue-and-groove floor boards.

In the oval box industry at New Lebanon, a circular saw was in service by 1830, cutting out box components. Two years later a planing machine was in use, surfacing box parts. By 1844 an "improved" planing machine was in use in the same community. The word "improved" tells us much about the nineteenth-century American inventive mind and the progressiveness of the Shak-

ers. In 1863 the latest wood lathe, iron lathe (for turning metals), boring machine, planer, and "dressing" machine (jointer) were installed in a newly built chair factory at New Lebanon. In this industry increasing use was made of power machinery as it became available.

White pine was the wood most commonly used for furniture. It was readily available from Shaker woodlots, and grew to large diameters. It could be easily worked with hand tools and power machinery. All forms of benches, boxes, built-ins, chests, chests of drawers, counters, cupboards, shelves, stands, stools, and tables were made wholly or in part of pine. For "nice" furniture, as it was called, cherry, maple (often figured—curly, striped, or bird's-eye), and walnut were the preferred woods. Sewing cabinets and writing desks were in most cases made of mixed woods; cherry, maple, and pine were the principal materials. Furniture parts such as bedposts, chair members, stand pedestals, and table legs, all of which required strength, were constructed from rock or

sugar maple. Ash, hickory, and white oak were used for bent parts. The working qualities of butternut and chestnut were appreciated; they were often used for the entire piece, or selectively, as in panels for case pieces. Drawer pulls of apple and pear wood are also found, and imported mahogany and rosewood were used sparingly for trim on special pieces. The wearing properties of lignum vitae were known, for one early account tells of its being used for the handle of a try square.

Most Shaker furniture was given a finish coat of paint, stain, shellac, or varnish. Early pieces were finished with heavy opaque coats of paint but soon the practice of thinning the paint and using it as a stain or a wash coat was adopted. This allowed the grain figure to strike through, making the piece more attractive, especially on bland soft woods. Paint colors were low-keyed and harmonized nicely with the simple forms of the pieces. Because so many shades of red, orange, yellow, blue, and brown were used, it is incorrect to apply the word "Shaker" when describing a color, as "Shaker red" or "Shaker blue." During the second half of the nineteenth century varnish became a popular finish for furniture made for dwellings. Pumice stone was used to remove the unacceptable high gloss of varnish.

All but one of the eastern communities were established during the fourth quarter of the eighteenth century. In the first quarter of the nineteenth century western communities were organized and reached their peak and decline in membership earlier than those in the east. By 1922 all the western communities had been dissolved. The quantity of furniture produced in the west was small compared to that made in the eastern societies. Their furniture needs, like their membership, declined rather early and it is doubtful that much furniture was made after the middle of the nineteenth century.

Stylistic differences between eastern Shaker furniture and that made in the Ohio and Kentucky societies are considerable, probably because western converts were culturally rooted mainly in the mid-Atlantic states.

It was natural for Shaker cabinetmakers to build furniture along the designs they were accustomed to seeing. Another reason for style differences was the geograpihical separation of the western communities from the parent ministry in New Lebanon. This separation allowed them a degree of autonomy and greater freedom of expression in furniture design.

Distinguishing western Shaker furniture from furniture that was made locally by non-Shakers is very difficult, mainly because stylistic differences between western Shaker and regional country are not appreciable. However, western Shaker tends to be somewhat less ornate than regional country, and this fact can be helpful in authentication. Design features of western Shaker, in comparison to eastern, include an overall feeling of heaviness, superfluous turning on legs, liberal use of molded edges and applied moldings, use of contrasting woods for decoration, and free use of curves. Walnut, cherry, butternut, and poplar were the favored woods, with pine, maple, ash, and

oak used to a lesser extent. Stylistically, western Shaker has long been considered the "poor cousin" of eastern Shaker, and is often described as ostentatious, uncomely, and poorly constructed. Actually, most pieces are very well constructed, convey a feeling of strength, and, if "showy," are honest expressions of cabinetmakers working in a style they knew best.

Regardless of its style, whether primitive, classic, or Victorian, or its geographical origin, eastern or western, or its intended use, communal or commercial, Shaker furniture evokes the history of a unique experiment in communal living. Any large display of their furniture, whether gathered in a museum or a book, will demonstrate that the Shakers did not always create pieces that we would ordinarily call beautiful. Sometimes proportions may be awkward or eccentric, and ornamentation unnecessary. But any such display will also demonstrate that at times the Shaker artisans created objects for mundane use which are of lasting beauty, the legacy of a dedicated people who, in the words of Mother Ann, "put their hands to work and their hearts to God."

The Present Work

Very early in researching material for this volume, it became clear that no single system for dating Shaker pieces would be satisfactory. Their fine condition often belied their actual age. The Shakers treated their furniture, as part of their communal property, with respect, and the normal signs of wear and tear found on most furniture, which may offer helpful clues in determining age, are often missing. The practice of duplicating forms that they found served their purpose best also makes dating difficult. Similar pieces were produced over a considerable span of time, and therefore it is often difficult to distinguish a piece made in one generation from another made in the next. The New Lebanon factory chairs, an extreme example, were standardized in 1873, but continued to be produced until the mid-1930s.

Depending on what seems to most closely date a piece without misrepresentation, the following categories are therefore used: decade, quarter, half-century, and circa (c.). To avoid confusion, New Lebanon is always so designated, although between 1860 and 1931, when a post office was located there, it was known as Mount Lebanon.

Extensive efforts were made to determine the community origin of the furniture included in the study. Unless a piece is inscribed with the maker's name or community origin or has a documented history, determining its provenance can be difficult. The problem is compounded by the fact that the geographical proximity of certain communities fostered a sharing of furniture designs. Itinerant Shaker cabinetmakers assisted in this dissemination process, as did members who moved with furnishings from one community to another. In determining the probable provenance of some pieces, comparing them with similar, documented pieces and having a working knowledge of such details as chair finials, moldings, and

leg turnings proved helpful.

In all cases on site, care was taken to properly identify the woods that were used. However, without laboratory examination, positive identification was impossible in a few cases. Over a period of time, birch and maple can become almost indistinguishable, and it is quite likely that the former may also have been used extensively for parts of chairs. Ash, hickory, and oak have a similar appearance, especially when stained or painted, and although infrequently used, raised some doubt regarding positive identification in a few cases. Otherwise, identification should be accurate. Occasionally the author found that pieces long identified as of one material were actually of another.

Due to normal shrinkage, turned legs, posts, rungs, and pedestals assume in cross section a slightly elliptical shape.. The major axis is the original size, and is the dimension that has been recorded for the turned parts. Also, through shrinkage the original dimensions of boards have changed, particularly in thickness and width. Being so variable, allowances for this normal occurrence have not been added to the recorded dimensions.

Determining the kinds of wood joints that were used to assemble the various parts of Shaker furniture was a relatively easy matter. Either their components were exposed, as in dovetail joints, or the lines used to cut wood away to make joints were usually visible. When such physical evidence was absent, as in closed mortise-and-tenon joints, which were commonly used to assemble aprons to legs in table construction, their size was an educated guess based on the author's cabinetmaking experience.

In addition to their furniture, Shaker cabinetmakers produced a wide range of other articles made of wood. Domestic implements, coopers' ware, brooms, brushes, spinning wheels, looms, yarn winders, reels, swifts, clothes pins, and garment hangers, to name a few, were all products of their industry, and were made with the same concern for utility as their furniture. Not being classified as furniture, such pieces are omitted from this work. Clocks, however,

whose classification is disputed, have been included.

Unless otherwise noted, photographs are by the author. Permission to illustrate selected pieces of furniture with measured drawings was granted to the author by the owners, with the understanding that if such drawings were used to reproduce pieces, this use would be limited to the home craftsperson. The author is deeply grateful to the owners for their generosity. Those readers who wish to make reproductions for enjoyment and personal use are urged to sign and date their work. By so doing they indicate their respect for the integrity of the original works and prevent any possible confusion in the future between reproduction pieces and the original creations.

The following works contributed greatly to the development of this volume: Edward Deming Andrews, *The Community Industries of the Shakers* (New York State Museum Handbook 15); Edward Deming Andrews and Faith Andrews, *Religion in Wood: A Book of Shaker Furniture* (Indiana

University Press); Henri Desroche, *The American Shakers: From Neo-Christianity to Presocialism* (The University of Massachusetts Press); Theodore E. Johnson and John McKee, *Hands to Work and Hearts to God* (Bowdoin College Museum of Art); Marian Klamkin, *Hands To Work: Shaker Folk Art and Industries* (Dodd, Mead and Company); Robert F. Meader, *Illustrated Guide to Shaker Furniture* (Dover Publications); Marguerite Fellows Melcher, *The Shaker Adventure* (Princeton University Press); Charles R. Muller, *The Shaker Way* (Ohio Antique Review).

Finally, the author assumes full responsibility for whatever errors the volume may contain.

The Book of Shaker Furniture

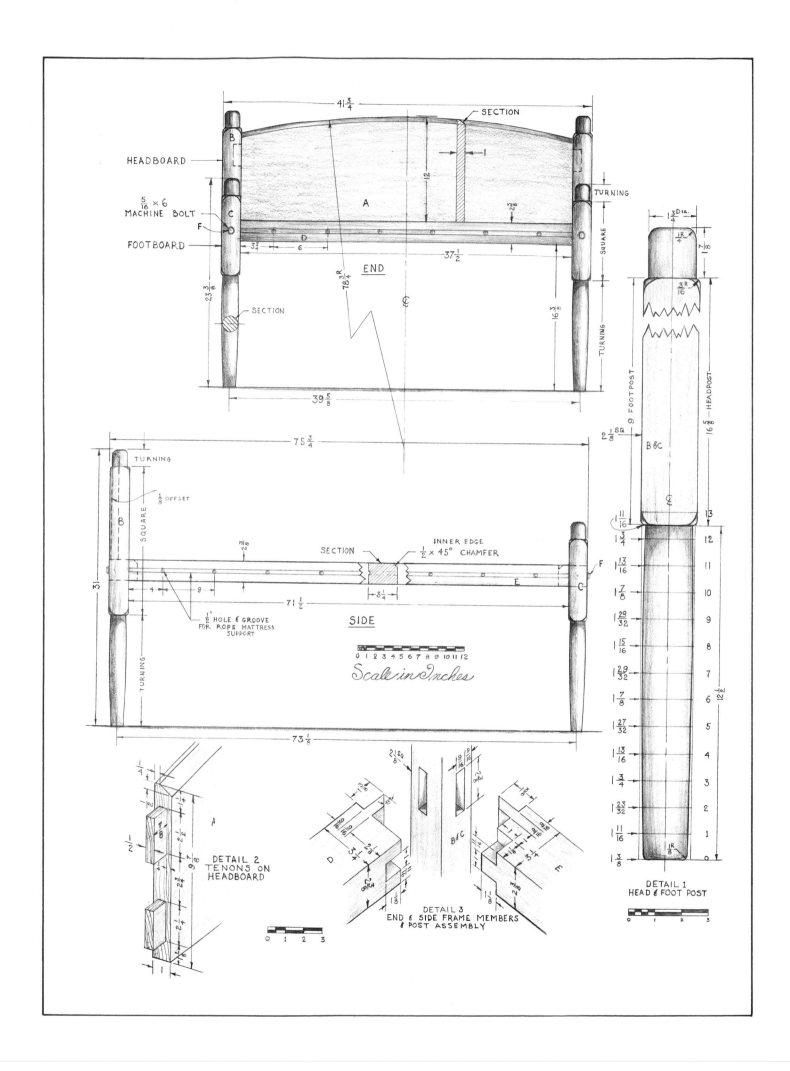

HEADBOARD

$\frac{5}{16} \times 6$
MACHINE BOLT

FOOTBOARD

END

SIDE

0 1 2 3 4 5 6 7 8 9 10 11 12
Scale in Inches

TURNING

SQUARE

TURNING

SECTION

SECTION

INNER EDGE
$\frac{1}{2} \times 45°$ CHAMFER

$\frac{1}{2}$" HOLE & GROOVE
FOR ROPE MATTRESS
SUPPORT

$\frac{1}{8}$ OFFSET

DETAIL 2
TENONS ON
HEADBOARD

DETAIL 3
END & SIDE FRAME MEMBERS
& POST ASSEMBLY

DETAIL 1
HEAD & FOOT POST

0 1 2 3

0 1 2 3

FOOTPOST

HEADPOST

Beds

Shaker writings reveal that in the formative years furniture, including beds, was in short supply. Believers slept crowded together on the floors of their hastily built, small cabins. Later, as societies organized and found time, small folding cots were made to provide some degree of comfort. Bedsteads with mattress supports of rope were the next development. These cottage, or hired-men's beds, were short and narrow, barely ever more than six feet long and three feet wide. Headboard surfaces were left plain and usually had a slightly curved upper edge, which in some examples had notched ends. Legs were lathe-turned, plain, rod-shaped posts, which in early examples rested directly on the floor, and in later types, on large wooden rollers. The Millennial Laws recorded in 1821 and revised in 1845 recommended that bedsteads be painted green; later examples were stained or varnished.

1. This clear-varnished, maple-and-pine bedstead is from New Lebanon (c. 1865). The upper edge of the pine headboard is curved and heavily chamfered. It is double-tenoned into the headpost and pinned from the back. Originally the side frame members (rails) were held, unsuccessfully, to the head- and footpost with wood screws, which were later replaced with lag screws which also failed; they now are held with draw bolts.

The lower, turned portion on the post is a typical Shaker form and was often used on corner posts of lidded chests (fig. 4), counters (fig. 6), and sewing desks (fig. 9). The frame members assemble to the post with an interesting but complicated form of joinery that, in good Shaker tradition, works. Collection of Mrs. Edward Deming Andrews.

H. 31, W. 41-3/4, L. 75-3/4.

Letter	No.	Name	Material	T	W	L
A	1	headboard	pine	1	12	39-1/4
B	2	headboard post	maple	2-1/8 sq.		31
C	2	footboard post	maple	2-1/8 sq.		23-3/8
D	2	end rail	maple	2-3/8	3-1/4	40-1/4
E	2	side rails	maple	2-3/8	3-1/4	74-1/4
Hardware						
F	4	machine bolts and nuts	NC 5/16-18 × 6" long			

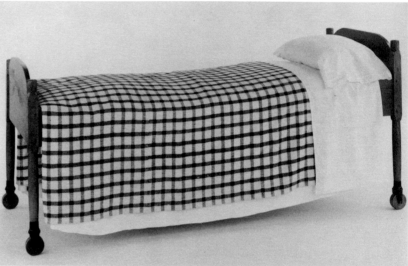

2. In mixed woods, this early nineteenth-century New Lebanon bedstead has chestnut posts, pine head- and footboards, and pine, stepped side rails. The posts have modified, pineapple-shape finials, and maple rollers let into nonswiveling metal castings. Wood slats support the mattress. The wooden parts, all left unfinished, have acquired a medium brown patina. Collection of the Henry Francis du Pont Winterthur Museum. Photograph courtesy of the museum.

H. 30-3/8, W. 27-7/8, L. 69-5/16.

3. Three different woods were used to make this mid-nineteenth-century bedstead from Hancock. There are pine head- and footboards, ash posts, and maple rails, all finished in clear varnish. Pine and "white wood" (bass, poplar, or tulip) were commonly used for head- and footboards because they were available in wide dimensions and were easily worked. The rails are tenoned on the ends and are held to the head- and footboards with wood screws. The high placement of the rails suggests that the bed was designed to be used in a nurse-shop or infirmary or to accommodate a trundle bed. The commercially made, iron swivel casters straddle the wooden rollers and rest on their axles. The counterpane is Shaker-woven and was intended for summer use. Collection of Philadelphia Museum of Art. Photograph by A. J. Wyatt.

H. 33-5/8, W. 30-1/2, L. 76.

4. Also of mixed woods, this bedstead was made in the first half of the nineteenth century in the New Lebanon society. The headboard, corner posts, bolt covers, and nonswiveling rollers are maple. Two chestnut cross braces help support twelve horizontal slats of pine. The slats are let into grooves cut into the head- and footboard frame members and are separated by small pieces of wood nailed in the grooves. The main components of the bedstead are assembled with bolts and nuts (mortise-and-tenon draw-bolt joints). Designed in this manner, the parts could be disassembled for storage within the community or for transporting to other communities for use or copying. The wood was lightly varnished and has turned a warm brown color. Author's collection.

H. 24-3/4, W. 35-7/8, L. 73-7/8.

5

6

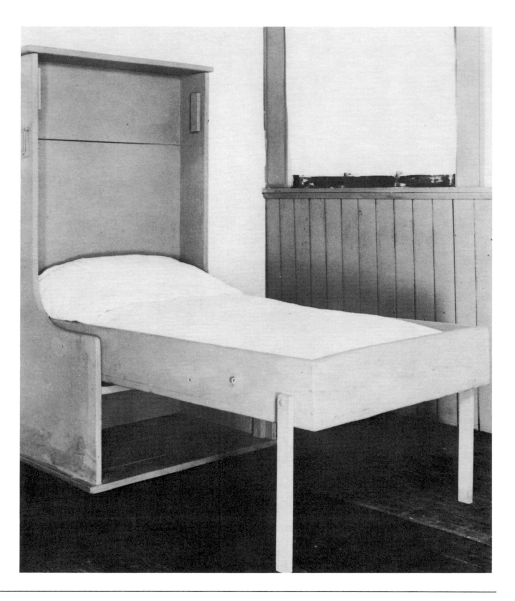

5. Although this bed has an institutional look, it also has a very appealing aesthetic. It was made in the late nineteenth century in the Pleasant Hill community. The wood is walnut and has a varnish finish. The overall shape of the posts, their heaviness, the shape of the turned portion at the lower end, the long inside taper, and rounded upper end are elements of form that give the piece an unmistakably western Shaker look. Collection of Shakertown at Pleasant Hill, Inc., Harrodsburg, Ky.

H. 34-7/8, W. 38-1/2, L. 73-1/2.

6. This bed and trundle bedstead was made in the first half of the nineteenth century at Union Village. Its frame is painted red, and its slats are pine. The double-pinned through-tenons on the rails and end slats indicate that the bed frames were not meant to be readily disassembled. Use of slats for mattress support followed the cross-rope-mattress period. On this bed a mild compromise with Shaker principles of plainness is seen in the bit of "excess" turning below the square portion of the bedposts. The wooden rollers on the trundle are let up into the bottom of the post, which increases the clearance at the top of the trundle and the underside of the bed. The casters do not swivel and predate the swiveling type. The coverlet (c. 1850) is Shaker-made. Collection of Warren County Historical Society Museum, Lebanon, Ohio.

Bed: H. 37-1/2, W. 32, L. 72.
Trundle: H. 15-1/2, W. 31, L. 64-1/2.

7. The wood in this child's folding bed is painted light blue and is most likely pine. The bed was made at the South Union community, probably during the second half of the nineteenth century. The legs swing down in place when the bed is lowered for use. When folded, a hook and eye hold the bed up, thus forming a rather narrow settle with storage space beneath. The nailed butt-joint construction is simple and suitable. Private collection. Photograph courtesy of Shaker Museum, South Union, Ky.

H. 57, W. 31-3/4, L. 55.

Benches

Benches were an important convenience in Shaker communities. They were used in workshops, farm buildings, laundries, schoolrooms, dwellings, and meetinghouses.

Pine, left natural, stained, or painted, was most often used. Some maple and a few walnut benches are extant. Construction was simple yet adequate.

1. This short utility bench from New Lebanon was made very early in the nineteenth century. The bench is pine stained brown and has an iron-rod brace. The legs are firmly and permanently fastened to the top with through, mortise-and-tenon joints, wedged. Collection of Mrs. Edward Deming Andrews.

H. 17-1/4, W. 20-7/8, D. 10-1/2.

Letter	No.	Name	Material	T	W	L
A	1	top	pine	3/4	10-1/2	20-7/8
B	2	legs	pine	3/4	10-1/2	17-1/4
C	4	wedges	pine	1/8	1	1/2
Hardware						
D	1	brace	iron rod	1/4 dia		28
E	4	wood screws	RH 5/8-6			

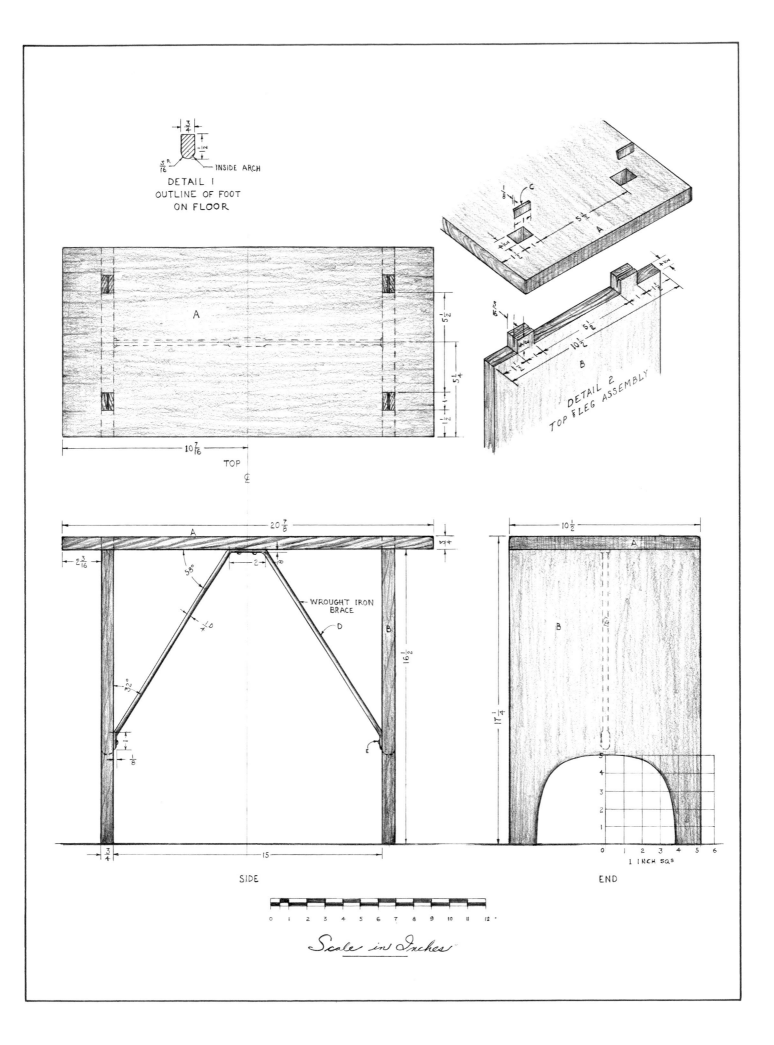

DETAIL 1
OUTLINE OF FOOT
ON FLOOR

INSIDE ARCH

C

A

DETAIL 2
TOP & LEG ASSEMBLY

B

TOP

A

5½

5¼

1½

10 7/16

20 7/8

A

2 3/16

58°

2

WROUGHT IRON
BRACE

D

32°

B

16½

E

¾

15

SIDE

10½

A

B

17¼

¼

5
4
3
2
1

0 1 2 3 4 5 6
1 INCH SQS

END

0 1 2 3 4 5 6 7 8 9 10 11 12

Scale in Inches

2. The relative lowness of this small bench or cricket, made at Hancock in the mid-nineteenth century, makes it difficult to classify. It could have seen service as a bench, a step-stool, or a footstool. It is made of pine, has a natural brown patina, and is varnished. The arc cutout at the floor end, the dadoes on the top, and especially the half dovetails on the four angled braces are typical Shaker forms. Glue and nails were used in assembling the piece. Collection of the Shaker Museum, Old Chatham, N. Y.

H. 10-1/4, W. 17, D. 7-7/8.

3. This small pine bench with butterfly-wing supports is stained orange-red and was made at the Hancock community during the first half of the nineteenth century. The joinery and level of craftsmanship are fine and equal to that found in other Shaker bench forms. Collection of Shaker Community, Inc., Hancock, Mass.

H. 16, W. 35-5/8, D. 9-1/2.

4. The medial stretcher on this pine bench from New Lebanon is permanently fastened to the legs with double-wedged through-tenons. The same method of joinery is used to fasten the top to the legs, thus eliminating the need for metal fasteners which in time could work loose. It is representative of types made at New Lebanon during the late eighteenth and nineteenth centuries. The pine has developed a warm brown patina. The slight arc on the stretcher harmonizes with the arc on the legs. Collection of Mrs. Edward Deming Andrews.

H. 18-1/4, W. 40-1/8, D. 9-1/2.

5. This pine bench was made in the first half of the nineteenth century in the Canterbury society. The legs are dadoed into the seat and the half-dovetailed, angled braces lock the seat to the legs. Shallow arc cutouts on the legs form feet. The edges of the arc cutouts are chamfered from both surfaces and come to an interesting pointed ridge at mid-thickness. Stokes Collection.

H. 17, W. 60, D. 9-7/8.

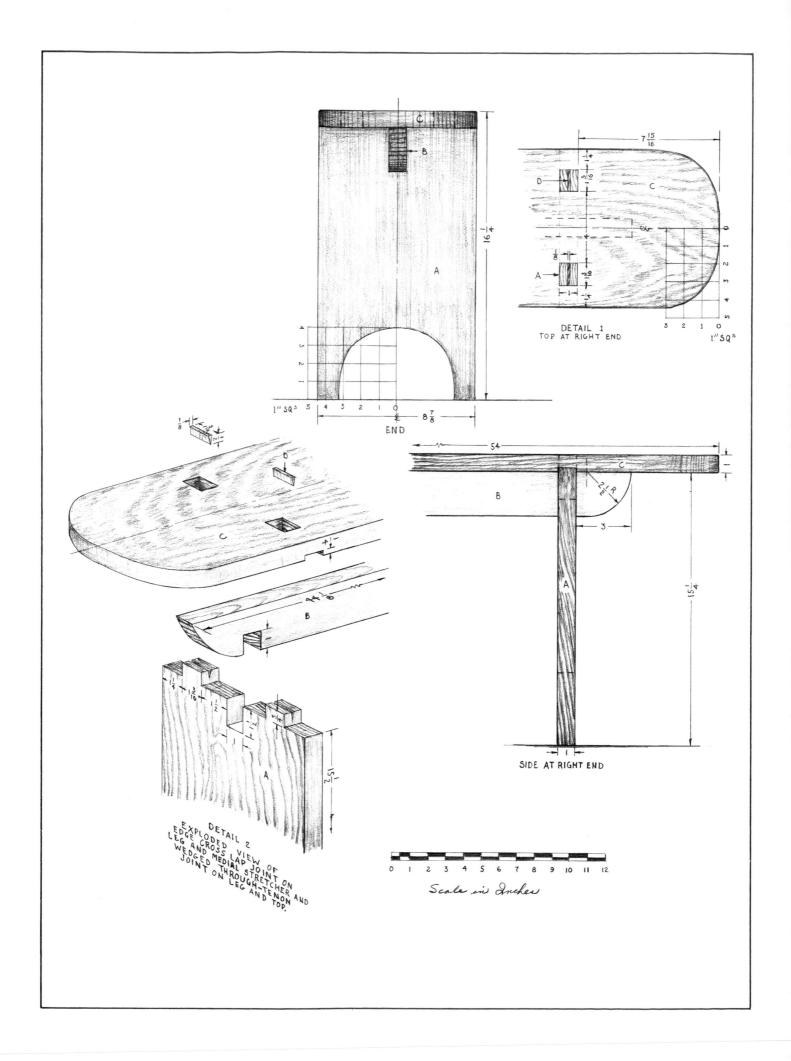

C

B

$16\frac{1}{4}$

A

$1"SQ^S$ 5   4   3   2   1   0 $8\frac{7}{8}$

END

$7\frac{15}{16}$

D $\frac{3}{16}$ C

$\frac{8}{}$ $\frac{3}{16}$ A $\frac{1}{}$

DETAIL 1
TOP AT RIGHT END

3   2   1   0   5 $1"SQ^S$

$\frac{1}{8}$ $\frac{3}{16}$

D

C

B $4\times\frac{1}{8}$

B

DETAIL 2
EXPLODED VIEW OF
EDGE CROSS LAP JOINT ON
LEG AND MEDIAL STRETCHER AND
WEDGED THROUGH-TENON
JOINT ON LEG AND TOP.

$\frac{1}{3}$ $1\frac{3}{16}$ $1\frac{1}{2}$ $1\frac{1}{2}$ $\frac{3}{4}$ 1 $15\frac{1}{2}$ A

54

C $2\frac{1}{2}$ R

B   3

A $15\frac{1}{4}$

1

SIDE AT RIGHT END

0 1 2 3 4 5 6 7 8 9 10 11 12

Scale in Inches

6. Constructed of unfinished walnut that has developed a natural patina, this medium-length bench was made at the South Union community during the first half of the nineteenth century. Probably because it was in greater supply, the Ohio and Kentucky societies used considerably more walnut for furniture than the eastern communities. Typically Shaker and structurally excellent are the edge cross-lap joints on the legs and medial stretcher (not visible in this photograph), the double-wedged through-tenons on the legs, and the dado joints on the underside of the top. The curved ends on the top and medial stretcher, and the cut-out curve on the ends at the floor line were probably made with a turning saw. The curves are most compatible and are aesthetically pleasing. Collection of Shaker Museum, South Union, Ky.

H. 16-1/4, W. 54, D. 8-7/8.

Letter	No.	Name	Material	T	W	L
A	2	legs	walnut	1	8-7/8	16-1/4
B	1	medial stretcher	walnut	1	2-1/2	44-1/8
C	1	top	walnut	1	8-7/8	54
D	4	wedges	walnut	1/8	1-3/16	1/2

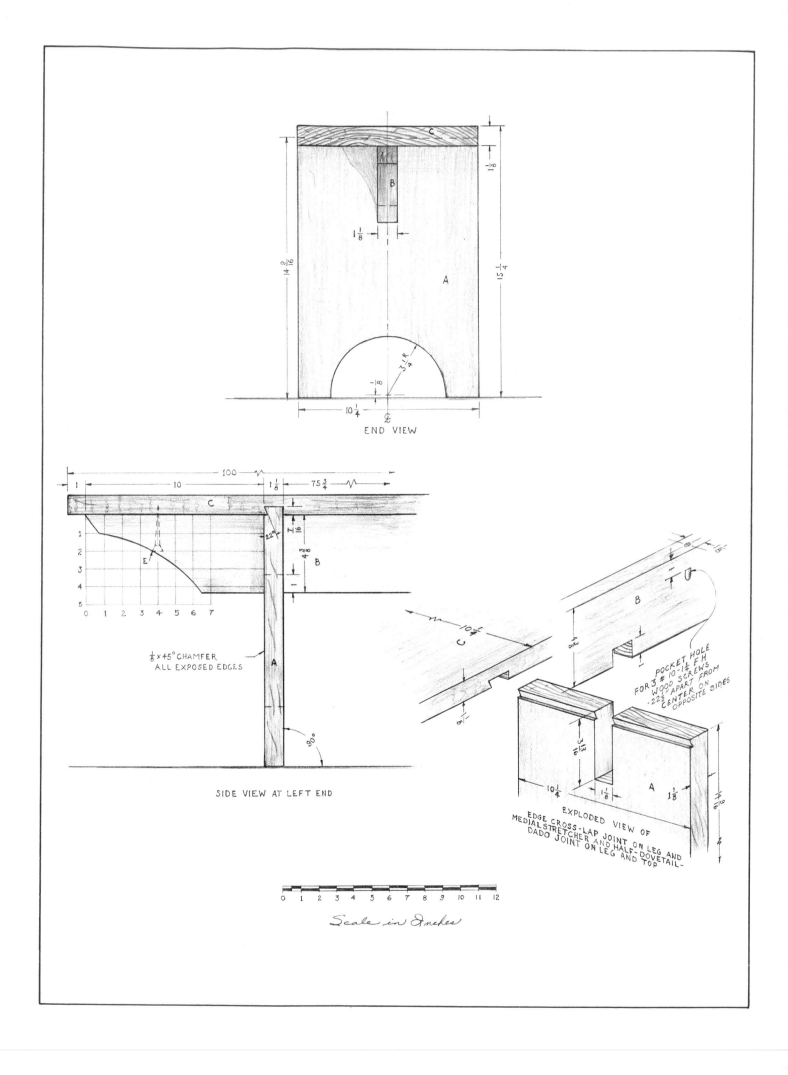

C

B

A

$14\frac{9}{16}$

$15\frac{1}{4}$

$1\frac{1}{8}$

$1\frac{1}{8}$

$3\frac{1}{4}R$

$\frac{1}{8}$

$10\frac{1}{4}$

℄

END VIEW

100

1

10

$1\frac{1}{8}$

$75\frac{3}{4}$

C

B

A

$\frac{7}{16}$

$4\frac{3}{8}$

1

22°

90°

E

$\frac{1}{8} \times 45°$ CHAMFER
ALL EXPOSED EDGES

SIDE VIEW AT LEFT END

B

C

A

$10\frac{1}{4}$

$\frac{1}{16}$

$4\frac{3}{8}$

$\frac{1}{8}$

$\frac{9}{16}$

$3\frac{13}{16}$

$10\frac{1}{4}$

$1\frac{1}{8}$

$1\frac{1}{8}$

$14\frac{9}{16}$

POCKET HOLE
FOR 3 # 10-1¼ F.H.
WOOD SCREWS
-22½" APART ON
CENTER ON
OPPOSITE SIDES

EXPLODED VIEW OF
EDGE CROSS-LAP JOINT ON LEG AND
MEDIAL STRETCHER AND HALF-DOVETAIL-
DADO JOINT ON LEG AND TOP

0 1 2 3 4 5 6 7 8 9 10 11 12

Scale in Inches

7. In this Hancock meeting-room or meetinghouse bench, the legs, stretcher, and top are held firmly together by the use of closely fitted locking joints and five wood screws. The screws go through the stretcher into the underside of the top. To facilitate disassembly for storage or transportation, the parts were assembled without glue. Benches of this type were made in quantity and used late into the nineteenth century. The necessary quantity and late manufacture indicate that while some hand-tool work was required, power woodworking equipment was principally employed in their production. The bench is maple which has turned a natural, warm brown color. The wood selected was most appropriate for it is heavy, hard, and strong—physical properties that contribute to increased serviceability. Collection of Shaker Community, Inc., Hancock, Mass.

H. 15-1/4, W. 100, D. 10-1/4.

Letter	No.	Name	Material	T	W	L
A	2	legs	maple	1-1/8	10-1/4	14-9/16
B	1	medial stretcher	maple	1-1/8	4-3/8	98
C	1	top	maple	1-1/8	10-1/4	100
Hardware						
D	3	wood screws		FH 1-3/4-10		
E	2	wood screws		FH 2-1/2-10		

8. Schoolroom benches of this type were produced in quantity during the first half of the nineteenth century and used in Shaker schoolrooms, usually in conjunction with multiple-place school desks. This bench is typical of those used at the New Lebanon and Hancock communities. It is pine painted with a light red wash. The legs are cut at the floor line in a semi-circular arc and the backrest is fastened to the legs with cleats. The application of a backrest to what is a basic plain bench is a classic example of Shaker ingenuity. Collection of Shaker Community, Inc., Hancock, Mass.

H. 26, W. 68-3/4, D. 14-1/2.

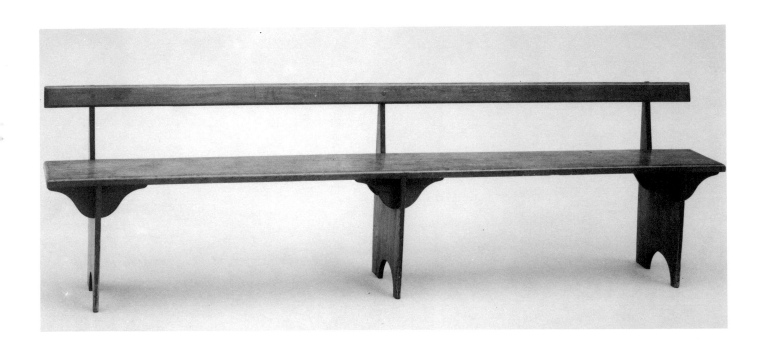

9. This communal dining-room bench was made at Hancock in the early nineteenth century. It is of pine with a wash coat of red paint and has three legs, six butterfly-wing supports, and a backrest. Supports are fitted to the legs with edge cross-lap joints and the top is fitted to the legs with dadoes. The backrest is formed by an upward extension of the legs. Collection of the Metropolitan Museum of Art, Purchase, 1966, Friends of the American Wing Fund. Photograph courtesy of the museum.

H. 26-1/2, W. 94, D. 12.

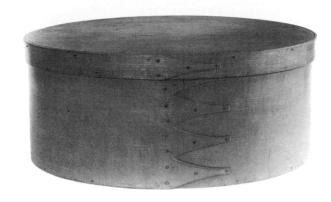

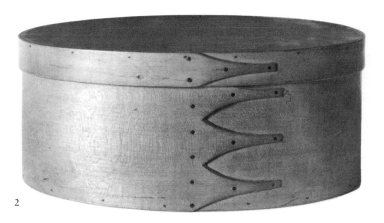

Boxes and Carriers

Oval and round boxes are craft items that were produced in great numbers and sold not only in Shaker stores, but peddled by brothers as far as Boston and New York. Though not furniture, they were included in this book because they are a well-known Shaker product and are readily associated with the Shaker sect. Oval boxes were first made about 1798 and continued to be produced in most all the communities throughout the nineteenth century.

Brother Delmar Wilson (1873–1961) of the Sabbathday Lake society made hundreds of boxes and carriers (boxes with handles) and produced them almost until his death. Brother Delmar was the last male Shaker; prior to his passing he recommended, and the surviving sisters agreed, that the Shaker rolls should forever be closed to new members.

At first, boxes were made entirely by hand with hand tools; later, powered circular saws were used to cut the sides, rims, tops, and bottoms. The "fingers" or "lappers" were cut with either a knife or fret saw. In

making a box more than eighteen processes had to be done carefully by hand.

The sides and rims were usually made of maple and the bottoms and tops (for dimensional stability) of quarter-sawn pine. The edges of the graceful fingers were beveled and the opposite end was edge-tapered almost to a knife point to form a scarf joint when assembled. The sides and rims were soaked in hot water and/or steamed until they were pliable and could be bent around a wooden mold. Copper nails held the ends together, forming a graceful oval shape. The ends of the nails were driven against a metal plate embedded into the side of the mold which caused them to peen over. Oval discs were carefully fitted and fastened in place at bottoms and tops, at first with wooden pegs, later with copper nails. The boxes were finished with clear varnish or shellac, also many were painted. Yellow, green, blue, and red were the colors most often used. The technology involved in producing oval carriers is the same as that for making oval boxes.

Boxes were made in graduated sizes and

were first sold singularly or in nests of twelve, then nine, and later, seven and five. Around 1833 the sizes were standardized and numbered; the smallest, number eleven, sold for three dollars a dozen or twenty-five cents apiece, and the largest, number one, cost nine dollars a dozen or seventy-five cents each.

Of the oval boxes and carriers, those with the most pleasing form and detail and of the best craftsmanship were made for communal use; boxes and carriers made for sale, though well crafted, have an easily recognized mass-production aesthetic.

This section also includes boxes that were made exclusively for communal use. They are candle boxes, general utility boxes, and boxes designed to hold kindling and firewood.

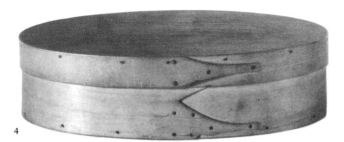

1. The letters *D.M.* stenciled on the cover of this medium-size oval box stand for David Meacham (1766–1847). Brother David was a trustee at the New Lebanon society and his initials were used as a trade-mark on certain items made for sale, such as dry measures and spinning wheels. The trade-mark may also have been a method of quality control; inspected pieces found substandard were not stenciled and sold. This box was made during the second quarter of the nineteenth century and is maple and pine painted green. Collection of Jean Sladek Popelka.

H. 2-1/4, W. 6-3/16, D. 3-7/8.

2. This large, well-proportioned, late nineteenth-century maple and pine oval box from New Lebanon has beautifully shaped, beveled, tapered fingers. Collection of Jean Sladek Popelka.

H. 5, W. 11-7/8, D. 8-5/16.

3. Exceptionally large and in fine condition, this New Lebanon nineteenth-century oval box has its original yellow wash paint. Private collection.

H. 6, W. 15, D. 11.

4. This unusually shallow oval box in maple and pine may have been designed to hold sewing-thread spools. It was made at New Lebanon, and its date is unknown. Collection of Donald Weeks.

H. 2-1/4, W. 8-13/16, D. 6.

5. Fewer round boxes than oval were produced over the years. This one was made at Canterbury during the first half of the nineteenth century and has a wash coat of brown paint. Private collection.

H. 3-3/4, Dia. 5-5/8.

6. Large round boxes fitted with a reinforcing metal or wood rim, as in this example, were to the Shakers what the brass spittoon was to the world. Referred to as "spit boxes" they were filled with sawdust or shavings and used in brethrens' retiring-rooms and shops. Several communities made them and some were sold to the world. This box is from the Harvard society and, as were most, was produced during the first half of the nineteenth century. They were usually painted yellow or (as in this example) orange. The box has a pine bottom and a maple rim and side. Spit box parts were prepared and assembled with the same care and in the same way as were oval boxes and carriers. Collection of Suzanne Courcier and Robert Wilkins.

H. 5-1/4, Dia. 12-1/8.

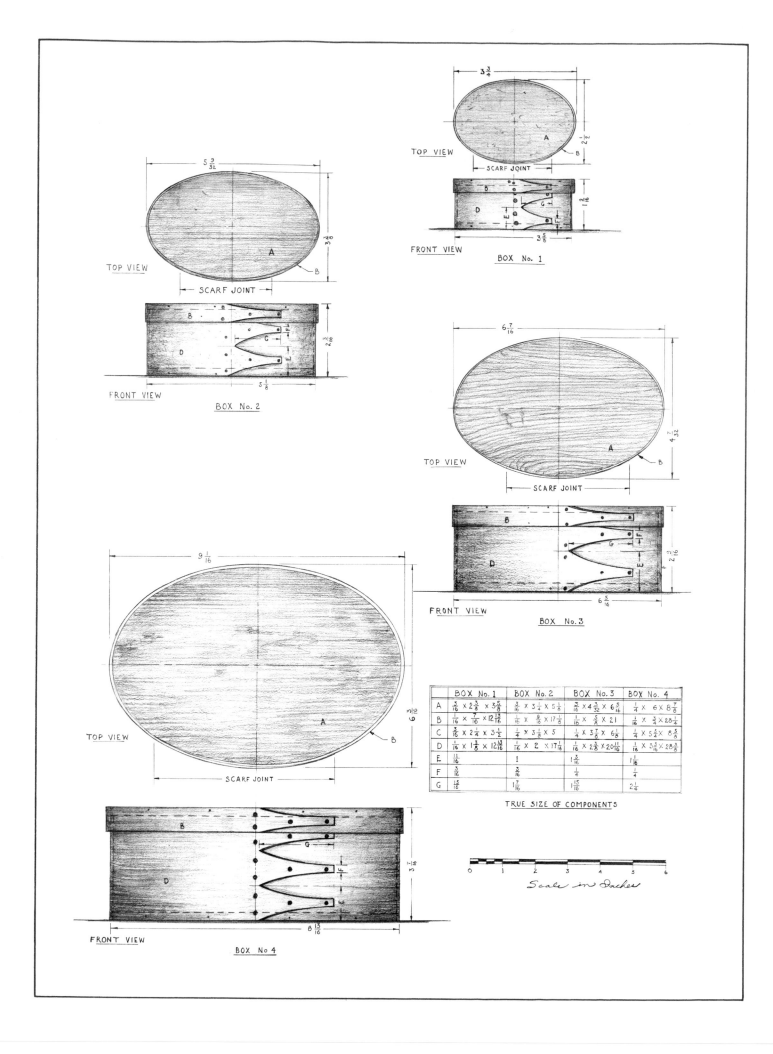

TOP VIEW

$3\frac{3}{4}$

$2\frac{1}{2}$

B

SCARF JOINT

FRONT VIEW

B

D

E

G

$1\frac{5}{16}$

$3\frac{5}{8}$

BOX No. 1

TOP VIEW

$5\frac{9}{32}$

$3\frac{3}{8}$

A

B

SCARF JOINT

FRONT VIEW

B

D

G

F

E

$2\frac{3}{16}$

$5\frac{1}{8}$

BOX No. 2

TOP VIEW

$6\frac{7}{16}$

$4\frac{7}{32}$

A

B

SCARF JOINT

FRONT VIEW

B

D

G

F

E

$2\frac{3}{16}$

$6\frac{5}{16}$

BOX No. 3

TOP VIEW

$9\frac{1}{16}$

$6\frac{3}{16}$

A

B

SCARF JOINT

FRONT VIEW

B

D

G

F

E

$3\frac{7}{16}$

$8\frac{13}{16}$

BOX No 4

	BOX No. 1	BOX No. 2	BOX No. 3	BOX No. 4
A	$\frac{3}{16} \times 2\frac{3}{8} \times 3\frac{5}{8}$	$\frac{3}{16} \times 3\frac{1}{4} \times 5\frac{1}{8}$	$\frac{3}{16} \times 4\frac{3}{32} \times 6\frac{5}{16}$	$\frac{1}{4} \times 6 \times 8\frac{7}{8}$
B	$\frac{1}{16} \times \frac{7}{16} \times 12\frac{1}{16}$	$\frac{1}{16} \times \frac{9}{16} \times 17\frac{7}{8}$	$\frac{1}{16} \times \frac{5}{8} \times 21$	$\frac{1}{16} \times \frac{3}{4} \times 28\frac{1}{4}$
C	$\frac{3}{16} \times 2\frac{1}{4} \times 3\frac{1}{2}$	$\frac{1}{4} \times 3\frac{1}{8} \times 5$	$\frac{1}{4} \times 3\frac{7}{8} \times 6\frac{1}{8}$	$\frac{1}{4} \times 5\frac{1}{4} \times 8\frac{5}{8}$
D	$\frac{1}{16} \times 1\frac{3}{8} \times 12\frac{13}{16}$	$\frac{1}{16} \times 2 \times 17\frac{1}{8}$	$\frac{1}{16} \times 2\frac{3}{8} \times 20\frac{11}{16}$	$\frac{1}{16} \times 3\frac{3}{16} \times 28\frac{3}{8}$
E	$\frac{11}{16}$	1	$1\frac{3}{16}$	$1\frac{1}{16}$
F	$\frac{3}{16}$	$\frac{3}{16}$	$\frac{1}{4}$	$\frac{1}{4}$
G	$1\frac{3}{16}$	$1\frac{7}{16}$	$1\frac{15}{16}$	$2\frac{1}{4}$

TRUE SIZE OF COMPONENTS

0 1 2 3 4 5 6

Scale in Inches

7. Assembled here is a sampler of oval boxes showing a variety of sizes from small (background, no. 1) to large (foreground, no. 4). All have maple sides with pine tops and bottoms and were made in eastern communities during the nineteenth century. The first box (no. 1) was originally painted red-orange and is inscribed on the underside of the cover, "For H. Francies From Hanna S Williams 1874." Sister Hanna (1793–1883) lived at the Hancock village. Another fine example (box no. 2) has a natural finish of clear varnish, as do the remaining two boxes. The top and bottom of the next box (no. 3) are held in place with small wooden pegs rather than with copper nails. A lengthy inscription on the inside of this box tells that it was made at Canterbury, owned for many years by R. A. Shepard, and given to her niece, Mattie S. Baker, in July 1887. On the last box (no. 4) the finger on the cover is perfectly aligned with those on the base, and the nails are all precisely placed. Attention to such details makes the box most desirable. Private collection.

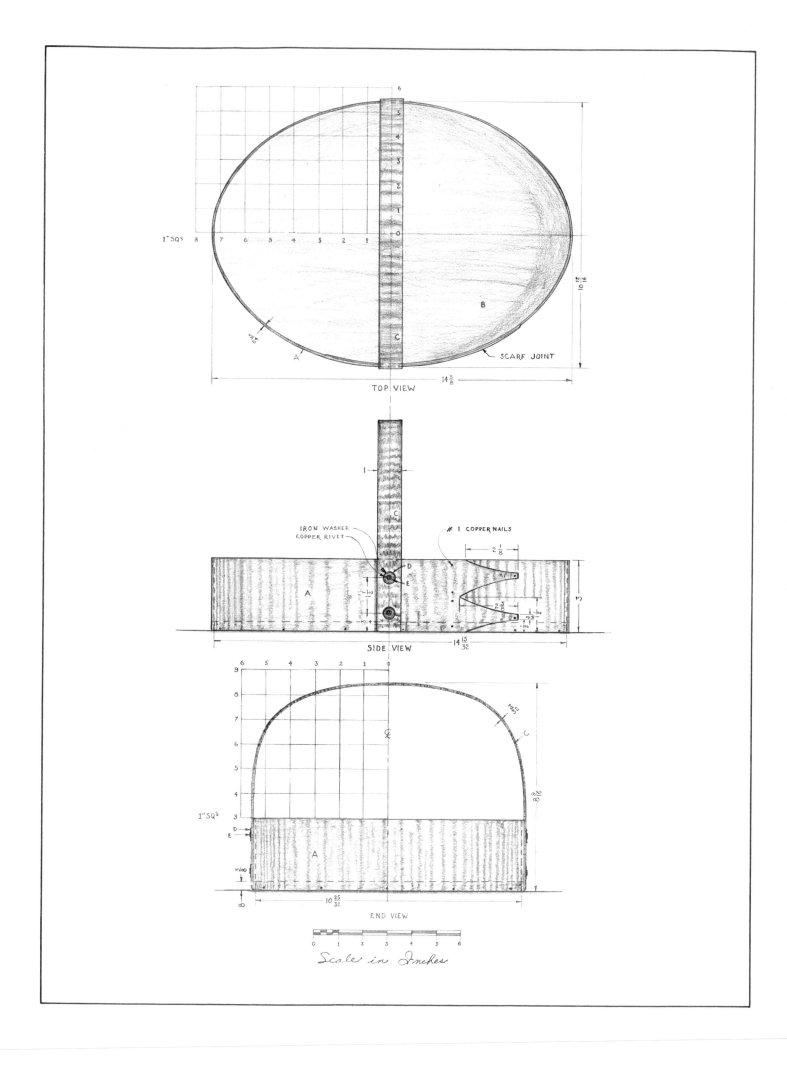

1" SQS

6
5
4
3
2
1
0

8 7 6 5 4 3 2 1

$10\frac{12}{16}$

B

C

A

SCARF JOINT

$14\frac{5}{8}$

TOP VIEW

I

C

IRON WASHER
COPPER RIVET

I COPPER NAILS

$2\frac{1}{8}$

D
E

A

$1\frac{1}{2}$

3

$2\frac{3}{4}$

$14\frac{15}{32}$

SIDE VIEW

6 5 4 3 2 1 0

9
8
7
6
5
4
3

$\frac{3}{32}$

C

$8\frac{9}{16}$

1" SQ's

D
E

A

B

$10\frac{25}{32}$

END VIEW

0 1 2 3 4 5 6

Scale in Inches

8. This oval carrier made in the late nineteenth or early twentieth century at either New Lebanon or Hancock is typical of hundreds that were mass produced and sold in Shaker stores. Edge-grained pine was used for the bottom and, in this example, tigerstripe maple was used for the side and bail. The ends of the side are scarf-jointed and fastened with copper nails, the points of which are peened on the inside. The bottom is also nailed in place. The plain (unsculptured) bail is attached to the side with rather unattractive washers and copper rivets. Collection of Dr. and Mrs. Thomas Kane.

H. 8-9/16, W. 14-5/8, D. 10-15/16.

Letter	No.	Name	Material	T	W	L
A	1	side	maple	5/64	3	48
B	1	bottom	pine	1/4	10-25/32	14-15/32
C	1	handle	maple	3/32	1	24-1/2
Hardware						
D	8	washers	iron			
E	4	rivets	copper			

9. Also of mixed woods is this oval carrier from Canterbury or Enfield, New Hampshire. It dates from the second half of the nineteenth century. Edge-grained pine was used for the bottom, maple, because of its strength, was used for the side and the bail was fashioned of hickory. The length-to-width ratio of the nicely shaped fingers (lappers) on the side is well proportioned. The ends of the sides are scarfed and fastened together with copper nails and the bottom is nailed in place with small brads. The changing shape of the bail contributes a great deal to the exceptionally graceful form of the carrier. Inscribed on the bottom are the names of two Canterbury sisters, Margaret Appleton (1866–1944) and Mary Bassford (1841–1929). It seems safe to assume that the carrier was used by these women. Collection of Philadelphia Museum of Art. Photograph by A. J. Wyatt.

H. 8, W. 11, D. 8.

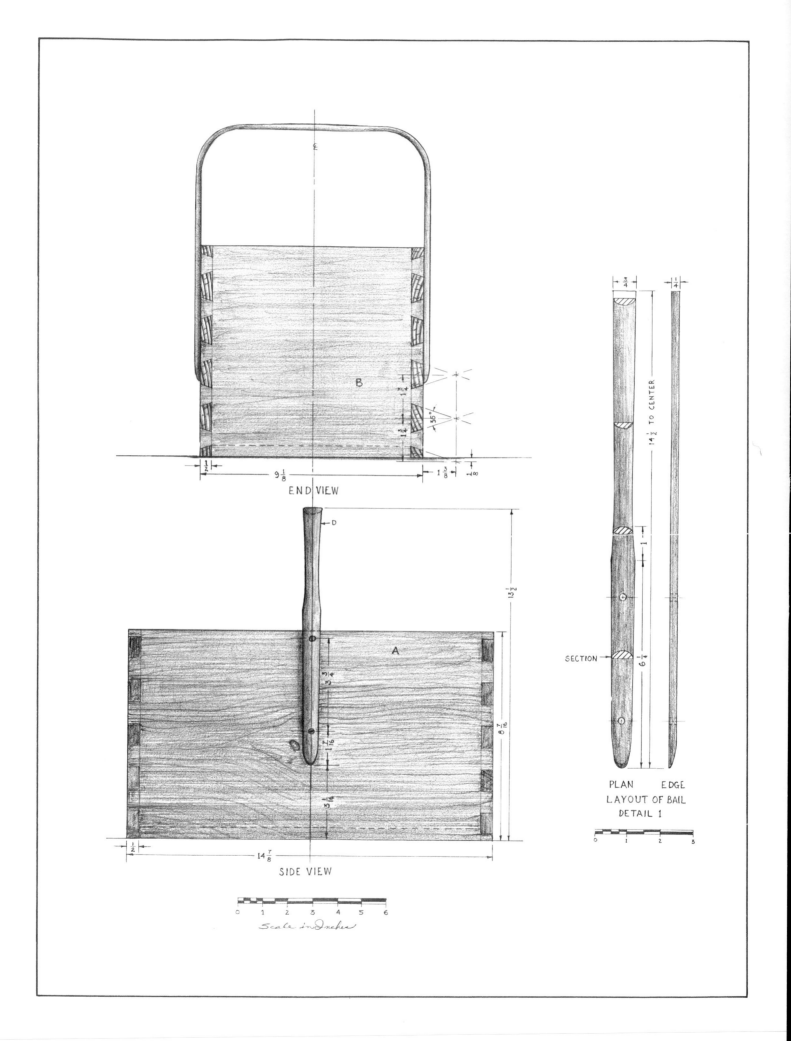

END VIEW

$9\frac{1}{8}$

$\frac{1}{2}$

$1\frac{3}{8}$

$\frac{1}{8}$

B

$\frac{3}{4}$

$\frac{3}{4}$

$35°$

D

A

$3\frac{3}{4}$

$1\frac{7}{16}$

$3\frac{1}{16}$

$8\frac{7}{16}$

$13\frac{1}{2}$

$\frac{1}{2}$

$14\frac{7}{8}$

SIDE VIEW

0 1 2 3 4 5 6
Scale in Inches

$\frac{3}{4}$

$\frac{1}{4}$

$14\frac{1}{2}$ TO CENTER

1

SECTION

$6\frac{1}{4}$

PLAN   EDGE
LAYOUT OF BAIL
DETAIL 1

0   1   2   3

10. Referred to as a chip-box, this early nine-teenth-century oblong carrier of pine was used to collect wood shavings and kindling for starting fires in Shaker stoves at the Canterbury society. The corners are neatly dove-tailed, the bottom is let into the sides, and the bail is nicely sculptured; all are finished in a red-orange stain. Collection of Shaker Village, Inc., Canterbury, N. H.

H. 8-7/16, H. to top of bail, 13-1/2, W. 14-7/8, D. 9-5/8.

Letter	No.	Name	Material	T	W	L
A	2	sides	pine	1/2	8-7/16	14-7/8
B	2	ends	pine	1/2	8-7/16	9-1/8
C	1	bottom	pine	1/2	8-1/8	13-7/8
D	1	bail	hickory	1/4	3/4	29

11. The community origin of this mid-nine-teenth-century oblong carrier of pine and ash and the nature of its service over the years are unknown. The molded edges of the bottom, the corner dovetails, and—the most interesting part—the ash bail, all show a high degree of craftsmanship. Examination of the shape of the bail shows it continuously changes throughout its length. A wash coat of yellow paint was applied to the inner surface of the carrier while the outside was left unfinished and has since acquired a nice natural brown patina. Private collection.

H. 10-1/4, W. 12, D. 10-1/8.

STAPLE HINGE

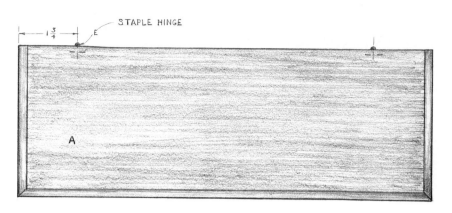

1 3/4

E

A

TOP

CHAMFER 1/4 × 45°

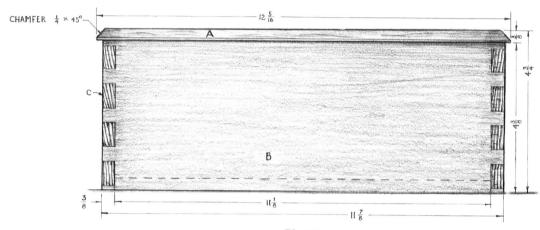

12 5/16

A

3/8

4 3/4

4 3/8

C

B

3/8

11 1/8

11 7/8

FRONT

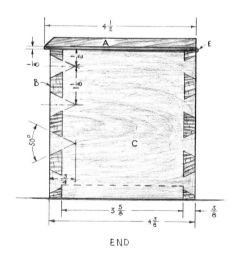

4 1/2

A

E

1/8

1/2

1/16

B

50°

C

3/4

3 5/8

3/8

4 3/8

END

E

DETAIL 1
STAPLE HINGE

0   1   2   3   4   5   6

Scale in Inches

13

12

14

12. This pine candle box (c. 1790) with natural brown patina was made in an unknown eastern community. It has well-made dovetailed corners, chamfered edges on the lid, and staple hinges. Collection of Mrs. Edward Deming Andrews.

H. 4-3/4, W. 12-5/16, D. 4-1/2.

Letter	No.	Name	Material	T	W	L
A	1	top	pine	3/8	4-1/2	12-5/16
B	2	front and back	pine	3/8	4-3/8	11-7/8
C	2	sides	pine	3/8	4-3/8	4-3/8
D	1	bottom	pine	3/8	3-5/8	11-1/8
Hardware						
E	2	staple hinges	iron wire			

13. The purpose of this small rectangular box is not known, but possibly it was used to store candles. It was made in the late eighteenth or early nineteenth century in an eastern community and is pine with its original yellow wash paint. The sides are rabbeted and the ends and bottom are nailed in place. The lid is hinged with leather strips and the box is fitted with a lock. Private collection.

H. 4, W. 11, D. 6.

14. Simply constructed with open dovetailed corners, this candle box from Hancock or New Lebanon is in pine with natural patina, and was made in the first half of the nineteenth century. Private collection.

H. 4-1/4, W. 12-7/8, D. 4.

15. The generous size of this candle box indicates it was designed to hold a good supply of candles. It has a sliding top and dovetailed corners and was made at Canterbury during the first half of the nineteenth century. It is poplar painted a yellow wash. Collection of the Shaker Museum, Old Chatham, N. Y.

H. 7, W. 13-1/4, D. 9-1/4.

16. The turned maple knobs at each end of this poplar box were used no doubt to transport the box and its contents. The box is in original yellow wash paint. It was made in the late eighteenth or early nineteenth century at New Lebanon. The lid has a small chamfer on its front edge and ends and is hinged with small pieces of leather. It is secured with a commercially made hook-and-eye purchased from the world. The ends were let into the front and back with nailed rabbet joints, and the bottom was simply nailed to the edges. Private collection.

H. 8, W. 19, D. 10.

17. The quarter-round molding on the top and bottom of this small, early nineteenth-century walnut box is similar to that used on firewood boxes made at Hancock, and possibly was made in that community. Private collection.

H. 5-3/16, W. 7-7/8, D. 7-3/4.

18. This wood-box was made at Hancock and dates from the first half of the nineteenth century. It is pine stained brown and has a Shaker-made bracket and stove implements. The well-made dovetailed corners reflect a high level of craftsmanship. The edge molding on the top and the bottom is a modified half round rather than the more common quarter round. Private collection.

H. 25, W. 26, D. 17.

19. Also from Hancock is this lidded wood-box of pine stained brown. It was made during the first half of the nineteenth century and is typical of many produced in this community. The long row of corner dovetails is exceptionally well made. (Missing from the right side are two small pegs, used for hanging a dustpan and brush.) The inner vertical partition separates kindling from larger wood. A quarter-round molding finishes the front edge and ends of the top and bottom. Collection of Shaker Community, Inc., Hancock, Mass.

H. 24, W. 25-1/4, D. 16-5/8.

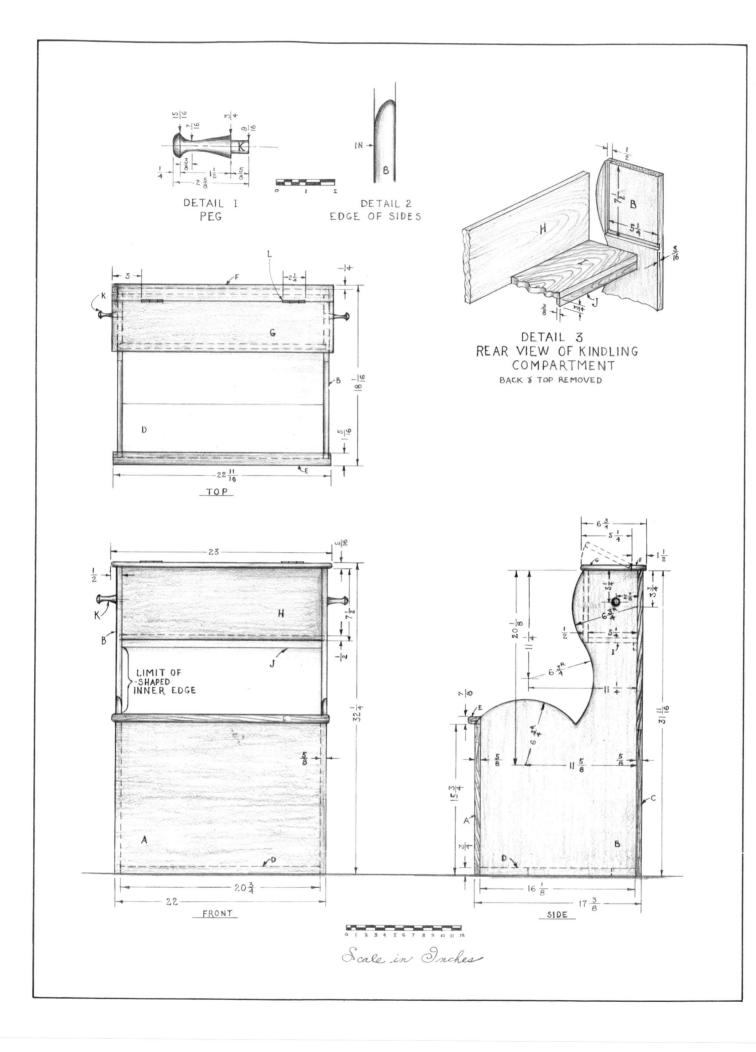

DETAIL 1
PEG

DETAIL 2
EDGE OF SIDES

DETAIL 3
REAR VIEW OF KINDLING
COMPARTMENT
BACK & TOP REMOVED

TOP

LIMIT OF
SHAPED
INNER EDGE

FRONT

SIDE

Scale in Inches

20. This wood-box from Pleasant Hill is of poplar painted red and is a good example of western Shaker craftsmanship. It was made during the first half of the nineteenth century and it has a kindling compartment, parts of which have been restored. Each side of the box is a single board, although this is not exceptional considering the girth of poplar trees. The front is fastened to the sides with wood screws, the back is nailed to the sides, and the bottom is let into the sides and nailed in place. The S-curve and arc cuts on each side are a pleasing change in form from the predominantly straight lines of the rest of the box. Single pegs on each side were used to hold stove implements. Collection of Shakertown at Pleasant Hill, Inc., Harrodsburg, Ky.

H. 32-1/4, W. 23, D. 18.

Letter	No.	Name	Material	T	W	L
A	1	front	poplar	5/8	15-3/4	22
B	2	sides	poplar	5/8	16-1/8	31-11/16
C	1	back	poplar	5/8	31-11/16	22
D	1	bottom	poplar	3/4	16-1/8	20-3/4
E	1	front cap	poplar	7/8	1-5/16	22-11/16
Kindling compartment						
F	1	fixed top	poplar	9/16	1-1/2	23
G	1	hinged top	poplar	9/16	5-1/4	23
H	1	front	poplar	1/2	7-1/2	21-1/8
I	1	bottom	poplar	1/2	5-1/4	21-1/8
J	1	cleat	poplar	3/8	3/4	20-3/4
K	2	pegs	walnut	15/16 dia		2-5/8
Hardware						
L	2	butt hinges	steel	1/2	2-1/4	

21. The drawer at the base of this wood-box was used for kindling. The box was made in the first half of the nineteenth century at Pleasant Hill and, like many other boxes from western communities, it is built of poplar. Originally painted blue-green, the box now shows its attractive, natural wood color. Designed for end loading, the box could hold long pieces of firewood that were used in fireplaces. The curves on the upper ends of the sides are an example of function influencing form. They probably facilitated loading and minimized damage to the exposed ends. The curve is pleasingly repeated on the cutout at the floor line. Unsophisticated nail joinery does not detract from its classic Shaker lines. Collection of Shakertown at Pleasant Hill, Inc., Harrodsburg, Ky.

H. 36, W. 26, D. 14-1/2.

22. From the South Union community, this large capacity wood-box of pine was made in the first half of the nineteenth century, and was probably used in a shop, dining, or meeting room. The simple nail construction was reinforced with strips of strap metal. Collection of Shaker Museum, South Union, Ky.

H. 32, W. 31-1/2, D. 16-1/4.

23. The turned legs on this wood-box (c. 1830) are applied to the underside of the box and are made of chestnut, while other parts of the box are pine; all are painted in a yellow wash. The sides and ends are held with corner dovetails and the hinged lid has bread-board ends. Collection of The United Society of Shakers at Sabbathday Lake, Maine. Photograph by David W. Serette

H. 30-1/2, W. 26-1/2, D. 20-1/2.

Built-ins and Cupboards

The Shakers' desire for neatness and order is evident in the fact that great numbers of built-in drawers and cupboards were an ar chitectural feature in nearly all their buildings. To get some idea of their importance, a dwelling at the Enfield, New Hampshire, society, built during the middle of the nineteenth century, has 860 built-in drawers. Often entire walls had built-ins composed of integrated cupboards, closets, and chests which, when all the units were closed, presented an orderly arrangement of vertical and horizontal planes accentuated only by rows of small pulls. Built-ins were often designed back-to-back in adjoining rooms; in this way, their contents could be used from either room. Cupboard-door frames were assembled with pinned mortise-and-tenon joints and drawers were carefully dovetailed. Pine was most often used; however, in special buildings other woods were employed for the exposed portions. The wood was lightly painted, stained, or simply clear varnished.

As with built-ins, Shaker cupboards vary in size from small wall units suspended from pegboards to monumental free-standing pieces that barely clear the ceiling. Communal living imposed a different set of demands on furniture and, therefore, in the quest for efficiency and order, considerable variation in forms was made. Large cupboards were not exceptionally overwhelming because the arrangement of their drawers, doors, and pulls generally presented a harmonious design of lines and mass. Stools with two or more steps were used to reach upper drawers and cupboards. The configuration of drawers and cupboards followed no prescribed pattern. While cupboards were usually placed at the top, examples exist where cupboards were installed in the middle or at the base. The decision as to the placement and size of cupboards and drawers within the case frame was determined by the purpose of the piece. Cupboard-door panels were either flat or fielded (raised) and door frames were assembled with mortise-

and-tenon joints, usually double pinned. Eastern cupboards were invariably made of pine finished in a wash coat of red or yellow paint. Walnut and cherry were species often used in Ohio and Kentucky pieces, and were generally finished in clear varnish.

1. This built-in cupboard and drawers is in a work room in the sisters' shop of the Upper Canaan family. The family, a branch of the New Lebanon North family, was started in 1813, fully organized by 1821, and dissolved in 1897. The sisters' shop built in 1854 still stands and is currently a private residence. The two-story building originally had eight rooms, with four on each floor, and each contained identical built-ins. On the ground floor a wall separating two rooms was removed and a fireplace added by the owner. The built-ins are made of pine that has mellowed to a warm brown. The flat, paneled doors have pinned mortise-and-tenon joints and the drawers are constructed with shouldered dovetails at the front corners and open dovetails at the back. The undersurface of the bottoms is tapered and let into grooves cut into the drawer sides and front. The doors and drawers still open and close with ease. The brass cupboard-door latches were commercially manufactured and purchased by the Shakers. Collection of John S. Roberts.

H. 98-3/4, W. 44-5/8, D. 21.

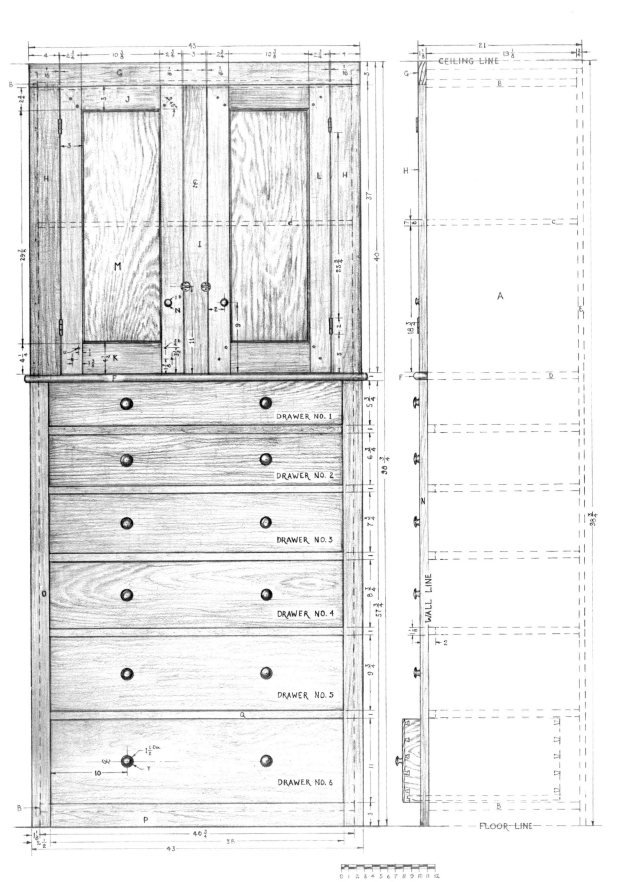

DRAWER NO. 1

DRAWER NO. 2

DRAWER NO. 3

DRAWER NO. 4

DRAWER NO. 5

DRAWER NO. 6

CEILING LINE

WALL LINE

FLOOR LINE

0 1 2 3 4 5 6 7 8 9 10 11 12
Scale in Inches

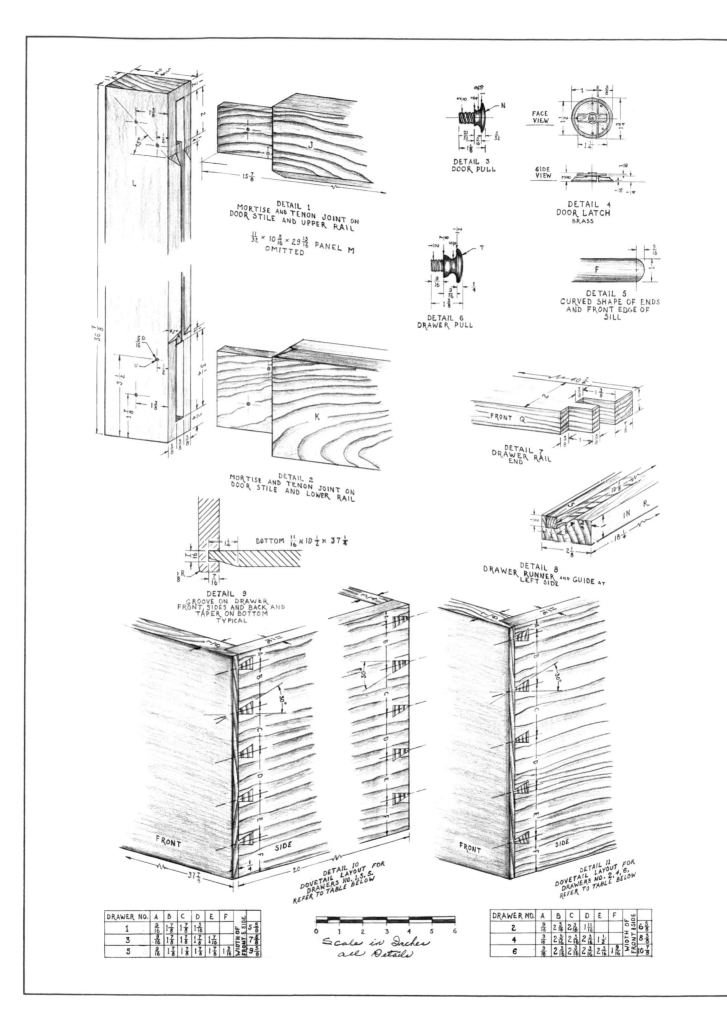

DETAIL 1
MORTISE AND TENON JOINT ON
DOOR STILE AND UPPER RAIL

$\frac{11}{32} \times 10\frac{5}{16} \times 29\frac{13}{16}$ PANEL M
OMITTED

DETAIL 2
MORTISE AND TENON JOINT ON
DOOR STILE AND LOWER RAIL

DETAIL 3
DOOR PULL

DETAIL 4
DOOR LATCH
BRASS

FACE VIEW

SIDE VIEW

DETAIL 5
CURVED SHAPE OF ENDS
AND FRONT EDGE OF
SILL

DETAIL 6
DRAWER PULL

DETAIL 7
DRAWER RAIL
END

DETAIL 8
DRAWER RUNNER AND GUIDE AT
LEFT SIDE

BOTTOM $\frac{11}{16} \times 10\frac{1}{2} \times 37\frac{1}{4}$

DETAIL 9
GROOVE ON DRAWER
FRONT, SIDES AND BACK AND
TAPER ON BOTTOM
TYPICAL

FRONT

SIDE

DETAIL 10
DOVETAIL LAYOUT FOR
DRAWERS NO. 1, 3, 5,
REFER TO TABLE BELOW

FRONT

SIDE

DETAIL 11
DOVETAIL LAYOUT FOR
DRAWERS NO. 2, 4, 6,
REFER TO TABLE BELOW

Scale in Inches
all Details

DRAWER NO.	A	B	C	D	E	F	WIDTH OF FRONT & SIDE
1	$\frac{9}{16}$	$1\frac{7}{8}$	$1\frac{7}{8}$	$1\frac{3}{16}$			$5\frac{5}{16}$
3	$\frac{9}{16}$	$1\frac{1}{8}$	$1\frac{1}{8}$	$1\frac{1}{2}$	$1\frac{7}{8}$		$7\frac{3}{16}$
5	$\frac{9}{16}$	$1\frac{7}{8}$	$1\frac{7}{8}$	$1\frac{1}{8}$	$1\frac{7}{8}$	$1\frac{3}{16}$	$9\frac{5}{16}$

DRAWER NO.	A	B	C	D	E	F	WIDTH OF FRONT & SIDE
2	$\frac{9}{16}$	$2\frac{5}{16}$	$2\frac{3}{16}$	$1\frac{11}{16}$			$6\frac{5}{16}$
4	$\frac{9}{16}$	$2\frac{5}{16}$	$2\frac{3}{16}$	$2\frac{3}{16}$	$1\frac{1}{2}$		$8\frac{3}{16}$
6	$\frac{9}{16}$	$2\frac{5}{16}$	$2\frac{3}{16}$	$2\frac{3}{16}$	$2\frac{5}{16}$	$1\frac{9}{16}$	$10\frac{7}{8}$

Figure 1

Letter	No.	Name	Material	T	W	L
A	2	sides	pine	1-1/8	19-7/8	98
B	2	top and bottom	pine	1-1/8	19-1/8	40-3/4
C	1	cupboard shelf	pine	7/8	19-1/8	40-3/4
D	1	cupboard bottom	pine	1	19-1/8	40-3/4
E	1	back (5 pcs t-and-g)	pine	3/4	40-3/4	98
F	1	sill	pine	1	1-7/8	44-5/8
G	1	cupboard frame rail	pine	1-1/8	3	43
H	2	stiles	pine	1-1/8	4	37
I	1	center stile	pine	1-1/8	3	37
J	2	door upper rail	pine	1-1/8	3	15-7/8
K	2	door lower rail	pine	1-1/8	4-1/2	15-7/8
L	4	door stiles	pine	1-1/8	3	36-7/8
M	2	door panels	pine	11/32	10-5/16	29-13/16
N	2	door pulls	maple	1 dia		1-1/8
O	2	drawer frame stiles	pine	1-1/8	2-1/2	57-3/4
P	1	drawer frame rail	pine	1-1/8	3	40-3/4
Q	5	drawer rails	pine	1	2	40-3/4
R	10	drawer runners	pine	1	2-1/8	18-1/4
S	12	drawer guides	pine	1/2	1/2	19-1/8
T	12	drawer pulls	maple	1-1/2 dia		1-3/8
U	16	pins	pine	5/16 dia		1-1/8
Drawer 1						
	1	front	pine	7/8	5-5/8	37-7/8
	2	sides	pine	11/16	5-5/8	20
	1	back	pine	3/4	4-7/8	37-3/4
	1	bottom	pine	11/16	19-1/2	37-1/4
Drawer 2						
	1	front	pine	7/8	6-5/8	37-7/8
	2	sides	pine	11/16	6-5/8	20
	1	back	pine	3/4	5-7/8	37-3/4
	1	bottom	pine	11/16	19-1/2	37-1/4
Drawer 3						
	1	front	pine	7/8	7-5/8	37-7/8
	2	sides	pine	11/16	7-5/8	20
	1	back	pine	3/4	6-7/8	37-3/4
	1	bottom	pine	11/16	19-1/2	37-1/4
Drawer 4						
	1	front	pine	7/8	8-5/8	37-7/8
	2	sides	pine	11/16	8-5/8	20
	1	back	pine	3/4	7-7/8	37-3/4
	1	bottom	pine	11/16	19-1/2	37-1/4
Drawer 5						
	1	front	pine	7/8	9-5/8	37-7/8
	2	sides	pine	11/16	9-5/8	20
	1	back	pine	3/4	8-7/8	37-3/4
	1	bottom	pine	11/16	19-1/2	37-1/4
Drawer 6						
	1	front	pine	7/8	10-7/8	37-7/8
	2	sides	pine	11/16	10-7/8	20
	1	back	pine	3/4	10-1/8	37-3/4
	1	bottom	pine	11/16	19-1/2	37-1/4
Hardware						
	2 pr	butt hinges	iron		1	2
	2	door latches	brass			

2. Typical of nineteen others in the brick dwelling house of the Hancock Church family is this built-in cupboard and drawers storage system. All are beautiful examples of the cabinetmaker's art. The dwelling was built in 1830 to accommodate a growing population and housed nearly one hundred Believers. The building contains 245 cupboard doors and 369 drawers. These storage units were placed in the corners of the rooms and by the sides of chimneys. The cupboards are pine and the drawer fronts are butternut, all stained warm brown. Pine was used for all interior construction. The flat cupboard-door panels required less time and skill to make than the fielded type and were most often used in built-ins. Collection of Shaker Community, Inc., Hancock, Mass.

H. 102, W. 68, D. 21.

3. This built-in cupboard and drawers is in the South Union center house which was built in 1824. This western Shaker community was formed in 1807, reached a peak population of 400 in the decade 1830–1840, gradually declined, and was dissolved in 1922. Fireplaces for heating buildings were common architectural features in western communities; however, with few exceptions, northern Shaker buildings were designed with smaller chimneys which adequately accommodated the small Shaker-designed, cast-iron stoves. The cupboard frame, doors, drawer fronts, and pulls are cherry; the interior construction is pine and poplar. Collection of Shaker Museum, South Union, Ky.

H. 91-1/2, W. 35, D. 17.

4. The labels on the cupboard doors and drawers of this built-in imply they stored a variety of herbs no doubt used in the manufacture of herbal medicines. The building that contained this built-in is unknown and probably no longer stands, but the unit is not unlike those found in New Lebanon. The medicinal herb industry was established in that community in 1800, flourished throughout the century and was still processing and marketing herbs in 1933. Photograph courtesy of the Smithsonian Institution, Washington, D. C.

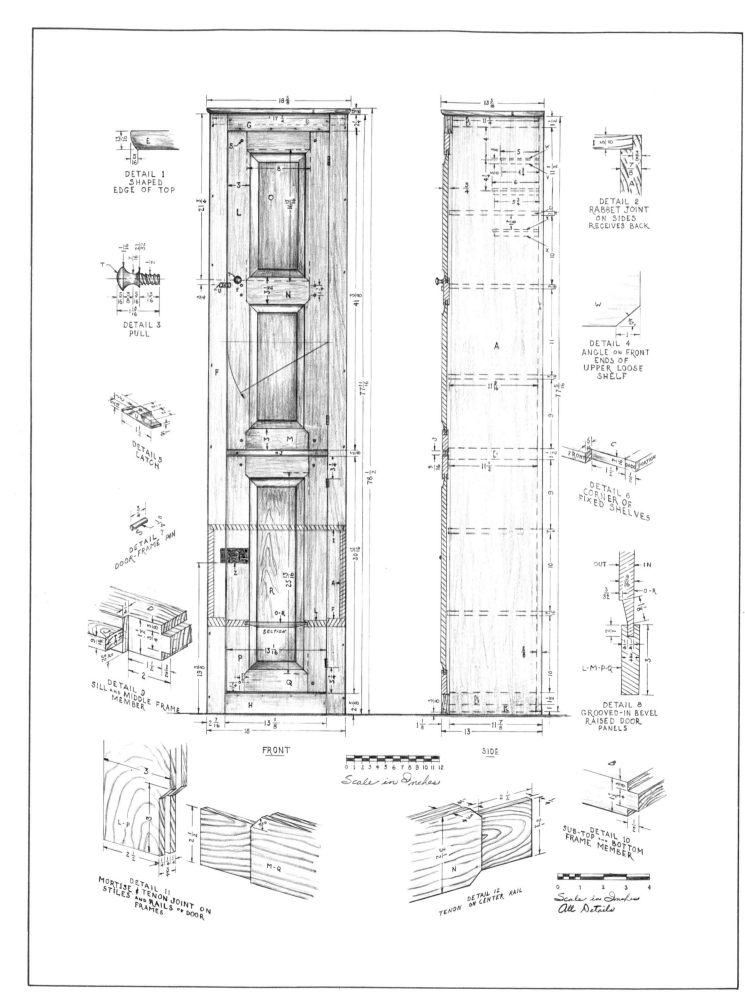

DETAIL 1
SHAPED
EDGE OF TOP

DETAIL 3
PULL

DETAIL 5
LATCH

DETAIL 7
DOOR-FRAME PIN

DETAIL 9
SILL AND MIDDLE FRAME
MEMBER

DETAIL 2
RABBET JOINT
ON SIDES
RECEIVES BACK

DETAIL 4
ANGLE ON FRONT
ENDS OF
UPPER LOOSE
SHELF

DETAIL 6
CORNER OF
FIXED SHELVES

DETAIL 8
GROOVED-IN BEVEL
RAISED DOOR
PANELS

FRONT

SIDE

Scale in Inches

DETAIL 11
MORTISE & TENON JOINT ON
STILES AND RAILS OF DOOR
FRAMES

DETAIL 12
TENON ON CENTER RAIL

DETAIL 10
SUB-TOP AND BOTTOM
FRAME MEMBER

Scale in Inches
All Details

Letter	No.	Name	Material	T	W	L
A	2	sides	pine	7/8	11-7/8	77-11/16
B	2	sub top and bottom	pine	1-1/2	11-1/4	17-1/4
C	5	shelves	pine	7/16	11-9/16	17-1/4
D	1	middle frame member	pine	1-1/2	11-1/2	17-1/4
E	1	top	pine	13/16	13-5/16	18-5/8
F	2	frame stiles	pine	1-1/8	2-7/16	77-11/16
G	1	top frame rail	pine	1-1/8	2-1/4	13-1/8
H	1	bottom frame rail	pine	1-1/8	2-5/8	13-1/8
I	1	back	pine	5/8	17-1/4	77-5/16
J	1	sill	pine	9/16	7/8	13-1/8
K	2	cleats	pine	1	1	11-1/4
Upper door						
L	2	stiles	pine	3/4	3	41-3/8
M	2	rails	pine	3/4	3	13-1/16
N	1	center rail	pine	3/4	3-1/2	13-1/16
O	2	panels	pine	9/16	8	16-15/16
Lower door						
P	2	stiles	pine	3/4	3	30-13/16
Q	2	rails	pine	3/4	3	13-1/16
R	1	panel	pine	9/16	8	25-13/16
S	12	pins	pine	1/4 dia		3/4
T	1	pull	pine	1-1/16 dia		1-13/16
U	1	latch	pine	5/16	1/2	1-1/2
V	2	shelf supports	pine	7/16	5/8	4-3/4
W	1	shelf	pine	3/8	5	16-1/4
X	4	shelf supports	pine	7/16	5/8	5-3/4
Y	2	shelfs	pine	3/8	6	16-1/4
Hardware						
Z	1	cupboard latch	steel		2	3-5/8
	4	butt hinges	steel		3/4	1

5. Free-standing, tall, narrow cupboards, though not rare, are somewhat uncommon. They probably were designed to fit a given space and to house specific items. This New Lebanon cupboard of pine painted dark red dates from the first half of the nineteenth century and was made to hold tinware. The two cupboard doors are interesting and puzzling; while nearly equal in length, the upper door has two fielded panels whereas the lower, only one. Also unusual and more complicated to make are the mitered corners on the square-shouldered mortise-and-tenon joints of the door-frame members. Five fixed shelves are rabbeted and glued into the sides, and the front frame and back are nailed in place. Collection of the Metropolitan Museum of Art, Purchase, 1966, Friends of the American Wing Fund. Photograph courtesy of the museum.

H. 78-1/2, W. 18-5/8, D. 13-5/16.

6. The lower part of this two-door cupboard contains one shelf while the upper portion has three. It is pine painted red on the outside and off-white (oyster) on the inside. The cupboard was made in the first half of the nineteenth century at Hancock. Double-pinned mortise-and-tenon joints on the door-frame corners hold the fielded panels securely. The purchased brass pulls are delightfully small for such large doors. The back fits flush with the sides and is nailed in place. Private collection.

H. 85-3/8, W. 35-1/2. D. 13-1/8.

7. On the back of this three-door cupboard from New Lebanon is the following written in red crayon, "January 26, 1837 for J. H." (attempts to identify J. H. have been unsuccessful). The single upper door made using wide stiles necessary, which makes the cupboard facade visually interesting. This portion of the cupboard has a single fixed shelf while the lower part has three shelves, each vertically subdivided into ten large pigeonholes. This suggests that the unit was designed to hold papers, records, and ledgers, and therefore was possibly used in an office. The cupboard is pine that has been left natural, and has developed an attractive honey-colored patina. The maple pulls are original to the piece. The frames of the flat panel doors are assembled with pinned mortise-and-tenon joints. There is a suggestion of a small sill between the doors. The cupboard top has a plain rounded-over molded edge. The unit, including the rabbeted back, is nail assembled. Collection of the Shaker Museum, Old Chatham, N. Y.

H. 53, W. 32, D. 13.

8. The door frame holding the two beaded panels on this pine cupboard is held together with single pins through the corner mortise-and-tenon joints. Although the practice is not rare, generally these joints were double pinned to give greater strength and also to prevent sagging. The cupboard contains shelves and was made in the Enfield, Connecticut, colony, during the first half of the nineteenth century. It has arc cutouts at the base which form legs, a beaded molding on the front corners, and an applied molding on the front and ends of the top. The piece has a clear varnish finish. Collection of Mrs. Edward Deming Andrews. Photograph courtesy of the Smithsonian Institution.

H. 51, W. 20, D. 15.

9. The purpose of this small, single-door, two-shelf cupboard of pine is unknown, as is the function of its single peg. It is painted light brown and was made during the first half of the nineteenth century in the Upper Canaan family. The pins on the door frame are located contrary to customary positioning. Private collection.

H. 40-3/4, W. 15-7/8, D. 11-1/2.

10. This cupboard-chest in pine painted red was made during the first half of the nineteenth century at Watervliet, New York. It has six drawers and two cupboard doors. Of the drawers, the lowest two are the same depth, the middle two are two inches shallower, and the top two are yet more shallow, although not of equal depth. The end stiles were designed to allow the cupboard doors to move laterally in the event the unit expanded or contracted. This is a fine indication of the Shaker craftsman's knowledge of wood and a concern to produce a well-crafted, functional, and lasting piece of furniture. Locks were installed on three drawers and on the right-hand cupboard door. The left door was secured with an inside latch. The cherry pulls are original to the piece. Private collection.

H. 75-1/4, W. 47-7/8, D. 19-3/4.

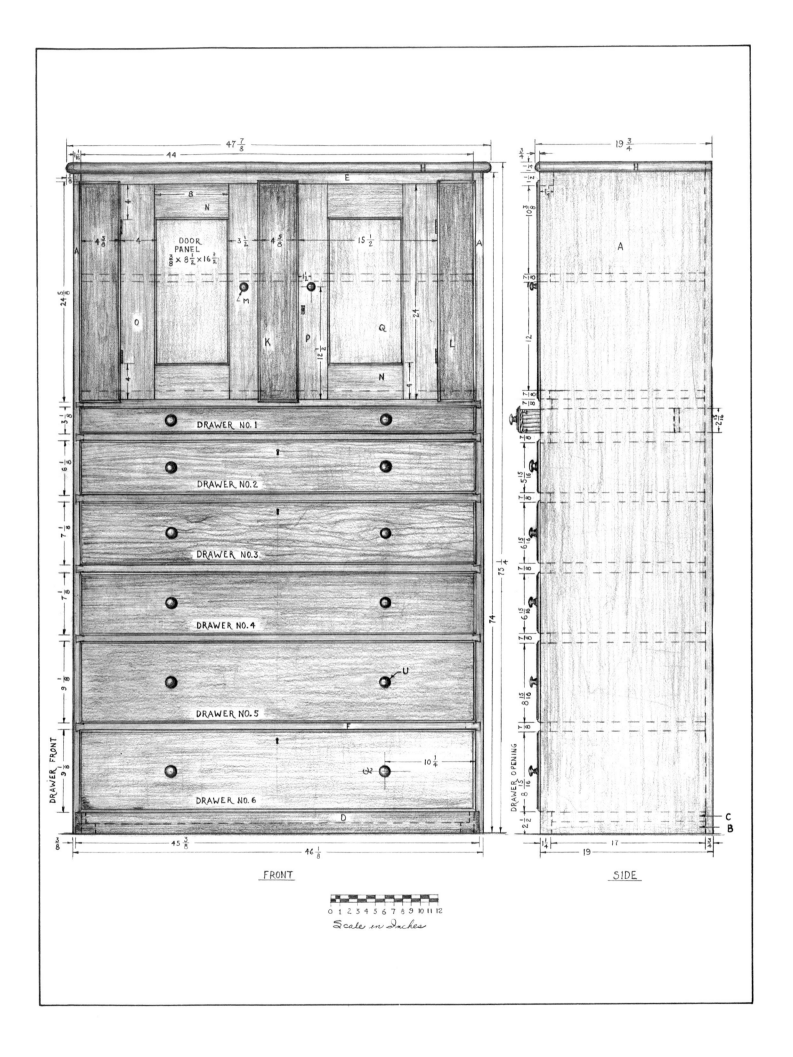

FRONT

SIDE

Scale in Inches

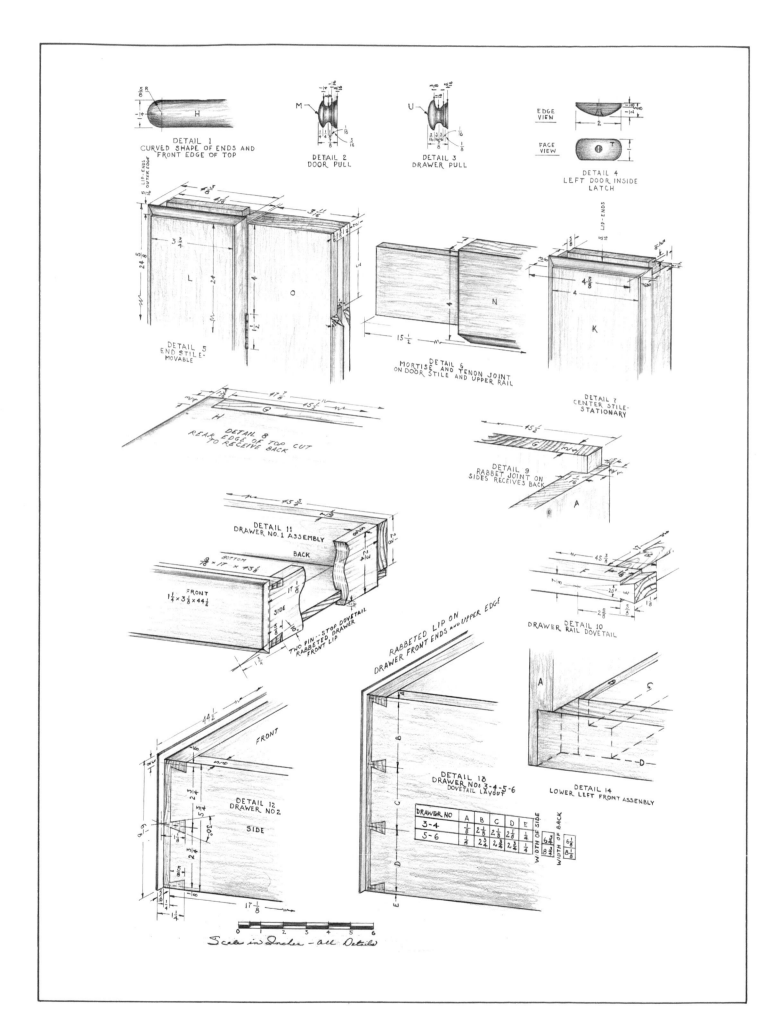

DETAIL 1
CURVED SHAPE OF ENDS AND
FRONT EDGE OF TOP

DETAIL 2
DOOR PULL

DETAIL 3
DRAWER PULL

EDGE VIEW
FACE VIEW

DETAIL 4
LEFT DOOR INSIDE
LATCH

DETAIL 5
END STILE-
MOVABLE

DETAIL 6
MORTISE AND TENON JOINT
ON DOOR STILE AND UPPER RAIL

DETAIL 7
CENTER STILE-
STATIONARY

DETAIL 8
REAR EDGE OF TOP CUT
TO RECEIVE BACK

DETAIL 9
RABBET JOINT ON
SIDES RECEIVES BACK

DETAIL 11
DRAWER NO. 1 ASSEMBLY

BACK

FRONT
$1\frac{1}{4} \times 3\frac{1}{2} \times 44\frac{1}{2}$

BOTTOM
$\frac{3}{16} \times 17 \times 43\frac{5}{8}$

SIDE

TWO PIN - STOP DOVETAIL
RABBETED DRAWER
FRONT LIP

DRAWER DETAIL 10
RAIL DOVETAIL

DETAIL 12
DRAWER NO.2

FRONT

SIDE

RABBETED LIP ON
DRAWER FRONT ENDS AND UPPER EDGE

DETAIL 13
DRAWER NOS. 3-4-5-6
DOVETAIL LAYOUT

DETAIL 14
LOWER LEFT FRONT ASSEMBLY

DRAWER NO	A	B	C	D	E	WIDTH OF SIDE	WIDTH OF BACK
3-4		$2\frac{1}{8}$	$2\frac{1}{8}$				$6\frac{1}{8}$
5-6		$2\frac{3}{4}$	$2\frac{3}{4}$	$2\frac{3}{4}$			$6\frac{1}{8}$

0 1 2 3 4 5 6
Scale in Inches — all Details

Figure 10

Letter	No.	Name	Material	T	W	L
A	2	sides	pine	1-1/16	19	74
B	2	cleat bottom				
		supports	pine	1-1/4	2-1/2	17
C	1	bottom	pine	1-1/8	17	43-1/8
D	1	lower rail	pine	1-1/4	2-1/2	45-3/8
E	1	upper rail	pine	1-1/4	1-1/2	45-3/8
F	6	drawer rails	pine	7/8	1-1/8	45-3/8
G	1	back—6 boards span				
		width	pine	3/4	75-1/4	45-1/2
H	1	top	pine	1-1/4	19-3/4	47-7/8
I	1	cupboard shelf	pine	7/8	17-1/4	44
J	1	cupboard bottom	pine	7/8	17-1/4	44
K	1	center stile	pine	1-3/8	4-5/8	24-5/8
L	2	outer stiles	pine	1-3/8	4-3/8	24-5/8
M	2	pulls	maple	1-1/4 dia		7/8
N	4	door rails	pine	1	4	15-1/2
O	2	door stiles—hinge	pine	1	4	24
P	2	door stiles—lock	pine	1	3-1/2	24
Q	2	panels	pine	3/8	8-1/2	16-1/2
R	10	drawer runners	pine	7/8	1-1/8	17
S	2	cupboard bottom				
		supports	pine	7/8	1-1/8	17
T	1	door latch	maple	5/8	1	2
U	12	drawer pulls	maple	1-3/8 dia		7/8
Drawer 1						
	1	front	pine	1-1/4	3-1/8	44-1/2
	2	sides	pine	5/8	2-3/4	17-1/8
	1	back	pine	7/16	2-1/8	43-3/4
	1	bottom	pine	9/16	17	43-1/8
Drawer 2						
	1	front	pine	1-1/4	6-1/8	44-1/2
	2	sides	pine	5/8	5-3/4	17-1/8
	1	back	pine	7/16	5-1/8	43-3/4
	1	bottom	pine	9/16	17	43-1/8
Drawers 3, 4						
	2	fronts	pine	1-1/4	7-1/8	44-1/2
	4	sides	pine	5/8	6-3/4	17-1/8
	2	backs	pine	7/16	6-1/8	43-3/4
	2	bottoms	pine	9/16	17	43-1/8
Drawers 5, 6						
	2	fronts	pine	1-1/4	9-1/8	44-1/2
	4	sides	pine	5/8	8-3/4	17-1/8
	2	backs	pine	7/16	8-1/8	43-3/4
	2	bottoms	pine	9/16	17	43-1/8
Hardware						
	4	butt hinges	brass		1/2	1-1/2
	1	door lock	iron			
	3	drawer lock	iron			

11. Also from Watervliet, New York, is this pine and poplar cupboard-chest in natural finish. It dates from the first half of the nineteenth century and has an applied molding at the top that is characteristic of cupboards produced in that community. The flat door panels are let into frames that have single-pinned mortise-and-tenon joints. The left door is secured with an inside latch and the right door is fitted with a lock. Collection of the Shaker Museum, Old Chatham, N. Y.

H. 72, W. 43-1/4, D. 21-1/4.

12. Community origin of this early nineteenth-century, two-door, six-drawer cupboard-chest of pine painted red (retouched) is unknown but it is similar to those made in the New Lebanon and Hancock communities. The cupboard doors have fielded panels, pinned mortise-and-tenon frames, finely made small pulls—as do the drawers—and friction door keepers fashioned from metal straps. At one time the right-hand door was fitted with a lock. The six drawers are the same depth, have molded-lip fronts, dovetailed corners, and let-in bottoms. Pegboards at each side have a single peg, the purpose of which is unknown. Collection of Mr. and Mrs. David Castleman.

H. 83, W. 38, D. 19-1/2.

13. The front baseboard on this pine cupboard-chest is hinged to facilitate cleaning under the chest and is an obvious expression of Shaker concern for cleanliness. It was made in the early part of the nineteenth century at New Lebanon and has a varnish finish over natural wood; however, traces of red paint indicate that it was originally painted. The drawers graduate slightly, have molded-lip edges, and are assembled with dovetails and let-in bottoms. Possibly not original to the piece are the uncomely large pulls. The wood grain pattern in the door panels is quite symmetrical and was probably carefully selected to create this effect. Collection of John S. Roberts.

H. 79-3/4, W. 31, D. 19-1/4.

14. The purpose of this small, three-drawer cupboard-chest is not known; however, in meeting the requirements of communal living, it no doubt served many different purposes over the years. The cupboard, made during the first half of the nineteenth century, is pine, stained red-brown, varnished, and assembled with nails. It has slightly curved, molded edges on the top which are in keeping with the relatively plain lines of the piece. A thumb molding on the edge of the drawer front and the porcelain pulls, which were probably installed when the cupboard was made, decorate the drawer fronts. An early iron cupboard-door latch, identical to the one on the cupboard shown in figure 5, secures the door. Normally butt hinges are not surface mounted as they are on this piece, but rather are let into gains cut into the edges of the stile and door. While the ones installed on this piece may not be attractive, they do allow the door to be opened to its fullest width. Private collection.

H. 33, W. 17, D. 10.

15. This New Lebanon cupboard-chest of pine stained brown dates from the second half of the nineteenth century. The piece is a very large free-standing office unit and was probably used by the church trustees. The large graduated drawers have an interesting series of six small drawers above, whose purpose is unknown. Four hinged doors hide interior shelves. Collection of Darrow School, New Lebanon, N. Y.

H. 74-1/4, W. 48, D. 24.

16. The arrangement of the graduated drawers and paneled doors on this exceptionally tall cupboard-chest is harmoniously elegant. The cupboard was used in the New Lebanon school (built in 1839) and dates from that period. The doors are hinged in the middle so that they may be partially or totally opened. Shelves, some vertically divided, line the cupboard and held books. Charts or maps were hung from the two pegs at the top. Collection of Mr. and Mrs. David Andrews. Photograph courtesy of the Smithsonian Institution.

H. 95-1/2, W. 30, D. 15-1/2.

17. Free-standing corner cupboards like the one shown here were not uncommon pieces of furniture in western Shaker communities; however, their use in eastern colonies is questionable. The reason for this may have been a disinclination on the part of members of eastern societies to arrange furniture other than along the walls. A quarter-round molding and grooves to hold the door panel were milled in the edges of the door rails and stiles. The panels were installed in the glued and pinned door frames without glue, so they could expand and contract freely. The cupboard dates from the third decade of the nineteenth century and has a walnut exterior with a varnish or shellac finish. The interior parts are poplar and the porcelain pulls appear to be original. The cove crown molding and scalloped cutouts at the base help make the cupboard an exceptionally attractive ex-

ample of western Shaker cabinetmaking. Collection of Otterbein Home, Lebanon, Ohio. Photograph by Charles R. Muller.

H. 72-1/4, W. across face, 33-1/2, W. overall, 42, D. 18-1/8.

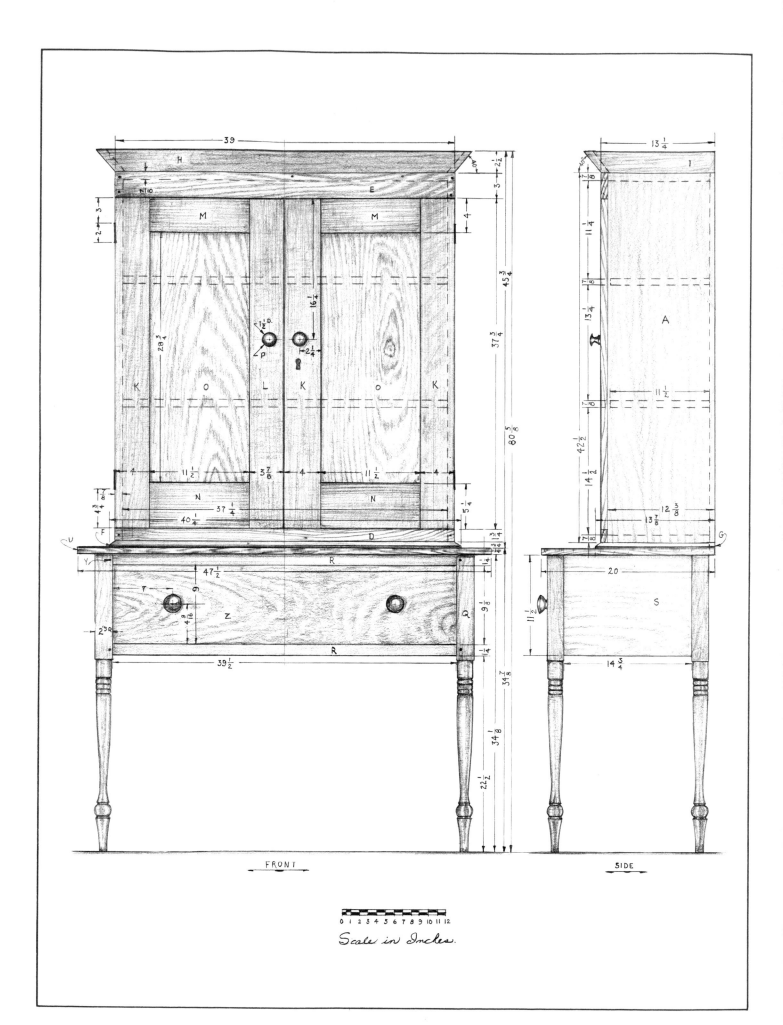

FRONT

SIDE

Scale in Inches.

18. Shaker press cupboards are quite possibly a furniture form made only in the western communities. Their purpose was to store cloth goods such as pillow cases, sheets, and towels after they were laundered and ironed into neatly folded stacks to further help the pressing process. The unit has two parts, a base with a drawer and a two-door shelved cupboard top. It was made in Pleasant Hill in the second half of the nineteenth century and is cherry with a clear varnish finish. The turned legs are mortised to accept triple bareface tenons which are cut on the back and side aprons. Construction of the drawer is typical. The cupboard sides, top, shelves, and bottom are nailed together and the back is rabbeted into the sides and is also nailed. Flat door panels are tapered on the inner surface and let into grooves cut into the mortise-and-tenoned door frames. A fixed crown molding caps the cupboard. Collection of the Shaker Museum, Old Chatham, N. Y.

H. 80-5/8, W. 47-1/2, D. 20.

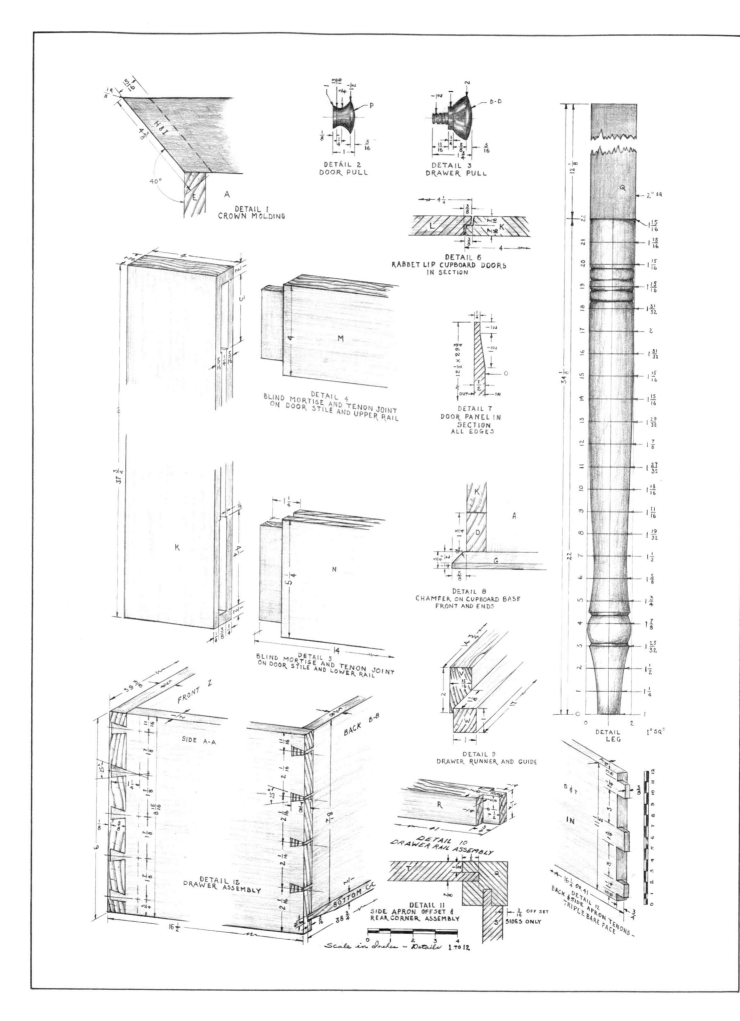

DETAIL 1
CROWN MOLDING

DETAIL 2
DOOR PULL

DETAIL 3
DRAWER PULL

DETAIL 6
RABBET LIP CUPBOARD DOORS
IN SECTION

DETAIL 4
BLIND MORTISE AND TENON JOINT
ON DOOR STILE AND UPPER RAIL

DETAIL 7
DOOR PANEL IN
SECTION
ALL EDGES

DETAIL 5
BLIND MORTISE AND TENON JOINT
ON DOOR STILE AND LOWER RAIL

DETAIL 8
CHAMFER ON CUPBOARD BASE
FRONT AND ENDS

DETAIL 9
DRAWER RUNNER AND GUIDE

DETAIL
LEG

FRONT Z

SIDE A-A

BACK B-B

DETAIL 10
DRAWER RAIL ASSEMBLY

DETAIL 12
DRAWER ASSEMBLY

DETAIL 11
SIDE APRON OFFSET &
REAR CORNER ASSEMBLY

DETAIL 12 APRON TENONS
BACK & SIDE APRON
TRIPLE BARE FACE

Scale in Inches - Details 1 TO 12

Figure 18

Letter	No.	Name	Material	T	W	L
Cupboard						
A	2	sides	cherry	7/8	12-3/8	42-1/2
B	2	top and bottom	cherry	7/8	11-3/4	37-1/4
C	2	shelves	cherry	7/8	11-1/2	37-1/4
D	1	bottom frame	cherry	15/16	1-3/4	39
E	1	top frame	cherry	15/16	3	39
F	1	base front	cherry	3/4	1-11/16	40-1/4
G	2	base sides	cherry	3/4	1-11/16	13-7/8
H	1	front crown molding	cherry	15/16	4-3/8	43-1/2
I	2	side crown moldings	cherry	15/16	4-3/8	15-1/4
J	1	back—4 boards span width	cherry	5/8	38-1/2	42-1/2
K	3	door stiles	cherry	7/8	4	37-5/8
L	1	door stile	cherry	7/8	4-1/4	37-5/8
M	2	door upper rails	cherry	7/8	4	14
N	2	door lower rails	cherry	7/8	5-1/4	14
O	2	door panels	cherry	1/2	12-1/2	29-3/4
P	2	door pulls	cherry	1-1/2 dia		1
Hardware						
	4	hinges	brass		1/2	2
Table						
Q	4	legs	cherry	2 sq		34-1/8
R	2	rails	cherry	7/8	1-1/4	41
S	2	side aprons	cherry	7/8	11-1/2	16-1/4
T	1	back apron	cherry	7/8	11-1/2	41
U	1	top	cherry	3/4	20	47-1/2
V	2	drawer guides	cherry	15/16	2	14-3/4
W	2	drawer runners	cherry	1	1	17
X	1	center guide	cherry	1	1-1/4	17-1/2
Y	4	pins	cherry	1/4 dia		1-3/4
Drawer						
Z	1	front	cherry	3/4	9	39-3/8
A-A	2	sides	poplar	1/2	8-15/16	16-1/2
B-B	1	back	poplar	5/8	8-1/4	39-1/4
C-C	1	bottom	poplar	1/2	16-1/8	38-3/4
D-D	2	pulls	cherry	2 dia		1-3/4

19. Another example of a Kentucky Shaker two-unit press cupboard is this one in varnished cherry. It was made in the South Union community and dates from the first half of the nineteenth century. The base has mildly elaborate, turned legs and a beaded molding on the drawer edges; both are a slight contradiction to the plain, square-edged top. It is assembled with mortise-and-tenon joints. The bottom of the cupboard unit is fastened to the sides with nails; six through-tenons are cut at the upper ends of each side to join corresponding mortises cut into the top. Collection of Shaker Museum, South Union, Ky.

H. 54, W. 43-1/2, D. 19.

20. Also from South Union is this two-unit press cupboard made in the first half of the nineteenth century. The walnut table base has a single drawer assembled with dovetails. Plainly turned legs, a form used in table legs (see Tables, figs. 14 and 15) are a contradiction to the generally accepted concept that western Shaker turnings were always worldly. It is possible that the three-shelf cupboard is not original to the base. The cupboard is poplar, stained walnut, and has mortise-and-tenon doors with fielded panels. The difference between the woods of the base and cupboard, as well as the different treatment of the top edges raises the question as to whether they were initially made to go together or if they are a marriage. If that is the case, it was most likely done by the Shakers. Collection of the Kentucky Library and Museum, Western Kentucky University, Bowling Green, Ky.

H. 57-1/2, W. 39-3/8, D. 19-3/4.

21. The origin of this finely proportioned beautiful sill cupboard of pine is presently unknown, yet its form, materials, construction, and finish are similar to cupboards made in several eastern communities during the first half of the nineteenth century. Four shelves are located in the upper part of the cupboard with the uppermost two each divided into six pigeonholes. The four small sill drawers are very interesting; the inner two are shallower from front to back than the flanking ones and have a secret drawer at their rear. In the chest portion, the drawers are graduated. The middle drawers are fitted with locks which, through an ingenious but simple mechanism, also lock the upper drawers. A rectangularly shaped piece of steel, embedded in the rail directly above the lock, is elevated by the lock bolt and seats into a slot cut into the bottom edge of the upper drawer fronts. The double arc cutout on the lower end of the sides is a rare form. Pigeonholes, secret drawers, and locks sug-

gest the piece was designed to be used in an office. Collection of the Golden Lamb Inn, Lebanon, Ohio.

H. 84-5/8, H. sill, 30-3/4, W. 48, D. base, 17-1/2, D. cupboard, 6-3/4.

22. The numerous pigeonholes in this sill cupboard suggest that this unit was also designed for shop or office use. Built in the first quarter of the nineteenth century in New Lebanon, it has four shelves, two doors, and four drawers, and is pine with a natural patina. The drawers are graduated, although the lower two are the same depth; each is assembled with dovetails and has lipped front edges and original pulls. The precise positioning of the pins on the plain-paneled door frames presents an interesting visual pattern. The upper corners of the cupboard are assembled with well-made open dovetails, an unusual but by no means rare form of construction. Other cupboard parts are assembled with nails. Collection of the Shaker Museum, Old Chatham, N. Y.

H. 80, W. 42-3/4, , D. base, 19-1/8, D. cupboard, 11-1/2.

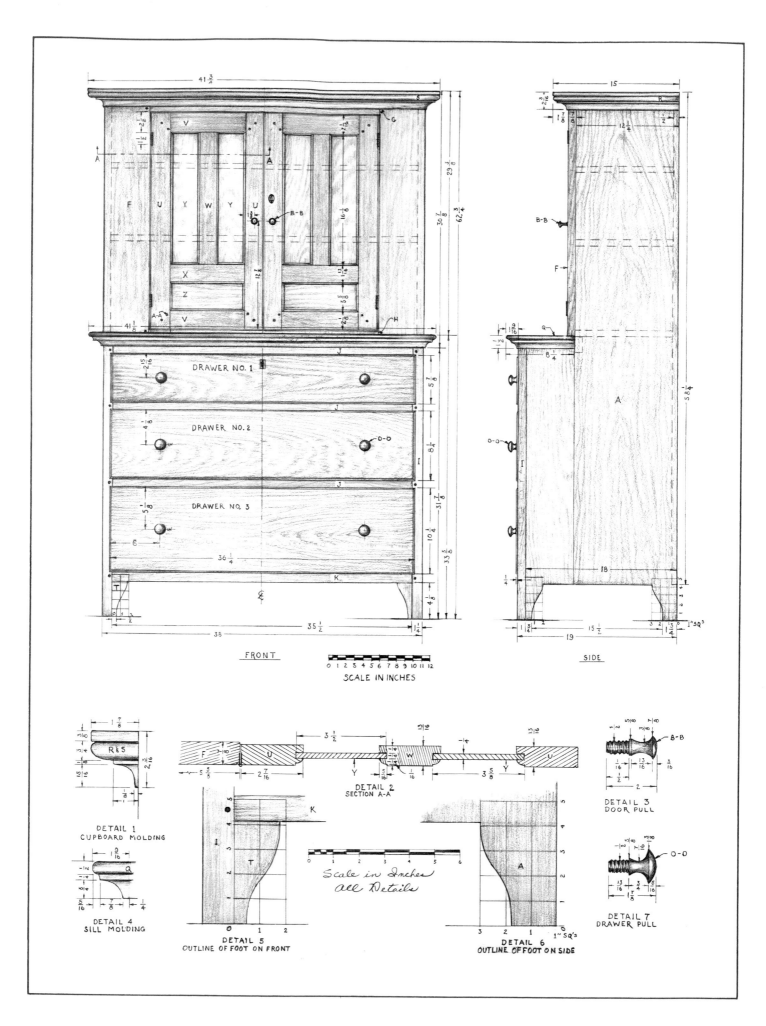

FRONT

SCALE IN INCHES
0 1 2 3 4 5 6 7 8 9 10 11 12

SIDE

DRAWER NO. 1

DRAWER NO. 2

DRAWER NO. 3

DETAIL 1
CUPBOARD MOLDING

DETAIL 4
SILL MOLDING

DETAIL 2
SECTION A-A

DETAIL 5
OUTLINE OF FOOT ON FRONT

Scale in Inches
all Details

0 1 2 3 4 5 6

DETAIL 6
OUTLINE OF FOOT ON SIDE

1" SQ's

DETAIL 3
DOOR PULL

DETAIL 7
DRAWER PULL

23. This two-door, three-drawer sill cupboard is from Watervliet, New York, and was made in the first half of the nineteenth century. The molding at the sill and top is very much like that on the cupboard in figure 11. The door stiles are characteristically wide; the double-pinned mortise-and-tenon joints on the door-frame corners are also typical. However, the divided door panels are a rare style. The graduated drawers are assembled with dovetails and have quarter-round molded lip edges. The pulls may not be original to the piece. If not, then the originals would be more nearly like those on the cupboard in figure 21. Ogee-shaped feet were cut from the sides; a small portion of the cut-away piece was inverted to make the nailed-on ogee foot at the front. Collection of Mrs. Edward Deming Andrews.

H. 62-3/4, W. 41-3/4, D. 20-9/16.

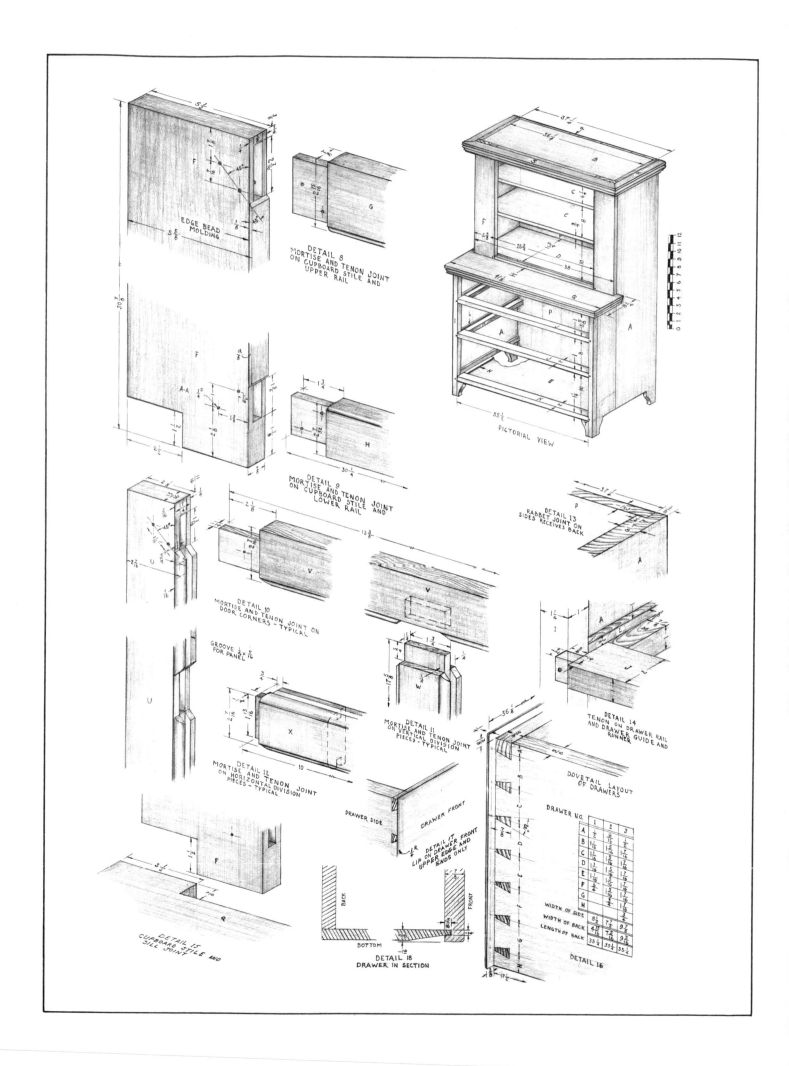

EDGE BEAD
MOLDING

DETAIL 8
MORTISE AND TENON JOINT
ON CUPBOARD STILE AND
UPPER RAIL

DETAIL 9
MORTISE AND TENON JOINT
ON CUPBOARD STILE AND
LOWER RAIL

DETAIL 10
MORTISE AND TENON JOINT ON
DOOR CORNERS - TYPICAL

GROOVE FOR PANEL

DETAIL 12
MORTISE AND TENON JOINT
ON HORIZONTAL DIVISION
PIECES - TYPICAL

DETAIL 11
MORTISE AND TENON JOINT
ON VERTICAL DIVISION
PIECES - TYPICAL

DETAIL 13
RABBET JOINT ON
SIDES RECEIVES BACK

DETAIL 14
TENON ON DRAWER RAIL
AND DRAWER GUIDE AND
RUNNER

PICTORIAL VIEW

DRAWER SIDE

DRAWER FRONT

DETAIL 17
LIP ON DRAWER FRONT
UPPER EDGE AND
ENDS ONLY

DETAIL 15
CUPBOARD STILE AND
SILL JOINT

DETAIL 18
DRAWER IN SECTION

BACK

FRONT

BOTTOM

DOVETAIL LAYOUT
OF DRAWERS

DETAIL 16

DRAWER NO.	1	2	3
A	1/2	3/8	5/8
B	1 1/16	1 1/4	1 1/4
C	1 1/4	1 5/16	1 5/16
D	1 1/16	1 5/16	1 1/4
E	1 1/16	1 5/16	1 1/4
F	5/8	1 5/16	1 1/4
G		7/8	1 1/16
H			1 1/16
WIDTH OF SIDE			
WIDTH OF BACK	5 1/2	7 1/2	9 1/2
LENGTH OF BACK	4 1/16	7 1/16	9 1/16
	35 1/2	35 1/2	35 1/2

Figure 23

Letter	No.	Name	Material	T	W	L	L
A	2	sides	pine	7/8	18	62-3/4	
B	1	top	pine	3/4	11-3/4	36-1/4	
C	2	cupboard shelves	pine	3/4	11-3/4	36-1/4	
D	1	cupboard bottom	pine	3/4	11-3/4	36-1/4	
E	1	bottom	pine	3/4	16-1/2	36-1/4	
F	2	cupboard end stiles	pine	7/8	5-5/8	30-7/8	
G	1	cupboard upper rail	pine	7/8	2-15/16	30-1/4	
H	1	cupboard lower rail	pine	7/8	2-7/32	30-1/4	
I	2	drawer end stiles	pine	1	1-1/4	31-7/8	
J	3	drawer rails	pine	1	2	37	
K	1	drawer lower rail	pine	1-1/8	2	37	
L	6	drawer guides	pine	3/8	1	17-1/2	
M	4	drawer runners	pine	7/8	1	16-1/2	
N	2	drawer runners	pine	3/8	7/8	16-1/2	
O	1	cupboard bottom support	pine	7/8	1-7/8	36-1/4	
P	1	back—5 boards t-and-g span width	pine	1/2	37-1/4	58-1/4	
Q	1	sill	pine	1-1/2	8-1/4	41-1/8	
R	2	cupboard molding —short	pine	1-7/8	2-3/16	15	
S	1	cupboard molding —long	pine	1-7/8	2-3/16	41-3/4	
T	2	bracket feet	pine	1	1-3/4	4-1/8	
Doors							
U	4	stiles	pine	13/16	2-7/16	25-11/16	
V	4	rails	pine	13/16	2-7/16	13-3/8	
W	2	vertical divisions	pine	13/16	2-7/16	17-5/8	
X	2	horizontal divisions	pine	13/16	2-7/16	10	
Y	4	panels	pine	1/2	3-1/2	16	
Z	2	panels	pine	1/2	3-1/2	9	
A-A	30	pins	pine	1/4 dia		7/8	
B-B	2	pulls	maple	7/8 dia		2	
Drawer 1							
C-C	1	front	pine	7/8	5-7/8	36-1/4	
D-D	2	sides	pine	5/8	5-1/2	17-1/2	
E-E	1	back	pine	5/8	4-15/16	35-1/4	
F-F	1	bottom	pine	1/2	17-1/8	34-1/2	
Drawer 2							
G-G	1	front	pine	7/8	8-1/4	36-1/4	
H-H	2	sides	pine	5/8	7-7/8	17-1/2	
I-I	1	back	pine	5/8	7-5/16	35-1/4	
J-J	1	bottom	pine	1/2	17-1/8	34-1/2	
Drawer 3							
K-K	1	front	pine	7/8	10-1/4	36-1/4	
L-L	2	sides	pine	5/8	9-7/8	17-1/2	
M-M	1	back	pine	5/8	9-5/16	35-1/4	
N-N	1	bottom	pine	1/2	17-1/8	34-1/2	
O-O	6	pulls	maple	1-3/8 dia		1-7/8	

24. This tall, four-drawer sill cupboard was also made in New Lebanon where it saw service in a weave shop. It dates from the first half of the nineteenth century and is made of pine that was originally painted red but since has been refinished natural. The conventionally made drawers were fitted with locks which implies that the contents required security. A very narrow cupboard door sets between very wide stiles and raises the question of how accessible small objects behind the stiles would be. As a weave shop piece, the problem probably was not a serious one. Collection of the Metropolitan Museum of Art, Purchase, 1966, Friends of the American Wing Fund. Photograph courtesy of the museum.

H. 73-1/4, W. 31-1/2, D. 13.

25. Impressive both for its massive size and plain lines is this double cupboard with sill from Enfield, New Hampshire. It is pine painted red and dates from the first half of the nineteenth century. The base has two banks of four graduated drawers and the cupboard unit has four two-panel doors that contain shelves. Woodstove implements probably hung from a small metal bracket (now missing) on the right side of the lower unit. The applied rectangular wooden plate offered some protection against scarring the cupboard side. Collection of the Golden Lamb Inn, Lebanon, Ohio.

H. 85, W. 70, D. base, 19 1/2, D. cupboard, 15-1/4.

26. One of a pair of sill cupboards made in New Lebanon and used in the North family infirmary to store medicinal herbs grown in the physic gardens. The wood is butternut and the piece dates from the first half of the nineteenth century. Each drawer is partitioned and its contents are appropriately labeled on the outside. The porcelain pulls may have been Shaker replacements for wooden ones. Collection of Mr. and Mrs. David Andrews. Photograph courtesy of the Smithsonian Institution.

H. 66, W. 47, D. base, 13-1/4, D. cupboard, 18-1/4.

27. The origin of this wall cupboard of poplar and pine painted red is not known; however, it dates from the early part of the nineteenth century. The corners are dovetailed and the door stiles and back are nailed in place. Of special interest are the early wire door hinges and the double chamfers on the curved portion of the back. The latch is a type found on many Shaker case pieces. Private collection.

H. 24-3/8, W. 13-1/4, D. 8-1/4.

Letter	No.	Name	Material	T	W	L
A	1	back	poplar	1/2	13-1/4	24-3/8
B	2	top and bottom	poplar	1/2	7	13-1/4
C	2	sides	poplar	1/2	7	17-3/8
D	2	stiles	pine	3/4	1-7/16	17-3/8
E	1	door	pine	3/4	10-5/16	17-3/8
F	1	shelf	poplar	7/16	7	12-5/8
G	1	latch	pine	3/8	7/16	1-1/4
Hardware						
H	1	wood screw		FH 3/4" × 6		

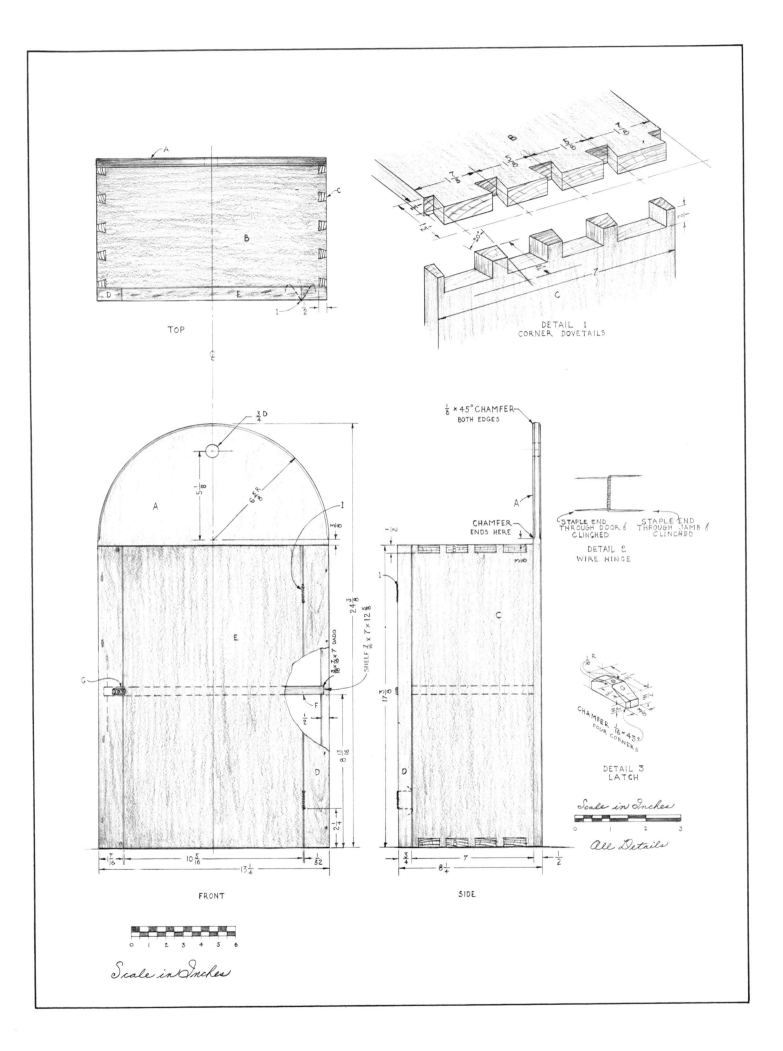

TOP

DETAIL 1
CORNER DOVETAILS

$\frac{1}{8}$ × 45° CHAMFER
BOTH EDGES

STAPLE END
THROUGH DOOR &
CLINCHED

STAPLE END
THROUGH JAMB &
CLINCHED

DETAIL 2
WIRE HINGE

CHAMFER
ENDS HERE

CHAMFER $\frac{1}{16}$ × 45°
FOUR CORNERS

DETAIL 3
LATCH

Scale in Inches

0   1   2   3

All Details

$\frac{3}{4}$ D

5$\frac{1}{8}$

6$\frac{5}{8}$ R

24$\frac{3}{8}$

SHELF $\frac{7}{16}$ × 7 × 12$\frac{5}{8}$

$\frac{7}{16}$ × 7 DADO

8$\frac{13}{16}$

2$\frac{1}{4}$

$\frac{7}{16}$ 10$\frac{5}{16}$ $\frac{1}{32}$

13$\frac{1}{4}$

FRONT

17$\frac{3}{8}$

$\frac{3}{4}$ 7 $\frac{1}{2}$

8$\frac{1}{4}$

SIDE

Scale in Inches

0 1 2 3 4 5 6

28. Few wall cupboards can match the pure Shaker lines of this example. It was made in New Lebanon in the first half of the nineteenth century and is of cherry refinished in clear varnish. The cupboard was used in a sisters' shop where it hung from a nail or pegboard. To keep the cupboard stable, strings were tied to the screw eyes at the top and anchored to adjacent pegs. Candle sconces and wall clocks were also stabilized in the same manner (see Clocks, fig. 6 and Shelves, fig. 7). The top and base have half-round molded edges and the projecting portion of the back is cut in a cyma curve. The cupboard has a shelf and an unnecessary inner bottom. All the components are nailed together. Collection of Shaker Community, Inc., Hancock, Mass.

H. 16-3/16, W. 11-1/2, D. 5-3/16.

29. This second-quarter nineteenth-century, two-shelf, two-door wall cupboard of cherry stained red was made in Pleasant Hill. The two hangers with their series of holes made it possible to adjust the cupboard's height. This suspension system was also used on Kentucky Shaker-made candle sconces (see Shelves, fig. 5) and seems to be an innovation limited to the Kentucky societies. The door frames are assembled with pinned mortise-and-tenon joints, and the flat door panels are in keeping with the cupboard's plain lines. The cupboard is assembled with nails. The cove molding at the cupboard top is mildly ornamental but attractive. Collection of Shakertown at Pleasant Hill, Inc., Harrodsburg, Ky.

H. 38 (includes hangers), W. 37, D. 10.

Cabinets

Four forms of furniture made by the Shakers seem not to have counterparts in furniture made by the world's people. They are sewing cabinets, tailor's and weaver's counters, sewing desks, and sewing stands. All are shop pieces designed to serve the sisters in their tailoring, weaving, and sewing occupations. With the exception of sewing stands (which have a single pedestal supported by three legs) all are case pieces that contain drawers and cupboards, arranged in no standard pattern. Sewing cabinets resemble sewing desks in size and, like desks, have multiple drawers, but do not contain the additional sliding work surface. The exposed parts of sewing cabinets (and sewing desks) were usually made from selected hardwoods and are fine examples of Shaker cabinet-making.

1. In mixed woods, this sewing cabinet from Hancock has eight drawers, all locked by an ingenious system of metal rods and wood cams activated by a key in the central drawer. The frame is cherry and the sides and back panels are pine stained to match. The drawer fronts and top are chestnut and the interior drawer components are of pine. The cabinet is a fine example of early nineteenth-century Shaker craftsmanship, employing the best traditional furniture-making practices. Pinned mortise-and-tenon joints hold the frame together, panels are loose fitted into grooves in the frame (which allows them to expand and contract without restriction), and the top is fastened to the base with wood screws in pocket holes. The drawers have quarter-round molded edges and cherry pulls. The three incised lines at the middle of the turned legs are purely decorative. Collection of Dr. and Mrs. Thomas Kane.

H. 29-1/8, W. 31-1/4, D. 22-3/4.

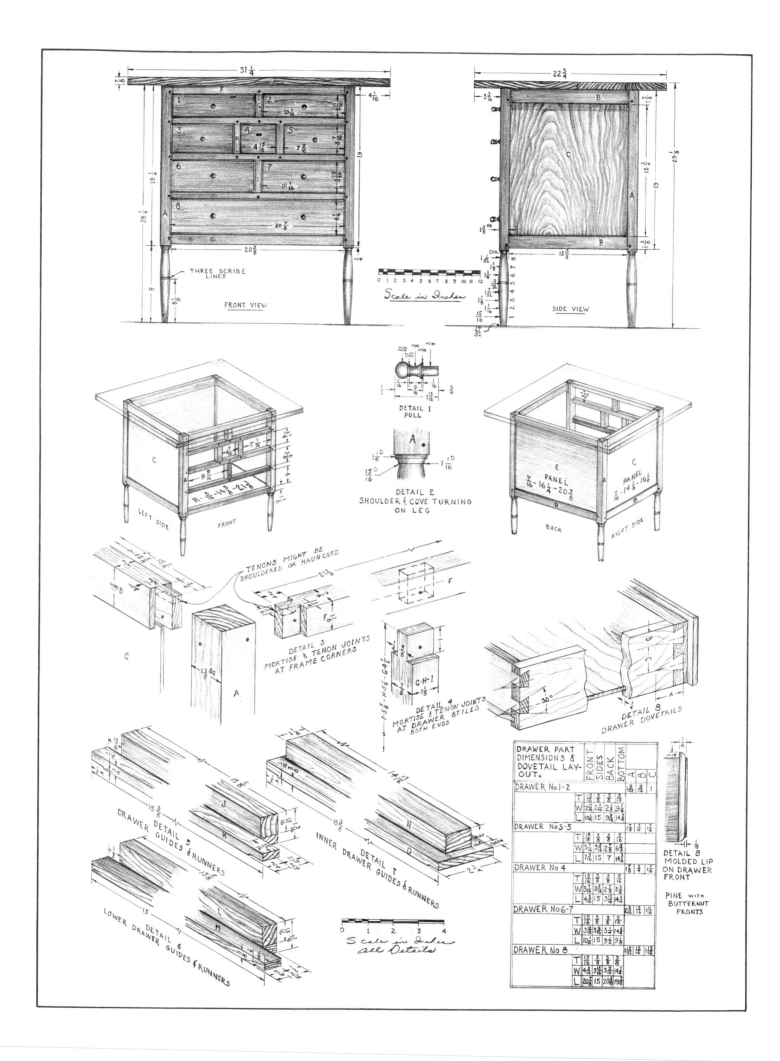

FRONT VIEW

THREE SCRIBE LINES

Scale in Inches

SIDE VIEW

DETAIL 1
PULL

DETAIL 2
SHOULDER & COVE TURNING
ON LEG

LEFT SIDE   FRONT

BACK   RIGHT SIDE

TENONS MIGHT BE
SHOULDERED OR HAUNCHED

DETAIL 3
MORTISE & TENON JOINTS
AT FRAME CORNERS

DETAIL 4
MORTISE & TENON JOINTS
AT DRAWER STILES
BOTH ENDS

DETAIL 8
DRAWER DOVETAILS

DETAIL 5
DRAWER GUIDES & RUNNERS

DETAIL 7
INNER DRAWER GUIDES & RUNNERS

DETAIL 6
LOWER DRAWER GUIDES & RUNNERS

Scale in Inches
all Details

DETAIL 9
MOLDED LIP
ON DRAWER
FRONT

PINE WITH
BUTTERNUT
FRONTS

DRAWER PART DIMENSIONS & DOVETAIL LAY-OUT.	FRONT	SIDES	BACK	BOTTOM	A	B	C
DRAWER No 1-2							
T							
W							
L							
DRAWER No 3-5							
T							
W							
L							
DRAWER No 4							
T							
W							
L							
DRAWER No 6-7							
T							
W							
L							
DRAWER No 8							
T							
W							
L							

Figure 1

Letter	No	Name	Material	T	W	L
A	4	posts	cherry	1-3/8	1-3/8	28-1/4
B	4	side rails	cherry	7/8	1-5/8	15-1/8
C	2	side panels	pine	7/16	14-1/8	16-1/4
D	2	back rails	cherry	7/8	1-5/8	21-7/8
E	1	back panel	pine	7/16	16-1/4	20-7/8
F	5	front rails	cherry	7/8	1-1/8	21-7/8
G	1	upper stile	cherry	7/8	1-1/8	4-1/2
H	2	middle stiles	cherry	7/8	1-1/8	5-1/4
I	1	lower stile	cherry	7/8	1-1/8	5-5/8
J	8	outer drawer guides	pine	11/16	13/16	13-5/8
K	8	outer drawer runners	pine	3/8	1-7/16	15-3/8
L	2	corner drawer guides	pine	1/2	13/16	13-5/8
M	2	corner drawer runners	pine	3/8	1-3/16	15
N	4	inner drawer guides	pine	3/4	1-1/8	14-13/16
O	4	inner drawer runners	pine	3/8	2-1/4	15-3/8
P	2	side supports for bottom	pine	3/8	7/16	13-5/8
Q	2	back and front supports for bottom	pine	3/8	7/16	20-3/8
R	1	bottom panel	pine	3/16	14-5/8	21-3/8
S	1	top	chestnut	7/8	22-3/4	31-1/4
T	30	pins	cherry		3/16 dia	1-11/16
U	8	pulls	cherry		22/32 dia	1-13/16

2. The exposed parts of this five-drawer sewing cabinet are made of maple and the internal parts are pine. The cabinet was made in Hancock and dates from the first half of the nineteenth century. Square, tapered legs are part of the corner posts; the sides of the cabinet are solid rather than paneled and the drop-leaf rests on two pullout supports. The drawers are constructed with traditional joinery. Their fronts have shouldered quarter-round lip edges and pulls of apple or pear. Collection of the American Museum in Britain, Bath, England. Photograph by Derek Balmer.

H. 27, W. 37, D. 15-3/4, D. with leaf up, 24-1/4.

3. Another exceptionally fine example of Shaker furniture is this six-drawer sewing cabinet. It was probably built by Brother James Smith, Jr. (1806–1880), of the New Lebanon community. Stamped along the front left, shouldered dovetails of the middle drawer is "Jas. X. Smith New-Lebanon N.Y" and the date 1843 is stamped at the other end. It is in mixed woods: the cabinet frame, top, and drawer fronts are cherry; the panels are butternut; and the interior parts are pine, basswood, and sycamore. The tapers on the inner surfaces of the corner posts form exceptionally pleasing legs and the quirk-bead molding on the frame members and around the drawer fronts are atypical Shaker work. The maple rim around the top has a portion of a yardstick applied to the front edge and probably was used for measuring cloth. Collection of the Metropolitan Museum of Art, Purchase, 1966, Friends of the American Wing Fund. Photograph courtesy of the museum.

H. 28, W. 32-1/2, D. 23-1/2.

Chairs

Included in this section are dining chairs, work chairs, side chairs, armchairs, rocking chairs, arm-rocking chairs, highchairs, and swivel chairs.

Shaker chair design grew out of the earlier slat-back or ladder-back chairs that were developed by seventeenth- and eighteenth-century New England chair makers. They were common pieces of furniture found in most every New England home, and, therefore, forms well known to early Shakers. A number of converts brought their slat-backs when they joined the order as well as some knowledge of how they were made. The slat-back chair was light and strong, functional and graceful, easily and quickly produced requiring few hand tools and a simple turning lathe. After the jigs and fixtures were made, they could be mass produced. Chairs were made for a specific purpose and in sizes to fit individuals for whom they were intended. Most were made of maple, sometimes curly or bird's-eye, but a few examples in cherry, birch, and walnut are extant. Many, if not all, Shaker communities made

chairs at one time or another. The earliest records of chairs made for sale are found in the New Lebanon Church family trustees' accounts and date from 1789. At first, production was small, sporadic, indeterminate, and limited to making side chairs for the community's use, with any excess sold to the world or to other Shaker families and colonies. Production continued to increase slowly until about 1852, when the need for greater standardization was recognized and implemented.

For many years Brother Robert Wagon (1833–1883) helped supervise chair making at the New Lebanon Second family chair factory. It was largely through his efforts that the foundation of a prosperous industry was established. Brother Robert realized that in order to meet the growing demand for Shaker chairs and to compete with their worldly counterparts, and also to discourage widespread imitation, it would be necessary to update factory equipment, increase production, and advertise widely. He therefore took over as elder of the newly established South

family and in 1873 had a factory built, and equipped with the latest woodworking machinery. He reorganized production methods and standardized the line by numbering chairs according to size. Zero was the smallest child's chair and number seven, the largest adult chair. The number was usually stamped on the back of the upper slat. They were finished in a mahogany or ebony color varnish-stain, or in the natural color of maple wood. Also, to protect the purchaser, the practice of marking chairs and foot benches with a gold decal trade-mark was initiated by this most capable brother. In case the purchaser found the label objectionable, instructions were supplied for its easy removal.

To advertise their line of chairs, an illustrated catalogue was issued by Elder Robert in 1874 (foot benches, chair cushions, and floor rugs were also included). Subsequent catalogues retained basically the same format and content for the next forty years. Production of factory chairs peaked sometime after the Philadelphia Centennial Exposition of 1876 where the Shakers had a display booth and exhibited chairs and footstools and were awarded a diploma and medal for combining strength, sprightliness, and modest beauty in their chairs. Chair making, at least in the New Lebanon community (which eventually became the center of the industry for the entire society), seems to have gone through three more or less distinct styles and chronological periods. The first, from 1789 to about 1815, is marked by chairs that are sturdy, physically heavy, and somewhat crude in form; the middle period ran to 1863 during which the finest examples were produced; and the final phase —the era of "mass production" which lasted until about 1935 when chair production was terminated—is distinguished by a sameness in Shaker design. Although well built and attractive, chairs of this final phase reflect an erosion of folk craftsmanship.

The number of slats in a chair back was determined by the height of the back; dining and work chairs were made with one or two slats, side chairs were usually made with three slats, and armchairs had three, four, and, less frequently, five slats. The number of slats in rocking chairs was decided by the same condition. For greater strength, slats were never sawn to a curve but were steamed and bent around a mold and allowed to dry. In some cases, the profile and shape of the upper edge of the slat can be helpful in ascertaining the origin and date of a chair.

To secure the slats to the posts usually only the top slat was pinned, from the back. However, on some early examples all the slats were pinned. The cross-sectional shape of these pins is another helpful clue in establishing the approximate age of a chair. The earliest were whittled out by hand and are irregularly shaped, whereas later pins were machine made and are uniformly cylindrical. On late period chairs, flat-head wood screws were used for the same purpose.

The pattern of rung arrangement usually has one rung at the rear and two on the sides and front. The rungs of the earliest chairs and often middle period chairs were largest at mid-point and tapered in a gentle curve down to a dowel at each end. Immediately prior to the Civil War and thereafter, tapered rungs were superseded by straight, dowellike rungs, although the two front rungs remained tapered for strength. Rungs were made from ash, hickory, and, later, maple.

The upper end of the back posts of Shaker slat-backs terminates, in most examples, in comely finials. Some styles have been labeled as nipple, candle-flame, and acorn, with the last having manifold forms. Certain styles have become associated with specific communities and are used as aids in determining the age and community provenance or at least the regional origin of a chair.

A few rocking chairs were made at New Lebanon before 1800, but did not become popular until the early years of the nineteenth century when the Believers began producing them on a limited scale. The first rocking chairs were made from regular chairs whose posts and legs had been modified to hold runners. Originally intended for aged or infirm brothers and sisters, they soon were part of the prescribed furnishings in every retiring-room. Shaker rocking chairs, by the nature of the arms, may be classified into three groups: the mushroom-finial type, the scroll-arm type, and the rolled-arm type. The sewing rockers (rocking chairs without arms) and the later cushion-rail type are two other groups. On late period factory chairs the shape of the thin, flat arm was standardized and retained until the end of production.

The method by which runners were attached to the chair varied. The earliest type was fitted up into slots cut in the legs and posts. On other examples, the runners were pinned to notches cut on the sides of the legs and posts. In yet another style, the bottoms of the legs and posts were tapered and doweled into flat runners, and pinned from the side of the runners. Runners were cut to no fixed pattern. On early chairs they are a high-cradle or "sled" runner shape which usually did not project beyond the front legs and extended only a few inches behind the back posts. On others, runners are abruptly wide where they join the legs and post. Probably the most attractive are those whose thickness is not much more than ¼ inch with a rounded-over, short projecting front, a

continuous graceful curve between the leg and post, and an equally attractive but much shorter curve at the rear projecting end. The runner form which eventually became a standard by 1863 can be traced from about the middle of the nineteenth century.

Like most furniture made during the early formative years of the society, side, arm, and rocking chairs were painted, ussually a dark red. This practice soon gave way to using thinned paints in different colors as a stain or wash coat. Also clear varnish, shellac, and various oils were used. Production chairs were dipped in vats of home-made stains and were available in mahogany, walnut, ebony, and natural color.

Materials used to upholster seats of chairs made during the initial and second period were splint, rush, woven straw, cane, and (rarely) leather. Starting about 1830 mild colored, narrow, worsted tape called "listing" was made of home-grown wool on Shaker-made looms and woven in different patterns for chair seats and backs. Later, catering to worldly taste, brightly colored cotton canvas tapes and plushes (a thick,

deep pile fabric) were used as upholstery materials.

Late period chairs were made in several styles and sizes and retailed on the grounds and wholesaled in major cities along the Atlantic seaboard and as far west as Chicago. Thousands of chairs and footstools were produced in the New Lebanon chair factories (there were four during the life of this community, 1787–1947), most of which were made in the Second and South families.

Chairs made in the Ohio and Kentucky societies tend to be heavier than their eastern counterparts. The back posts on some chairs have finials, on others they are flattened on the front surface starting from above the seat to the top. The shape is referred to as "mule ears." The slats, as many as four, often have quarter-circle cutouts (corner notched) at each end where they joined the posts and are secured with metal pins, a practice unheard of in the east. Side and armchairs generally have posts that terminate at the floor line in a sharp taper much like the front legs of both eastern and western chairs. On chairs having side-scroll arms, the arms are often very wide.

1. This two-slat dining chair (c. 1830) is from Watervliet, New York. It is of maple stained light brown and has a splint seat. Long benches were first used in the large communal dining halls where the sisters and brothers took their meals at separate tables. Dining halls were located near the kitchen, usually on the first floor of the dormitory-type dwellings. Benches were replaced with one-slat low-back chairs. Later, two-slat chairs were made for greater support. These low-back chairs could easily be moved for cleaning the floor or hung out of the way on pegrails. When placed under the table they made setting, serving, and clearing the table easier and gave an ordered appearance to the dining hall. The high placement of the stretcher on trestle tables, a Shaker innovation, made this convenience possible. On this chair, the upper ends of the back posts and front legs were simply rounded over. The lower ends of the front legs are tapered whereas the back posts terminate at the floor line in a straight, full diameter. All rungs are taper-turned except the front seat rung which is elliptical in cross section, designed to impart greater structural strength and longer life to the seating material. The back slats were curved for greater comfort. Collection of the Shaker Museum, Old Chatham, N. Y.

H. 25-5/8, W. 18-13/16, D. 14-11/16.

Letter	No.	Name	Material	T	W	L
A	2	back posts	maple	1-7/16 dia		25-5/8
B	2	front legs	maple	1-7/16 dia		17-1/8
C	2	slats	maple	1/4	2	13-1/4
D	1	seat—back stretcher	maple	13/16	1-1/2	13-9/16
E	1	back rung	maple	3/4 dia		13-9/16
F	2	seat—side stretchers	maple	13/16	1-1/2	13-9/16
G	4	side rungs	maple	3/4 dia		13-9/16
H	1	seat—front stretcher	maple	13/16	1-1/2	17-11/16
I	2	front rung	maple	13/16 dia		17-11/16
J	2	pins for slat	maple	1/4 dia		1-1/2

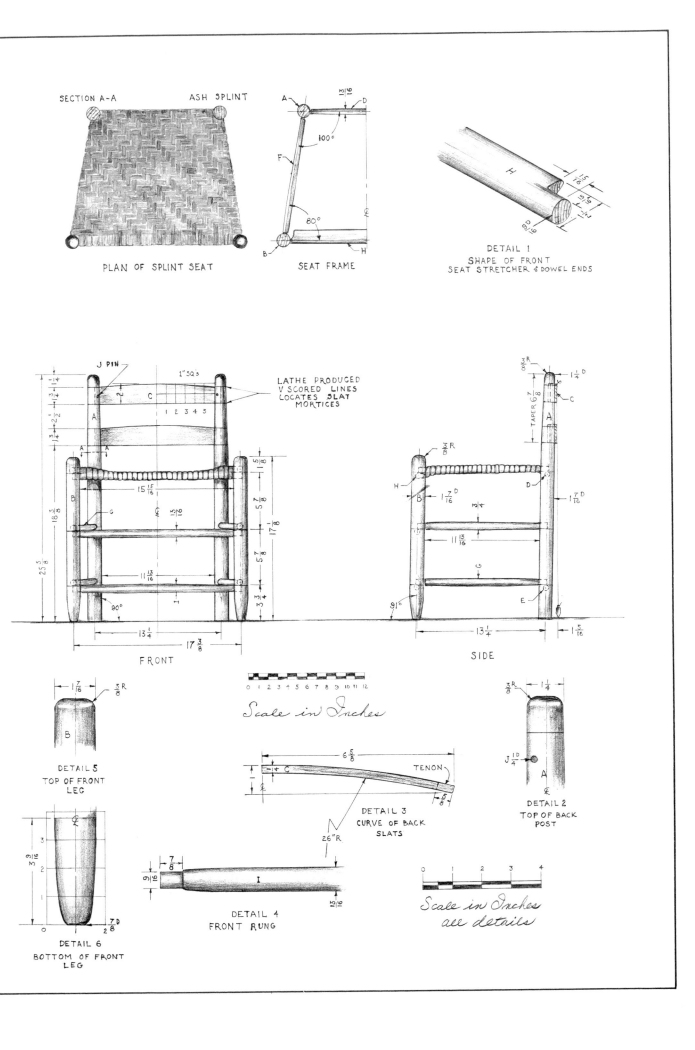

SECTION A-A   ASH SPLINT

PLAN OF SPLINT SEAT   SEAT FRAME

100°
80°
A
F
B
H
D
$\frac{13}{16}$

DETAIL 1
SHAPE OF FRONT
SEAT STRETCHER & DOWEL ENDS

H
$\frac{15}{16}$
$\frac{9}{16}$
$\frac{1}{2}$
D $\frac{9}{16}$

J PIN
1" SQ'S
LATHE PRODUCED
V SCORED LINES
LOCATES SLAT
MORTICES

$1\frac{1}{4}$
$1\frac{3}{16}$
$2\frac{1}{2}$
$3\frac{1}{4}$
C
A
A A
B
G
2
1 2 3 4 5
$15\frac{15}{16}$
$1\frac{5}{8}$
$\frac{15}{16}$
$18\frac{3}{8}$
$25\frac{5}{8}$
80°
$11\frac{13}{16}$
$5\frac{7}{8}$
$17\frac{1}{8}$
$5\frac{7}{8}$
1
$3\frac{3}{4}$
$13\frac{1}{4}$
$17\frac{3}{8}$

FRONT

$\frac{1}{8}$R
$1\frac{1}{4}$ D
TAPER $6\frac{7}{8}$
A
C
S
$\frac{3}{8}$R
H
B
D
$1\frac{7}{16}$ D
$\frac{3}{4}$
$1\frac{7}{16}$ D
$11\frac{13}{16}$
G
E
91°
$13\frac{1}{4}$
$1\frac{5}{16}$

SIDE

Scale in Inches
0 1 2 3 4 5 6 7 8 9 10 11 12

$1\frac{7}{16}$
$\frac{3}{8}$R
B

DETAIL 5
TOP OF FRONT
LEG

$6\frac{5}{8}$
C
TENON
$\frac{5}{8}$
DETAIL 3
CURVE OF BACK
SLATS
26"R

$\frac{3}{4}$R
$1\frac{1}{4}$
J $\frac{1}{4}$ D
A

DETAIL 2
TOP OF BACK
POST

$3\frac{9}{16}$
3
2
1
0
$\frac{7}{8}$ D
$2\frac{3}{8}$

DETAIL 6
BOTTOM OF FRONT
LEG

$\frac{7}{8}$
$\frac{9}{16}$
I
$\frac{13}{16}$

DETAIL 4
FRONT RUNG

0 1 2 3 4
Scale in Inches
all details

2. The origin of this one-slat dining chair is attributed to Hancock; however, the high arced, heavily beveled upper edge of the back slat and the nipple finials on the posts are forms that were also used on dining chairs made in the Watervliet, New York, community. The chair is made of maple and beech, finished with clear varnish. Collection of the Metropolitan Museum of Art, Purchase, 1966, Friends of the American Wing Fund. Photgraph courtesy of the museum.

H. 26, W. 17-1/4, D. 12-1/4.

3. Also from the Watervliet, New York, community is this two-slat dining chair. It dates from the mid-nineteenth century, is maple with a tape seat, and is especially interesting because of the tilting buttons ("tilters") on the back posts. Tilters are wooden half-balls that were installed in half-round sockets cut into the bottoms of the posts. The backward lean on early Shaker chairs made them comfortable for sitting but susceptible to tipping; therefore,the swiveling tilter, with its flat underside resting on the floor, tended to eliminate this problem; also, rugs and floors were spared from undue wear and marring. The buttons are held in place with a raw-hide thong knotted on the end and pulled through a hole in the button, and on through another hole in the bottom of the socket. A wooden peg is driven alongside the tautly pulled thong and the excess trimmed off. A conscious attempt was made to locate the exit hole for the leather thong at a point on the post where it would be least noticed. The place most suitable was on the

inside surface approximately 45 degrees from the back and side rungs.

To prevent the thin wall of the socket from breaking away, which was a common occurrence, Brother George A. Donnell invented and was granted a patent (no. 8771) in 1852 for a metal tilting button with a supporting metal ferrule. Very few of these chairs with patent tilters were made, possibly because Brother George left the order shortly thereafter.

Tilters on dining chairs seem odd considering Believers were denied the luxury of after-meal lounging. Private collection.

H. 28-5/8, W. 17-1/8, D. 15.

4. Made during the closing years of factory operation (c. 1930), this dowel-back dining chair from New Lebanon is maple finished with a dark mahogany varnish-stain. It has a Shaker decal and the tape seat is a replacement. The chair was probably a limited production model, possibly made by non-Shaker hired hands from standard chair and stool parts. The front legs are similar to those used in utility stools (see Stools, figs. 4 and 5) and the back posts could be a modification of those used in the tall work chairs (see Chairs, fig. 5). The substitution of dowels for bent-back slats and the elimination of mortises in the back posts simplified construction. At the time this would be an important factor, considering the steady decline in membership and the advanced ages of the mainly female members. The round finial is a variant of the acorn form. Author's collection.

H. 27-3/4, W. 17-1/2, D. 14-1/2.

5. This work chair from Canterbury was made in the second half of the nineteenth century. It is a type used at shop desks, laundry and ironing tables, weaving looms, tailors' counters, and similar work areas. The chair is maple in a red wash paint and has a cotton tape seat. Collection of the Shaker Museum, Old Chatham, N. Y.

H. 35-3/4, H. of seat, 25, W. 19, D. 16-7/8.

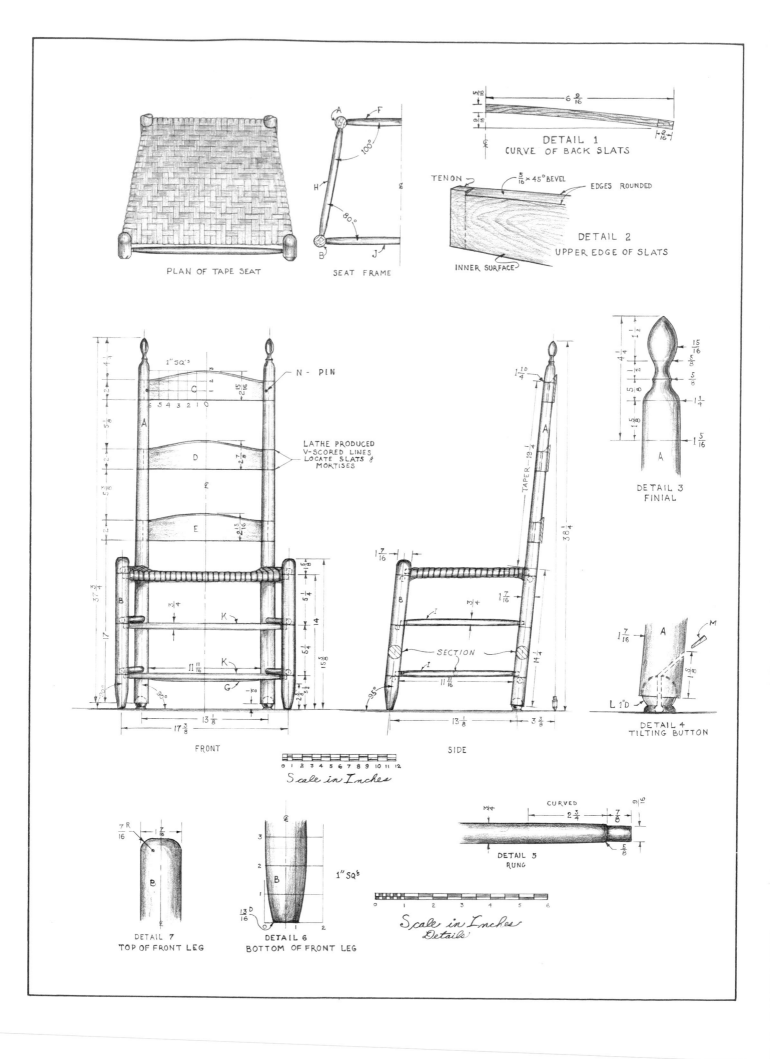

PLAN OF TAPE SEAT

SEAT FRAME

DETAIL 1
CURVE OF BACK SLATS

DETAIL 2
UPPER EDGE OF SLATS

TENON

5/16 × 45° BEVEL

EDGES ROUNDED

INNER SURFACE

N - PIN

LATHE PRODUCED
V-SCORED LINES
LOCATE SLATS &
MORTISES

1" SQ'S

DETAIL 3
FINIAL

FRONT

SIDE

Scale in Inches

SECTION

TAPER 19 1/4

DETAIL 4
TILTING BUTTON

DETAIL 7
TOP OF FRONT LEG

DETAIL 6
BOTTOM OF FRONT LEG

1" SQ's

DETAIL 5
RUNG

CURVED

Scale in Inches
Details

6. Chairs similar in style to this three-slat side chair from New Lebanon were also made in Hancock and Watervliet, New York. Dating from approximately 1830, they were produced in quantity for Believers' use with a few sold to the world. Evidence of premachine mass production shows in the slight difference in the size and shape of the individually lathe-turned parts. Further confirmation of early manufacture is in the style of the finial on the back posts and the cornered mortises for the back slats (not shown in photograph) which predate mortises with round ends. The chair is varnished maple, has a retaped seat, and is fitted with tilting buttons. Collection of Mrs. Edward Deming Andrews.

H. 38-1/4, W. 18-3/16, D. 17-1/4.

Letter	No.	Name	Material	T	W	L
A	2	back posts	maple	1-7/16 dia		37-3/4
B	2	front legs	maple	1-7/16 dia		15-5/8
C	1	upper slat	maple	5/16	2-15/16	13-1/8
D	1	middle slat	maple	5/16	2-7/8	13-1/16
E	1	lower slat	maple	5/16	2-13/16	13
F	1	seat—back stretcher	maple	13/16	1-3/8	13-3/16
G	1	back rung	maple	3/4 dia		13-3/16
H	2	seat—side stretchers	maple	13/16	1-3/8	13-3/16
I	4	side rungs	maple	3/4 dia		13-3/16
J	1	seat—front stretcher	maple	13/16	1-3/8	16-3/16
K	2	front rungs	maple	3/4 dia		16-3/16
L	2	titling buttons	maple	1 dia		1-1/4
M	2	pins for buttons	maple	1/8 dia		1/2
N	2	pins for ladder	maple	3/16 dia		5/8

7. The low seat of this apple-sorting chair from Canterbury eliminated the need for stooping in sorting or similar tasks. Three scribe lines on each leg locate the height of the chair rungs; however, the center ones and those on the outer back spindles are purely decorative. The sculptured pine-plank seat and maple components are protected with coats of orange shellac. The chair dates from the first half ot the nineteenth century. Collection of Shaker Village, Inc., Canterbury, N. H.

H. 22-3/8, H. of seat, 10, W. 14-5/8, D. 14-5/8.

8. Except for the height of the back, this spindle-back chair is similar to the one illustrated in figure 7. This particular style was referred to as a step-up chair. It was used much like a step-stool to reach upper cupboards or drawers. All parts are maple except the sculptured pine-plank seat. The origin of the chair is unknown, but it is similar to chairs made in Canterbury during the mid-nineteenth century. The legs have scribe lines at the intersecting points of the untapered rungs. Collection of the Philadelphia Museum of Art. Photograph courtesy of the museum.

H. 28-1/4, H. of seat, 15-3/4, W. 15, D. of seat, 13.

9. Also from New Lebanon and from the same period as figure 6 is this side chair of maple with cane seat and tilting buttons. The small size of the chair makes it rare and indicates that it probably was made for the children's order. The "4" stamped into the top right leg was a room designation. The finish is a natural patina. Author's collection.

H. 34-1/2, H. of seat, 12-1/2 front, 13-1/2 rear, W. 16-3/4, D. 15.

10. One of the finest Shaker chair styles is this side chair from Enfield, New Hampshire (c. 1850). It is made of birch, stained light brown protected with clear varnish. The cane seating is a material that was often used on chairs made in this community. A "13" stamped on the upper end of the front legs is a room designation. The usually well-defined taper on the leg below the lowest rung is only slightly suggested here. The back posts are fitted with tilters, have three slightly graduated slats, and a style of finial called "candle-flame" that is commonly associated with this New Hampshire community. Collection of the Shaker Museum, Old Chatham, N. Y.

H. 41-1/8, W. 18-3/8, D. 18-1/2.

11. This maple side chair is attributed to the Watervliet, New York, community, probably because of the characteristically high curve and the pronounced bevel on the upper edge of the back slats rather than because of the shape of its finials. The chair has been refinished natural—its original color. The seat has also been retaped. Of special note is the difference in width of the slats graduating from narrow to wide in ascending order. This arrangement was determined to give greater comfort and support to the back; therefore, the wider slat was put at the top where it was most needed. This practical detail is absent on later, commercially produced side chairs. Stamped on the upper end of the left front post is the word *Sick* which indicates that the chair was used in a nurse-shop or infirmary. The date 1840 is stamped on the upper end of the right front post. Collection of Robert F. W. Meader.

H. 40, W. 18-3/4, D. 15-3/4.

12. This side chair from New Lebanon
(c. 1860) has tilting buttons, acorn finials,
bent back posts, and tapered rungs, all in the
original—natural maple—finish. The wood
has developed a lovely golden patina and the
Shaker-made tape seat has faded attractive-
ly. A "3" is stamped into the back of the top
slat and is a size designation. Bent back posts
were a later development designed to add
greater comfort to side chairs. Collection of
Mr. and Mrs. Peter Marks.

H. 34-1/4, W. 18, D. 18-3/4.

13. This side chair of maple and birch was
purchased at the New Lebanon chair factory
in 1928. Its ebony finish is original but the
seat has been retaped. The finial shape is yet
another variant. The lack of a well-defined
taper on the back posts, the absence of tapers
on any rungs, and the general feeling of
heaviness make this chair style somewhat
less desirable than earlier forms. Collection
of Donald Weeks.

H. 40-1/2, W. 18, D. 19.

14. Also from New Lebanon and made during the closing years of factory production is this three-slat side chair. It is maple with a mahogany stain, has a decal (size undecipherable) and a retaped seat. The abrupt taper and reduced diameter on the lower end of the front legs are similar to those occasionally found on chairs from Ohio and Kentucky (see fig. 15). The absence of tapered rungs, the curved back post, and the acorn-style finial attest to its late manufacture. The ratio of the rather ample width to its short height gives the chair a rather unattractive, boxy look. Author's collection.

H. 33-1/4, W. 19-1/4, D. 18-1/4.

15. This three-slat side chair dates from the first half of the nineteenth century and was made at Pleasant Hill. It has maple legs, ash rungs, oak slats, and a tape seat (for another example of multiple woods used in a chair see fig. 27). All wooden parts are painted red. The finial shape on the back post is very similar to the candle-flame style used on chairs made at the Enfield, New Hampshire, community (see fig. 10). The short pronounced taper of the posts at the floor line is a form not commonly used on eastern chairs. Collection of Shakertown at Pleasant Hill, Inc., Harrodsburg, Ky.

H. 39-1/4, W. 18-1/2, D. 18-1/4.

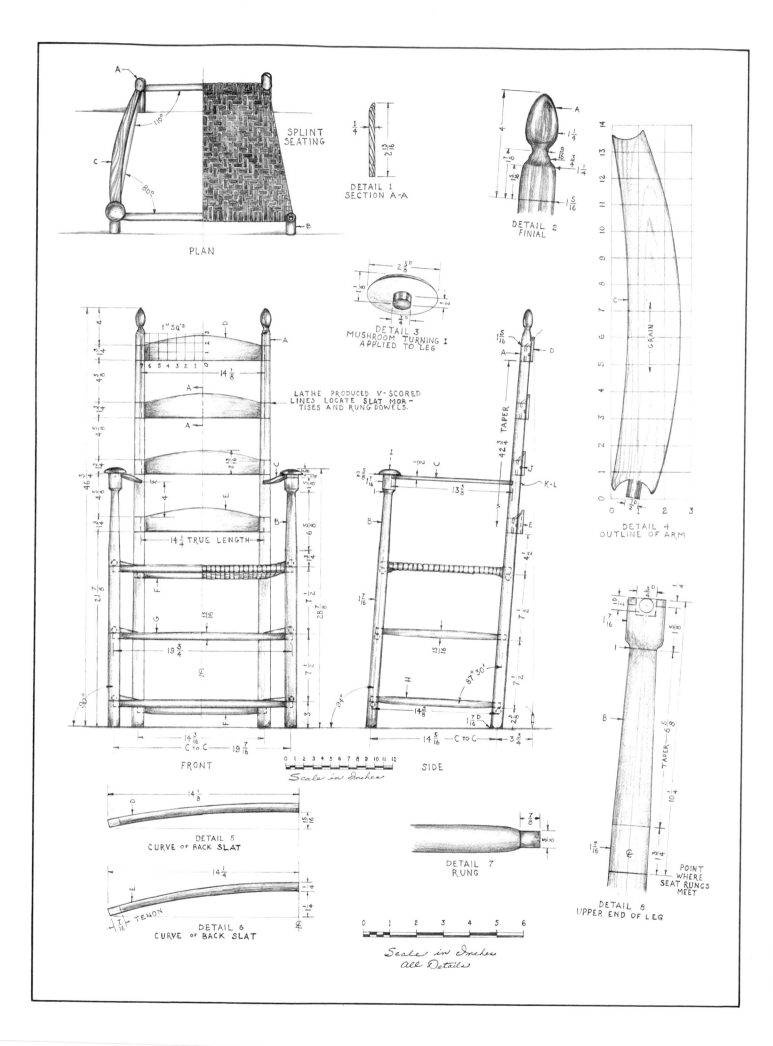

SPLINT SEATING

110°

80°

PLAN

DETAIL 1
SECTION A-A

DETAIL 2
FINIAL

DETAIL 3
MUSHROOM TURNING
APPLIED TO LEG

DETAIL 4
OUTLINE OF ARM

GRAIN

1" SQ'S

14 1/8

LATHE PRODUCED V-SCORED
LINES LOCATE SLAT MOR-
TISES AND RUNG DOWELS.

14 1/4 TRUE LENGTH

19 3/4

42 3/4 TAPER

13 5/8

14 5/16 C TO C

87° 30'

14 3/16
C TO C
19 7/16

FRONT

0 1 2 3 4 5 6 7 8 9 10 11 12
Scale in Inches

SIDE

DETAIL 5
CURVE OF BACK SLAT

14 1/8

DETAIL 6
CURVE OF BACK SLAT

14 1/4

TENON

DETAIL 7
RUNG

0 1 2 3 4 5 6
Scale in Inches
All Details

DETAIL 8
UPPER END OF LEG

TAPER 6 5/8

POINT
WHERE
SEAT RUNGS
MEET

16. The size of this armchair suggests that it was probably designed for brethrens' use. It is a fine example of an early nineteenth-century New Lebanon chair. The wood is maple stained a light orange-brown protected with a coat of varnish and the splint seat is original to the piece. The rungs are tapered, the back slats are extra thin and equal in size, and the mushroom-shaped finials were turned and applied to the legs (earlier practice was to turn the finials as part of the leg). Each slat is pegged from the back with crudely shaped pegs which help verify its early date of manufacture. Pegging was necessary to prevent separation of the post and slats; however, it was unnecessary to peg any but the uppermost slat for the others would be automatically locked in and, in addition, would be allowed to flex for added comfort. The sides of the arms straddle the legs and attach to them with their own dowel. Single wood screws go through each post into the arms to hold them in place. They are installed in a counterbored hole which is plugged. Private collection.

H. 46-3/4, W. 22-1/16, D. 18-25/32.

Letter	No.	Name	Material	T	W	L
A	2	posts	maple	1-7/16 dia		46-3/4
B	2	legs	maple	1-7/16 dia		28-7/8
C	2	arms	maple	1/2	2-9/16	13-5/8
D	3	slats	maple	1/4	2-13/16	14-1/8
E	1	slats	maple	1/4	2-13/16	14-1/4
F	2	back rungs	maple	15/16 dia		14-1/2
G	3	front rungs	maple	15/16 dia		19-3/4
H	6	side rungs	maple	15/16 dia		14-5/8
I	2	mushroom finials	maple	2-5/8 dia		1-1/8
J	8	pins	maple	1/8 dia		3/4
K	2	plugs	maple	1/4 dia		1/4
Hardware						
L	2	wood screws	FH 1-1/2-8			

17. This made-for-sale, three-slat armchair of maple stained carmel-color was made in the early part of the twentieth century at the New Lebanon community by Sister Lillian Barlow (1876–1942). Sister Lillian and Brother William Perkins (1861–1934) were the last Shakers to make chairs. (As male membership declined, the sisters took up the work in the shops and continued producing selected goods for sale.) The purity of the candle-flame finial form has been aesthetically weakened with the interruption of the ringed neck. The upper end of the leg passes through a hole in the arm and into the applied flat mushroom-shaped finial, holding all firmly in place. Private collection.

H. 41-1/2, W. 23-3/8, D. 21.

18. Similar to the chair shown in figure 17 is this exceptionally tall, five-slat armchair from New Lebanon. It was made about 1900 and is maple with birch rungs, all finished in clear varnish. The tape seat is a replacement.

In an 1875 New Lebanon Shaker chair catalogue the overall height of the largest production chair, "7," is 42½ inches; this chair is 8¾ inches taller. It can be assumed that this chair was not part of the production line; that probably not many were made; and that those made were done only on special order. (One reference has it they were made as presentation pieces and given to elders in recognition of their years of service to the order.) Collection of the Henry Francis du Pont Winterthur Museum. Photograph courtesy of the museum.

H. 51-1/4, W. 23-1/2, D. 20-1/4.

19. This three-slat child's armchair is probably a size "0," the smallest of the standard line manufactured at New Lebanon. It is finished in a mahogany-colored varnish-stain and has a Shaker-woven, ½-inch-wide, olive-and-blue tape seat. The word *Trade* (remnant of a decal) is barely decipherable on the back of the lower slat. Collection of Joanne Blois Russell.

H. 22-3/4, W. 14-1/8, D. 12.

20. The top slat of this four-slat New Lebanon production model armchair has a "6" stamped into its back and the bottom slat has a Shaker decal. The chair is maple finished with a mahogany-colored varnish-stain and has a scarlet-and-old-gold tape seat. It was probably made in the early part of the twentieth century. The acorn-shaped finials on the bent back posts, the curve on the upper edge of the back slats, the shape of the thin flat arms (with suggested wrist and elbows), the high-domed, mushroom-shaped applied finials, the urn-shaped turnings on the legs, and the straight rungs on the sides and back became standard forms in the last quarter of the nineteenth century and continued to be used to the end of chair manufacturing. Collection of Mr. and Mrs. William Hollinger.

H. 41-1/8, W. 24, D. 22-1/2.

21. The runner shape on this number three, three-slat rocking chair became a standard form in 1863 when the New Lebanon community reorganized the chair manufacturing industry. This chair could date from that period but more probably was made during the first quarter of the twentieth century. It is made of maple and is finished with a mahogany-colored varnish-stain. Collection of John S. Roberts.

H. 39-1/8, W. 18-1/4, D. 23-1/2.

Letter	No.	Name	Material	T	W	L
A	2	back posts	maple	1-5/16 dia		38-1/2
B	2	front legs	maple	1-1/4 dia		15
C	2	rockers	maple	5/16	3-1/4	23-1/2
D	1	upper slat	maple	1/4	2-1/2	14-1/4
E	1	middle slat	maple	1/4	2-3/8	13-3/4
F	1	lower slat	maple	1/4	2-3/8	13-1/2
G	1	seat—back rung	maple	11/16 dia		13-9/16
H	1	back rung	maple	5/8 dia		13-9/16
I	1	seat—front rung	maple	11/16 dia		17-1/2
J	2	front rungs	maple	11/16 dia		17-1/2
K	2	seat—side rungs	maple	11/16 dia		13-9/16
L	4	side rungs	maple	5/8 dia		13-9/16
M	2	pins	maple	1/8 dia		1
Hardware						
N	2	wood screws		FH 3/4-6		

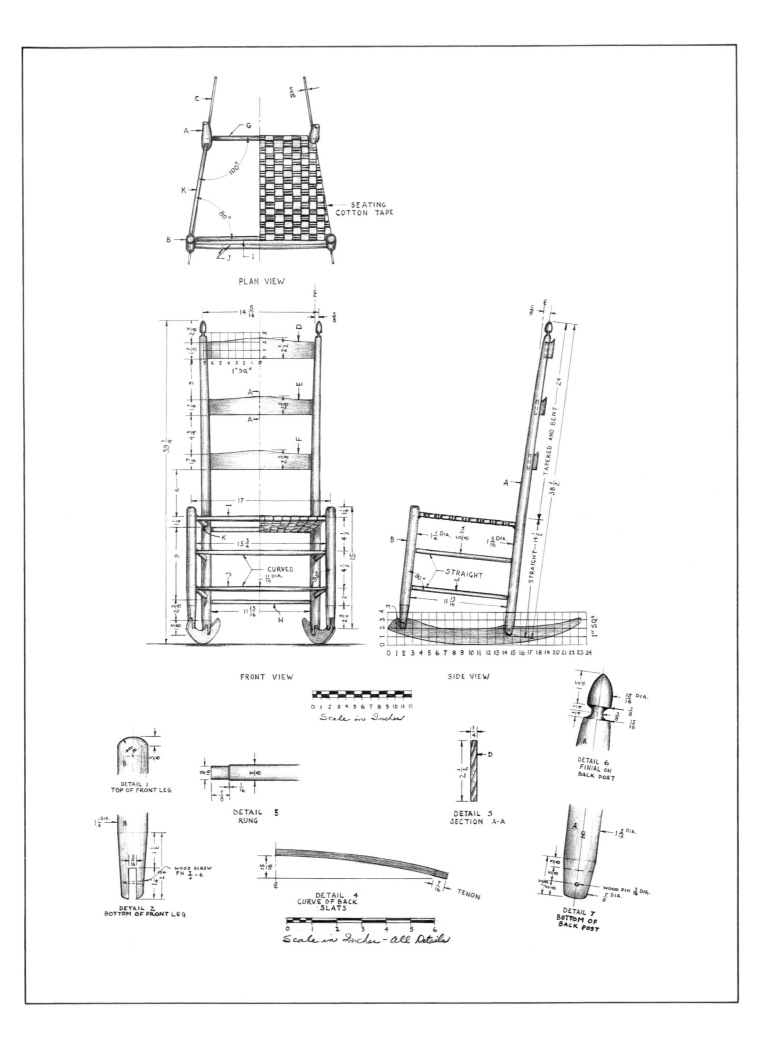

PLAN VIEW

SEATING COTTON TAPE

FRONT VIEW

SIDE VIEW

Scale in Inches

DETAIL 1
TOP OF FRONT LEG

DETAIL 3
RUNG

DETAIL 5
SECTION A-A

DETAIL 6
FINIAL ON BACK POST

DETAIL 2
BOTTOM OF FRONT LEG

DETAIL 4
CURVE OF BACK SLATS

TENON

DETAIL 7
BOTTOM OF BACK POST

Scale in Inches – All Details

22. The finial and runner shapes on this three-slat rocking chair are forms that were used on chairs made in the New Lebanon, Hancock, and Enfield, Connecticut, communities during the first quarter of the nineteenth century. The chair has a rush seat and is fabricated entirely from figured maple, obviously specially selected. Other examples of chairs made from this beautiful (but difficult to work) material exist and probably were made to be used only by the ministry. Special care was often taken in making furniture for this highest order of Shakerdom. In the case of this chair, its small size suggests it was made for eldresses' use. Collection of the Henry Francis du Pont Winterthur Musuem. Photograph courtesy of the museum.

H. 35-7/8, W. 16-1/4, D. 21-1/2.

23. Pasted on the back of the middle ladder of this chair is a paper label containing the word *Ministry's*. This would indicate that it was assigned (because of its small size) to the eldresses' quarters. It was made in New Lebanon in the early part of the nineteenth century and is maple in a natural light color with a tan-and-blue-gray cotton tape seat. Typical features found on early rocking chairs are tapered, turned rungs, scribe layout lines (for the slat mortises), and finials that show a slight variation in shape. The flat runners are a variant from the traditional "knife-blade" style. Collection of Philadelphia Museum of Art. Photograph by A. J. Wyatt.

H. 35-1/2, W. 18-1/2, D. 21.

24. The contrast between the black-and-orange tape seat and the ebony finish on this child's rocking chair is most attractive. The chair has a "0" stamped into the back of the upper slat and is an early twentieth-century New Lebanon chair factory product. Collection of Shaker Village, Inc., Canterbury, N. H.

H. 23, W. 13-1/8, D. 16-1/4.

25. A Shaker concern for improving the comfort of their chairs is reflected in the two outwardly curved back posts and the curved horizontal bars that hold the padded tape back. This chair is a number two and, according to an early Shaker chair catalogue, "[the No. 2 chair] is a trifle smaller than the No. 3 in the seat, but in every other respect it is the same." From New Lebanon (c. 1920), it is maple with a mahogany varnish-stain, and has a pomegranate-and-black replacement tape seat. All rungs are straight except the two at front, which, being more exposed to shoe abuse, are tapered and heavier. Acorn-shaped finials with a distinct, small neck became a standard form from the last quarter of the nineteenth century to the end of production. A decal is located on the inner surface of the left rocker near the back post. Author's collection.

H. 33-1/2, W. 17-5/16, D. 24-1/4.

26. Because of its large size, all the rungs on this number seven four-slat, tape-seat rocking chair of maple are, for added strength, extra large throughout their centers. The chair was made in New Lebanon during the last quarter of the nineteenth century and has tapered and bent back posts, acorn-shaped finials, and is finished in an ebony-colored varnish-stain. Collection of Green-field Village and the Henry Ford Museum, Dearborn, Mich. Photograph courtesy of the museum.

H. 41, W. 22, D. of seat, 18, D. of rocker, 29.

27. This three-slat rocking chair is from Pleasant Hill and is an example of the use of three different woods in a chair (for another example, see fig. 15). Originally painted red, the chair is now natural color wood, clear-varnished. Collection of Shakertown at Pleasant Hill, Inc., Harrodsburg, Ky.

H. 37-3/4, W. 19-1/4, D. 27-3/4.

28. The size of this arm-rocking chair (c. 1805) and its look of primitive sturdiness suggest it was made for male members' use. Although the chair is attributed to Hancock, its finials are similar to those found on chairs made during the same period at New Lebanon and Watervliet, New York. Of maple, originally painted red, it now is natural maple color, clear varnished with a retaped light olive seat. The high, cradle-shaped or "sled" runners originally had ends that projected beyond the legs, probably in a half-round form. It is not clear why they were removed, but it may have been to reduce the danger of the aged and infirm bumping into the projecting ends. The rungs are crudely fashioned, especially those at the front, and the large mushroom-shaped finials were turned as part of the legs. The flat, outwardly curved arms are doweled to the legs and posts and are locked in place with pins. The top edges of the slats are heavily beveled with the upper one pegged through its tenons. Collection of Donald Weeks.

H. 46-1/2, W. 22, D. 25.

29. This four-slat arm-rocking chair of maple (c. 1850) was made in the Canterbury society. Originally stained light orange-red, it now is finished natural with clear varnish. Unusual are the number of taper rungs—four instead of the customary seven—and the urn-shaped turnings on the legs, which terminate in a square with a tenon on the end that is pinned to the rolled arms. The back of the arms are also fastened with a pinned tenon. The unbeveled back slats are graduated in width, with the widest at the top. The shape of the candle-flame finial is more bulbous than the slightly later versions made in the Enfield, New Hampshire, society (see fig. 10), Collection of the Ohio Historical Society, Glendower, Lebanon, Ohio.

H. 47, W. 20-3/4, D. 23.

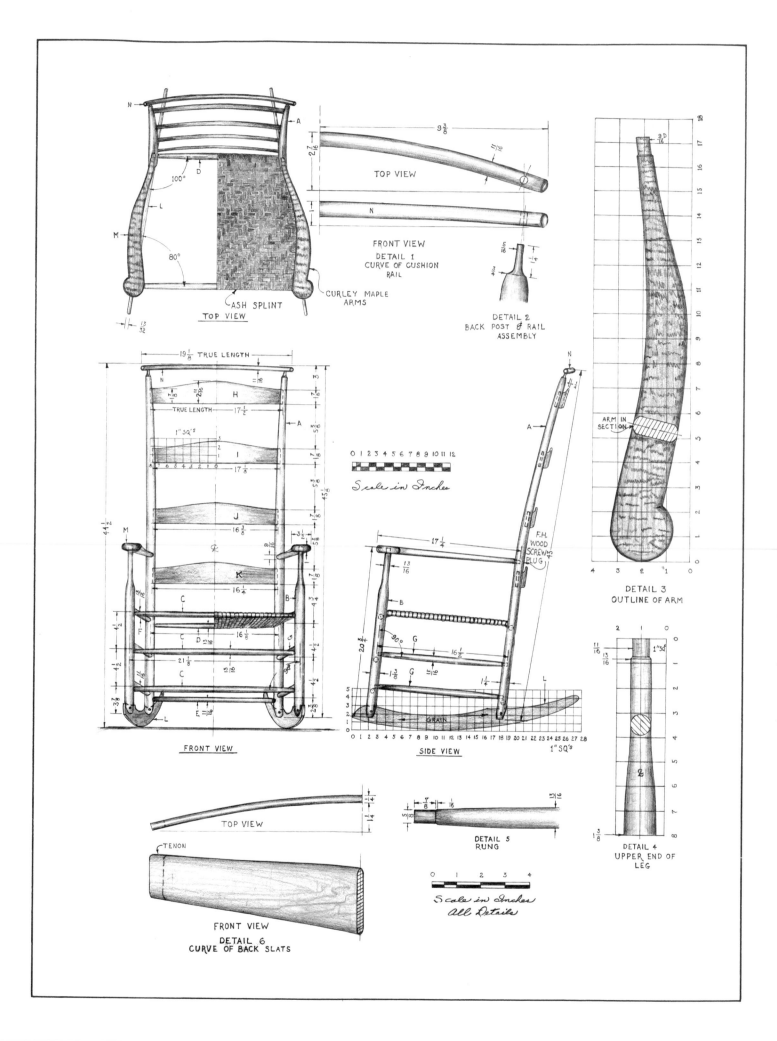

TOP VIEW

100°

D

L

M

80°

ASH SPLINT

CURLEY MAPLE ARMS

TOP VIEW

13/32

9 3/8

11/16

2 7/16

TOP VIEW

N

FRONT VIEW
DETAIL 1
CURVE OF CUSHION RAIL

5/16

1 1/4

4 3/4

DETAIL 2
BACK POST & RAIL ASSEMBLY

9 D/16

ARM IN SECTION

DETAIL 3
OUTLINE OF ARM

19 1/8 TRUE LENGTH

N

11/16

1 7/8

2 11/16

H

TRUE LENGTH — 17 1/2

A

1" SQ'S

I

17 1/8

J

16 3/8

K

16 1/4

C

B

M

3 1/2

F

C   D

16 1/8

G

21 1/8

13/16

C

44 1/2

43 5/8

4 1/2

4 1/2

3 3/8

2 3/8

E 1 1/16

L

FRONT VIEW

0 1 2 3 4 5 6 7 8 9 10 11 12

Scale in Inches

N

A

17 1/4

F.H. WOOD SCREW #3 PLUG

B

90°

G

16 1/2

G

1 3/4

1 1/16

1 1/4

20 3/4

13/16

L

GRAIN

0 1 2 3 4 5 6 7 8 9 10 11 12 13 14 15 16 17 18 19 20 21 22 23 24 25 26 27 28

SIDE VIEW   1" SQ'S

2   1   0

11/16

13/16

1" SQ

1 3/8

DETAIL 4
UPPER END OF LEG

TOP VIEW

7/8

1/16

13/16

5/8

DETAIL 5
RUNG

TENON

FRONT VIEW
DETAIL 6
CURVE OF BACK SLATS

0 1 2 3 4

Scale in Inches
All Details

30. The size of this arm-rocking chair suggests it was made for brethrens' use. It was made in New Lebanon and dates from the second quarter of the nineteenth century. The frame is maple, in a clear varnish finish, and the seat is ash-splint. Using figured-grained woods for the more obvious parts of furniture—in this case, curly maple for the arms—was not uncommon practice. Often entire chairs were made from this material (see fig. 22). The legs and post straddle the rockers and are held in place with metal pins. Usually the upper edges of the back slats were left square or, more often, beveled; in this chair they are rounded. Dowels turned on the ends of the posts hold the cushion tie bar (rail). Tie bars were used on rocking chairs of all sizes, both arm and armless, into the twentieth century (see figs. 31 and 34). The form of the turned legs immediately below the scroll or ladle-shaped arms helps date the piece. On earlier examples the arms penetrate a collar and on later styles this part is turned a lovely urn- or vase-shape (see figs. 33, 34, and 35). On this chair the legs, the taper of the arms, and the graceful bend of the slender back posts contribute elegance and harmony to this fine example of Shaker craftsmanship. Collection of John S. Roberts.

H. 44-1/2, W. 23, D. 27-5/8.

Letter	No.	Name	Material	T	W	L
A	2	back posts	maple	1-1/4 dia		43
B	2	front legs	maple	1-3/8 dia		20-3/4
C	3	seat—front rungs	maple	13/16 dia		21-1/8
D	1	seat—back rung	maple	13/16 dia		16
E	1	back lower rung	maple	11/16 dia		16
F	2	seat—side rungs	maple	13/16 dia		16-1/2
G	4	side rungs	maple	11/16 dia		16-1/2
H	1	upper slat	maple	1/4	2-11/16	17-1/2
I	1	second slat	maple	1/4	2-11/16	17-1/8
J	1	third slat	maple	1/4	2-11/16	16-3/8
K	1	lower slat	maple	1/4	2-11/16	16-1/4
L	2	runners	maple	13/32	3-1/2	27-5/8
M	2	arms	curly-maple	1	2-5/8	17-1/4
N	1	cushion rail	maple	11/16 dia		19-1/8

31. Though many of the components of this four-slat, number seven arm-rocking chair are similar to the chair shown in figure 30, it is not quite as classic in form. This chair was made in New Lebanon during the third quarter of the nineteenth century. Several parts are standard forms, but the large flat mushroom-shaped finials and the contour of the arms make the chair a transitional style. Collection of the Philadelphia Museum of Art. Photograph by A. J. Wyatt.

H. 39, W. 23-1/4, D. 28-1/2.

32. Another example of a transitional form is this arm-rocking chair, also from New Lebanon and made in the same time period as the chair in figure 31. The bulbous finials on the posts, the curve of the arms, and the high-crowned, mushroom-shaped finials on the legs are carry-over forms from earlier styles. The rest of the components are standard factory shapes (see fig. 20). The chair frame is maple, which has developed a warm brown patina, and the seat is wool listing. A "3" is stamped on the back of the upper slat. Eldress Rosetta Stevens (1850–1947) used the chair in the New Lebanon society. Collection of the Philadelphia Museum of Art. Photograph by A. J. Wyatt.

H. 35, W. 19-1/8, D. 23.

33. This number seven, four-slat arm-rocking chair was made about 1880 in New Lebanon. The frame is maple with a natural finish and the seat is red listing. With the exception of the tapered side and back rungs, all components of the chair are standard forms. Collection of the Henry Francis du Pont Winterthur Museum. Photograph courtesy of the museum.

H. 41-1/2, W. 24, D. 28-7/8.

34. Adult furniture was scaled down for children and was made from the beginning of communal living to the end of chair manufacturing. The side chair shown in figure 9 is an early nineteenth-century example. This one and the chair illustrated in figure 35 are twentieth-century factory products. This three-slat arm-rocking chair with cushion-tie bar is a number one and was made in New Lebanon (c. 1930). It is made of maple and has acquired an attractive medium brown patina. The tape seat is olive-and-carmine wool. The finials, mushroom-shaped, have a pronounced bead at their rims and make it another variant of the form. Collection of Shaker Museum, South Union, Ky.

H. 27, W. 16, D. 20.

35. The more comfortable tape-back rocking chair was made in all sizes. This example is a number one and was made about 1930 in New Lebanon. It has a gray and red-and-bayberry-stripe tape seat and back and is finished in a mahogany-colored varnish-stain. The runners are held to the legs and posts with wood pins. Author's collection.

H. 28-1/2, W. 16-1/4, D. 19-3/8.

36. Components of this arm-rocking chair from Pleasant Hill appear heavier than eastern equivalents and convey strength at the expense of grace. The chair is of mixed woods and dates from the second half of the nineteenth century. It has tapered rungs, candle-flame finials, ladle-shaped arms, rockers with an interesting profile which is heavier in width where the legs and post join, a seat of wool listing, and a four-slat back. The four slats have created a crowded look and are unwarranted on a chair of this height; however, they may have been supplied as an attempt to make the back more comfortable. Collection of Shakertown at Pleasant Hill, Inc., Harrodsburg, Ky.

H. 38-1/2, W. 20, D. 23.

37. This highchair from the New Lebanon chair factory is one of six made in 1880 for special friends of the Shakers. The finial shapes—bulbous acorns on the back posts and mushrooms on the front legs—are forms used on other types of Shaker-made chairs, as was the urn-shaped turning on the upper end of the legs. The chair is made of maple and appears to have been stripped of its original unknown finish. It now has a red maple-colored stain protected with clear varnish. It has been reseated with half-inch-wide red-and-black worsted tape woven in a checkerboard pattern. Other restorations include the addition of five inches to the ends of the cut-off legs to bring the chair to its original height and the total reconstruction of the footrest and its peg supports. Collection of the Shaker Museum, Old Chatham, N. Y.

H. 36, W. 17, D. 17.

38. In mixed woods, this highchair (c. 1850) has a footrest, an elevating rod, and a curved spindle back which is reminiscent of Windsor low back chairs. The origin of the chair is unknown, but except for the charming footrest it is very similar to swivel chairs made in several eastern societies. The chair has legs, rungs, and spindles of maple, a lathe-turned pine seat, and a curved back rail of hickory. The inside curve of the footrest clears the canted legs when the seat is rotated. Unfortunately this charming example of Shaker ingenuity now exists only as a photograph because it was destroyed by fire. Collection of Greenfield Village and the Henry Ford Museum, Dearborn, Mich. Photograph courtesy of the museum.

H.29, W. 16-1/2, D. 14.

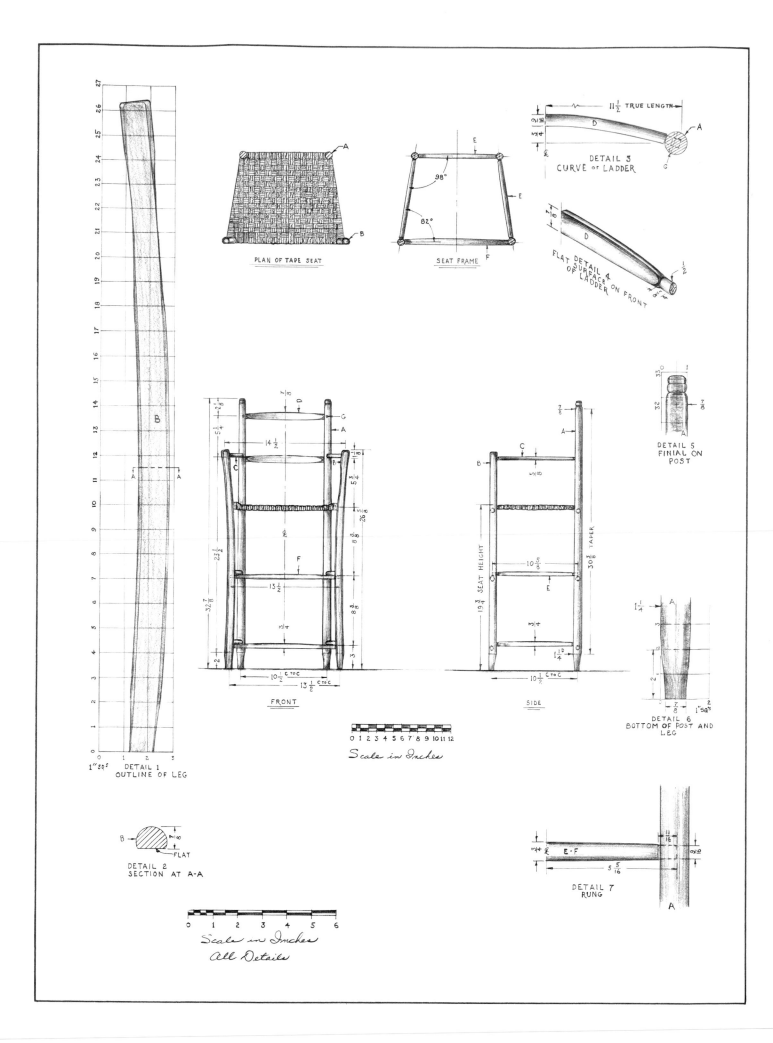

PLAN OF TAPE SEAT

SEAT FRAME

DETAIL 3
CURVE of LADDER

11½ TRUE LENGTH

FLAT SURFACE ON FRONT
OF LADDER
DETAIL 4

DETAIL 5
FINIAL ON
POST

DETAIL 1
OUTLINE OF LEG

1" SQS

FRONT

SIDE

DETAIL 6
BOTTOM OF POST AND
LEG

1" SQS

Scale in Inches

DETAIL 2
SECTION AT A-A

DETAIL 7
RUNG

0 1 2 3 4 5 6
Scale in Inches
All Details

39. The style of this highchair is not exclusively Shaker, for similar examples exist that were made by non-Shaker craftsmen. It dates from the first half of the nineteenth century and is of mixed woods painted red. The flat surfaces on the otherwise turned and bent front legs and back slats are curious forms. Collection of Shakertown at Pleasant Hill, Inc., Harrodsburg, Ky.

H. 32-7/8, W. 15-3/4, D. 10-5/8.

Letter	No.	Name	Material	T	W	L
A	2	posts	hardwood	1-1/4 dia		32-7/8
B	2	legs	hardwood	1-1/4 dia		26-5/8
C	2	arms	hardwood	5/8 dia		10-5/8
D	2	slats	hardwood	7/8 dia		11-1/2
E	9	side and back rungs	hardwood	3/4 dia		10-5/8
F	3	front rungs	hardwood	3/4 dia		13-1/2
G	2	pins	hardwood	1/8 dia		3/4

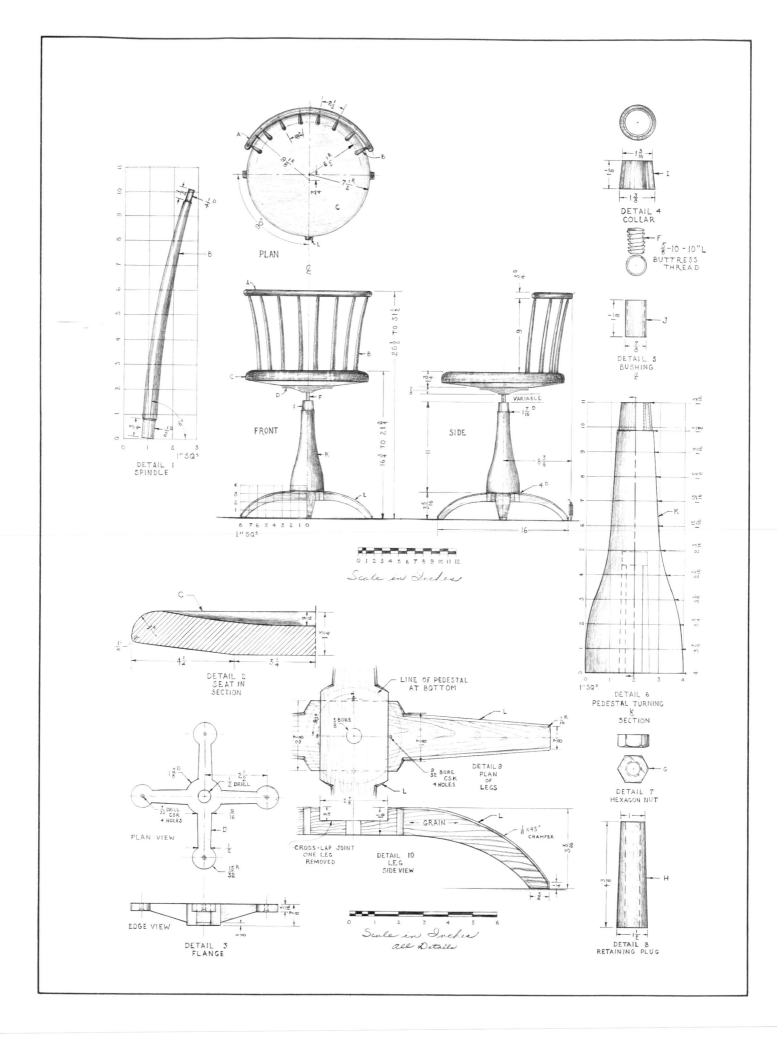

PLAN

DETAIL 1
SPINDLE

DETAIL 4
COLLAR

$\frac{5}{8}$-10-10"L
BUTTRESS
THREAD

DETAIL 5
BUSHING

FRONT

SIDE

Scale in Inches

DETAIL 2
SEAT IN
SECTION

DETAIL 6
PEDESTAL TURNING
& SECTION

DETAIL 7
HEXAGON NUT

LINE OF PEDESTAL
AT BOTTOM

PLAN VIEW

BORE

BORE
CSK
4 HOLES

DETAIL 9
PLAN
OF
LEGS

DRILL
CSK
4 HOLES

DRILL

EDGE VIEW

DETAIL 3
FLANGE

CROSS-LAP JOINT
ONE LEG
REMOVED

DETAIL 10
LEG
SIDE VIEW

GRAIN

$\frac{1}{8}$ x 45°
CHAMFER

Scale in Inches
All Details

DETAIL 8
RETAINING PLUG

40. Credit for the origin of the swivel chair has been given to Enfield, New Hampshire; however, they were also made at a later date in other communities, as was this example from Canterbury. The chair was made during the third quarter of the nineteenth century and is an elevating type. Chairs of this form were used in offices, shops, and schoolrooms and were referred to as "swivel-stools," "revolving stools," "revolving-chairs," "revolvers," and "turning chairs." All the wooden parts are maple except the pine-plank seat and the curved backrest rail of ash. The seat raises and lowers on a centrally located, buttress-threaded steel rod. The two slightly arced spiderlike feet were sawn from solid maple and assembled with a cross-half-lap joint. A "jacks"-shaped, cast-iron flang (without its vertical axis) is fixed with wood screws to the underside of the seat and holds the upper end of the elevating rod. Rotating the seat causes the elevating rod to turn in a nut embedded in the center of the pedestal. Eight taper-bent, Windsor-type spindles are doweled into the seat and curved back rail and form a sensitively light backrest which is somewhat incongruous in form with the strong, bold seat, pedestal, and legs. Collection of the Shaker Museum, Old Chatham, N. Y.

H. of seat range, 16-3/4 to 21-3/4, W. 16, D. 16.

Letter	No.	Name	Material	T	W	L
A	1	curved rail	ash	3/4 dia		19
B	8	spindle	maple	9/16 dia		10-1/4
C	1	seat	pine	1-3/4		15 dia
D	1	plug (retaining)	maple	1-1/4 dia	tapered to 1	4-3/8
E	1	pedestal	maple		4 dia	11
F	2	foot	maple	3-5/16	2-7/8	16
Hardware						
G	1	flange	cast iron	7/8	5-15/16	5-15/16
H	4	wood screws	steel	FH 12-1		
I	1	elevating rod	steel	5/8 dia	10 threads per 1"	12
J	1	nut	steel	5/8 hex		
K	1	collar	steel 18 GA	1-3/16 dia	tapered to 1-3/8	1-1/8
L	1	bushing	steel 18 GA		13/16 dia OD	1-1/8
M	4	wood screws	steel	FH 3-14		

41. This nonelevating swivel chair from New Lebanon probably predates the previous and following examples. The pedestal on the chair has a more Shaker-like form than the previous example. In mixed woods, it has maple feet, a chestnut spindle, a pine seat, metal back spindles, and a curved backrest rail of hickory. The two outer spindles penetrate through the rail. Private collection.

H. to top of rail, 26-3/4, Dia. of seat, 15-1/4.

42. The community origin of this nonelevating swivel chair is unknown; however, it probably was made in an eastern community during the second half of the nineteenth century. The decorative turnings are a worldly influence and help confirm the time of manufacture. It is made of mixed woods that have been stained dark cherry-red. Collection of Shaker Community, Inc., Hancock, Mass.

H. 27-1/2, W. 21-1/8, D. 15-1/8.

Chests

This section includes typical six-board lidded chests, lidded chests with one, two, or three drawers, and chests of drawers. Six-board lidded chests were made in the New Lebanon colony as early as 1790. Lidded chests with drawers and chests of drawers were also produced about the same time. Many lidded chests and chests of drawers were designed without feet and rested flush on the floor (which prevented dust from accumulating beneath the piece). Others had applied bracket feet or feet cut out of the four sides. Pine was the material commonly used because it was easily worked and was available in exceptionally wide boards.

Fitting chests with locks was not an uncommon practice but does seem to point to a contradiction, for Shaker societies were built on mutual trust and early church regulations discouraged the use of locks on furniture. It is quite possible their necessity was recognized by the leadership who had the responsibility of securing important spiritual and temporal documents.

1. This lidded storage chest in pine painted brown-red was made during the first half of the nineteenth century; its plain lines suggest it is possibly eastern, though its community origin is not known. The corners carry well-made dovetailed joints and the lid (or seat) has a quarter-round molding on the exposed edges. Somewhat unorthodox is the use of table-leaf hinges surface mounted on the lid, instead of the generally used butt hinges edge-gained. A hand-wrought iron hasp made it possible to secure the chest contents. The curved back—angled and supported by a piece of strong strap iron, with another under the lid—suggests that the chest was also designed to do service as a seat, possibly in a wagon. The nailed-on bottom was surface applied rather than let into the chest, which indicates either that it was not made to hold and transport heavy items or, if so used, was improperly designed. Collection of Shakertown at Pleasant Hill, Inc., Harrodsburg, Ky.

H. 21-1/2, W. 38-1/4, D. 19-1/8.

Letter	No.	Name	Material	T	W	L
A	1	hinged seat	pine	3/4	13-1/2	38-1/4
B	1	fixed seat part	pine	3/4	4-3/4	38-1/4
C	2	front and back	pine	3/4	14-1/2	37-3/4
D	2	sides	pine	3/4	14-1/2	18
E	1	bottom	pine	3/4	18	37-3/4
F	1	backrest	pine	3/4	5-1/2	37
Hardware						
G	2	table-leaf hinges	iron			1
H	1	back brace	iron	1/8	1	6
I	1	seat brace	iron	1/8	1	5
J	1	hasp	iron			
K	4	rivets	iron			
L	12	wood screws	iron	FH 5/8-8		

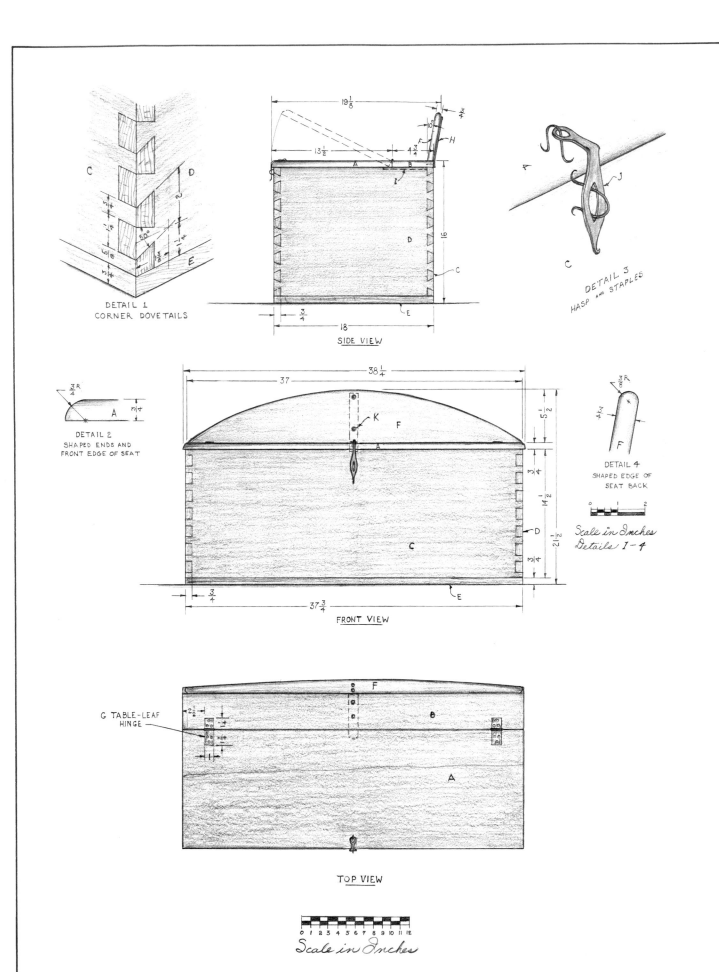

DETAIL 1
CORNER DOVETAILS

SIDE VIEW

DETAIL 3
HASP AND STAPLES

DETAIL 2
SHAPED ENDS AND
FRONT EDGE OF SEAT

DETAIL 4
SHAPED EDGE OF
SEAT BACK

Scale in Inches
Details 1-4

FRONT VIEW

G TABLE-LEAF
HINGE

TOP VIEW

Scale in Inches

2. This pine six-board lidded chest, painted red, is from Hancock and dates from the early part of the nineteenth century. It has corner dovetails, a thumb molding on the lid, and an early chest lock. The bottom on this chest was also nail applied. Private collection.

H. 14-3/8, W. 34-1/8, D. 13.

3. Many curved-top wooden chests or trunks were made by the "world's people"; however, this example is attributed to New Lebanon and dates from the first half of the nineteenth century. The chest is made of pine painted brown and has dovetailed corners, leather hinges, and small brass bail handles. Collection of the Shaker Museum, Old Chatham, N. Y.

H. 11-1/4, W. 23-1/2, D. 13-1/2.

4. The sides and ends of this six-board lidded chest are assembled to corner posts. All parts of the chest are cherry except the poplar bottom. It was made in the first half of the nineteenth century, at Pleasant Hill. The heavy lidded top and corner posts offer credence to its western attribution. Collection of Shakertown at Pleasant Hill, Inc., Harrodsburg, Ky.

H. 22, W. 35-1/4, D. 17.

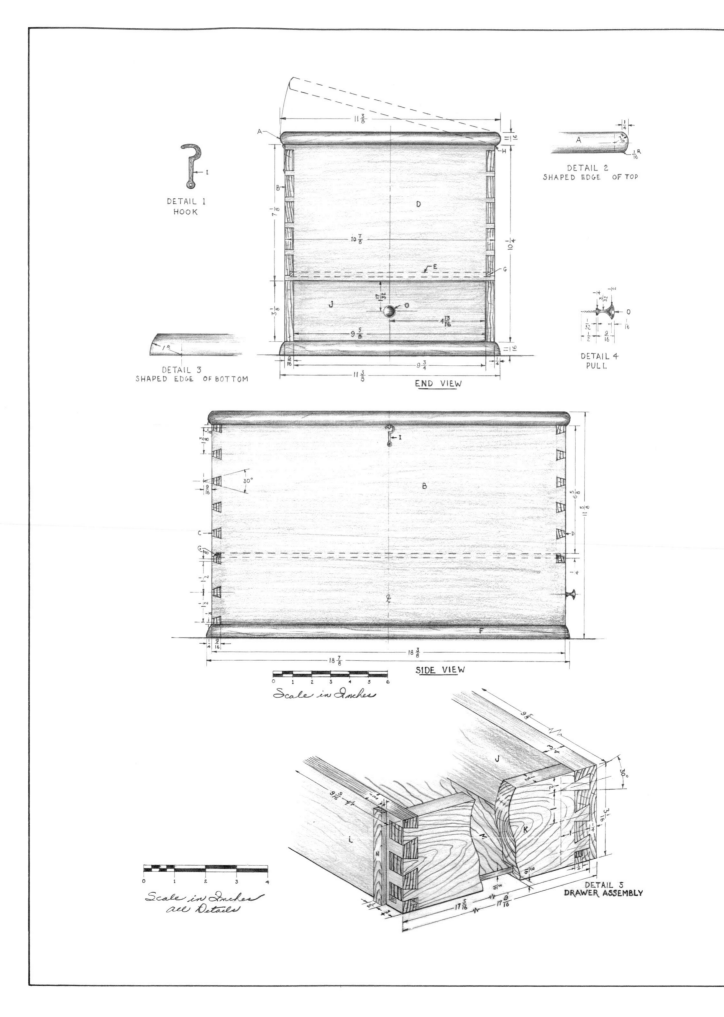

DETAIL 1
HOOK

DETAIL 2
SHAPED EDGE OF TOP

DETAIL 3
SHAPED EDGE OF BOTTOM

DETAIL 4
PULL

END VIEW

SIDE VIEW

Scale in Inches

Scale in Inches
all Details

DETAIL 5
DRAWER ASSEMBLY

5. The fine craftsmanship that went into making this small, single-drawer chest suggests that it was made to hold things of importance; precisely what cannot be determined. It was made in the New Lebanon community during the first half of the nineteenth century and is in unfinished pine, which has developed a warm brown patina. The chest has two bottoms: the upper one serves as the bottom for the lidded portion and is held in grooves milled into the inner surfaces of the sides and ends; the lower bottom constitutes the chest base and is nail applied. Properly sized dovetails hold the chest sides together. The edges of the lid have a half-round molding and the edges on the bottom are arc-molded. Grooves cut into the inner surfaces of the drawer sides hold the drawer bottom in place and stop-blocks nailed to the back of the drawer position the front so that it is flush with the edges of the chest when closed. The hinges, hook, and drawer pull are not Shaker-made. Private collection.

H. 11-5/8, W. 18-7/8, D. 11-3/8.

Letter	No.	Name	Material	T	W	L
A	1	top	pine	11/16	11-3/8	18-7/8
B	2	front and back	pine	9/16	10-1/4	18-3/8
C	1	left end	pine	9/16	10-1/4	10-7/8
D	1	right end	pine	9/16	7-1/8	10-7/8
E	1	chest bottom	pine	1/4	10-1/8	17-5/8
F	1	bottom	pine	11/16	11-3/8	18-7/8
G	8	filler plugs	pine	cut to size		
Hardware						
H	2	butt hinges	iron		9/16	1-3/4
I	1	hook and eye	brass	1-1/2		
Drawer						
J	1	front	pine	3/4	3-1/16	9-5/8
K	2	sides	pine	1/2	3-1/16	17-5/16
L	1	back	pine	1/2	3-1/16	9-9/16
M	1	bottom	pine	5/16	9	16-15/16
N	2	stop blocks	pine	1/4	1	3-1/16
Hardware						
O	1	pull	brass	1/2 dia		1-1/16

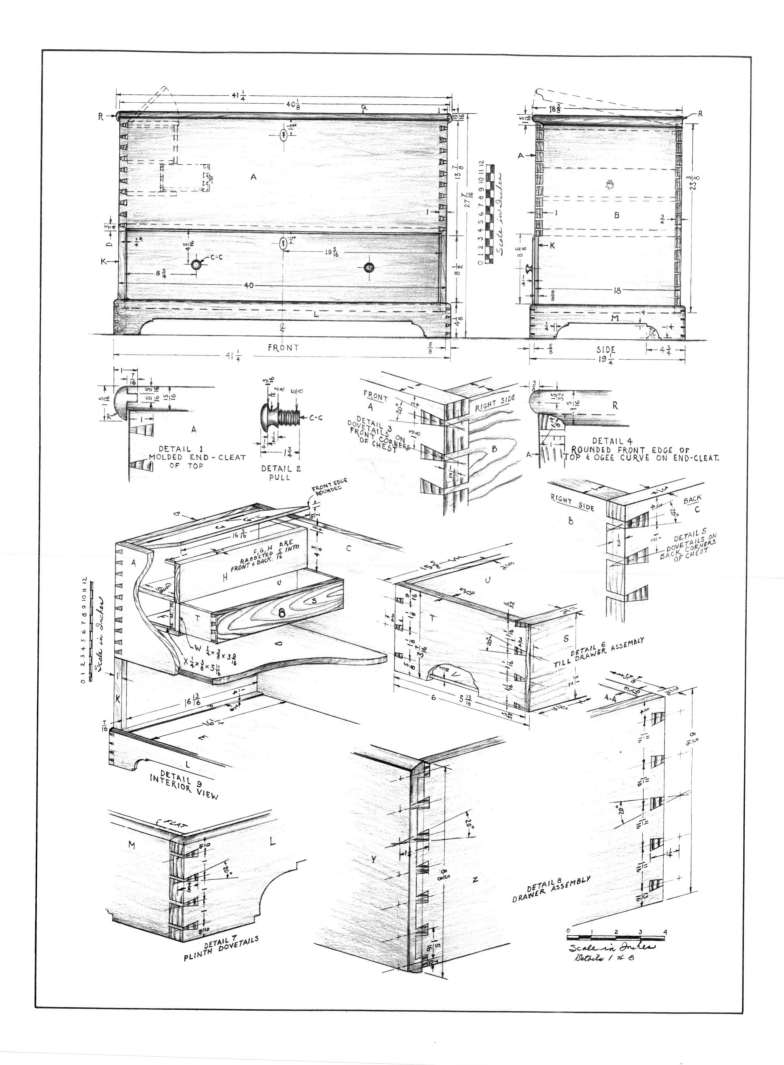

FRONT

SIDE

Scale in Inches

DETAIL 1
MOLDED END-CLEAT
OF TOP

DETAIL 2
PULL

DETAIL 3
DOVETAILS ON
FRONT CORNERS
OF CHEST

DETAIL 4
ROUNDED FRONT EDGE OF
TOP & OGEE CURVE ON END-CLEAT.

DETAIL 5
DOVETAILS ON
BACK CORNERS
OF CHEST

DETAIL 6
TILL DRAWER ASSEMBLY

F.G.H ARE
RABBETED 5/16 INTO
FRONT & BACK. 1/16

DETAIL 9
INTERIOR VIEW

DETAIL 8
DRAWER ASSEMBLY

DETAIL 7
PLINTH DOVETAILS

Scale in Inches
Details 1 to 8

6. Inscribed in burnt letters on the back of this one-drawer blanket chest of pine in original red paint is "made April, 1837 Canaan." The chest is attributed to Brother Gilbert Avery (1775–1853), a member of the Upper Canaan family, which was a part of the New Lebanon community. A plinth with dovetailed corners and convex cutouts raises the chest off the floor. Four corner blocks fastened to the inside corners lend added support. The sides and ends of the chest are held together with dovetails. A lidded till with a drawer beneath is at the inside left end. As an afterthought, a hole had to be cut in the chest bottom to allow air trapped behind the drawer to escape into the chest proper. The applied tongue-and-groove molding at the ends of the hinged top is typical of Shaker work. The key escutcheons are of bone. Collection of Mrs. Edward Deming Andrews.

H. 27-7/16, W. 41-1/4, D. 19-1/4.

Letter	No.	Name	Material	T	W	L
A	1	front	pine	1	13-7/8	40
B	2	sides	pine	1	23-3/8	18
C	1	back	pine	3/4	23-3/8	40
D	1	chest bottom	pine	3/4	16-1/2	38-5/8
E	1	bottom	pine	7/8	16-1/4	38-5/8
F	1	drawer shelf	pine	7/16	6-1/16	16-7/8
G	1	till bottom	pine	7/16	5-5/8	16-7/8
H	1	till front	pine	7/16	4-3/4	16-7/8
I	2	till lid supports	pine	1/4	3/8	5-5/8
J	1	till lid	pine	7/16	6-1/4	16-3/16
K	2	front filler pieces	pine	7/16	1	9-1/2
L	2	front and back plinths	pine	5/8	4-1/8	41-1/4
M	2	end plinths	pine	5/8	4-1/8	19-1/4
N	4	corner support blocks	pine	2	2	3-1/8
O	4	glue blocks	pine	1-1/4	1-1/4	2-1/2
P	2	drawer runners	pine	1/4	7/8	16-1/4
Q	1	top	pine	15/16	18-3/8	40-1/8
R	2	end cleats	pine	1	1-5/16	18-3/8

Letter	No.	Name	Material	T	W	L
Till Drawer						
S	1	front	cherry	11/16	3-1/2	15-11/16
T	2	sides	pine	5/16	3-7/16	5-13/16
U	1	back	pine	5/16	2-15/16	15-5/8
V	1	bottom	pine	5/16	5-1/2	15-1/4
W	2	fillers	pine	1/4	3/8	3-9/16
X	2	guides	pine	1/4	3/8	5-11/16
Drawer						
Y	1	front	pine	7/8	8-5/8	38-5/8
Z	2	sides	pine	9/16	8-5/16	17-1/8
A-A	1	back	pine	9/16	7-5/8	37-7/8
B-B	1	bottom	pine	1/2	16-7/8	37
C-C	2	pulls	maple	1-3/16 dia		1-3/4
Hardware						
	1	drawer ring pull	brass	5/8 dia ring		
	2	butt hinges	brass		3/8	1-3/4
	2	butt hinges	steel		3/4	2
	1	chest lock				
	2	key escutcheon	ivory	1/8	7/8	1-1/4

7. From New Lebanon, this two-drawer pine blanket chest is painted a yellow wash and dates from the first half of the nineteenth century. The bracket feet are cut on an angle at the front and sides. End cleats on the lidded top help keep it straight. The lipped edges on the dovetailed drawers are quarter-rounded and the pulls are probably maple. Collection of the Shaker Museum, Old Chatham, N. Y.

H. 36-1/4, W. 42-1/4, D. 18-1/4.

114

8. From Canterbury, this pine one-drawer blanket chest is also painted a yellow wash and dates from the second half of the nineteenth century. The chest is nailed at the corners and the plinth is assembled with corner dovetails. Still intact under the chest are drawer runners which supported an added-on drawer. Collection of Greenfield Village and the Henry Ford Museum, Dearborn, Mich. Photograph courtesy of the museum.

H. 33, W. 42-7/8, D. 19-1/4.

9. The evolution of the chest of drawers is shown in figures 7 and 8 and in this three-drawer blanket chest. In this example, the addition of another drawer would, for all practical purposes, eliminate the lidded chest portion of the piece. The chest dates from the first half of the nineteenth century and was made in the Enfield, New Hampshire, society. It is pine painted red and rests on a plinth dovetailed at the corners and cut in ogee curves which form feet. The graduated drawers have edge-molded fronts and are assembled with traditional joinery. A bead-and-cove molding was cut on the edges of the chest lid. Collection of the Shaker Museum, Sabbathday Lake, Maine. Photograph by Bill Finney.

H. 40, W. 43-1/4, D. 19.

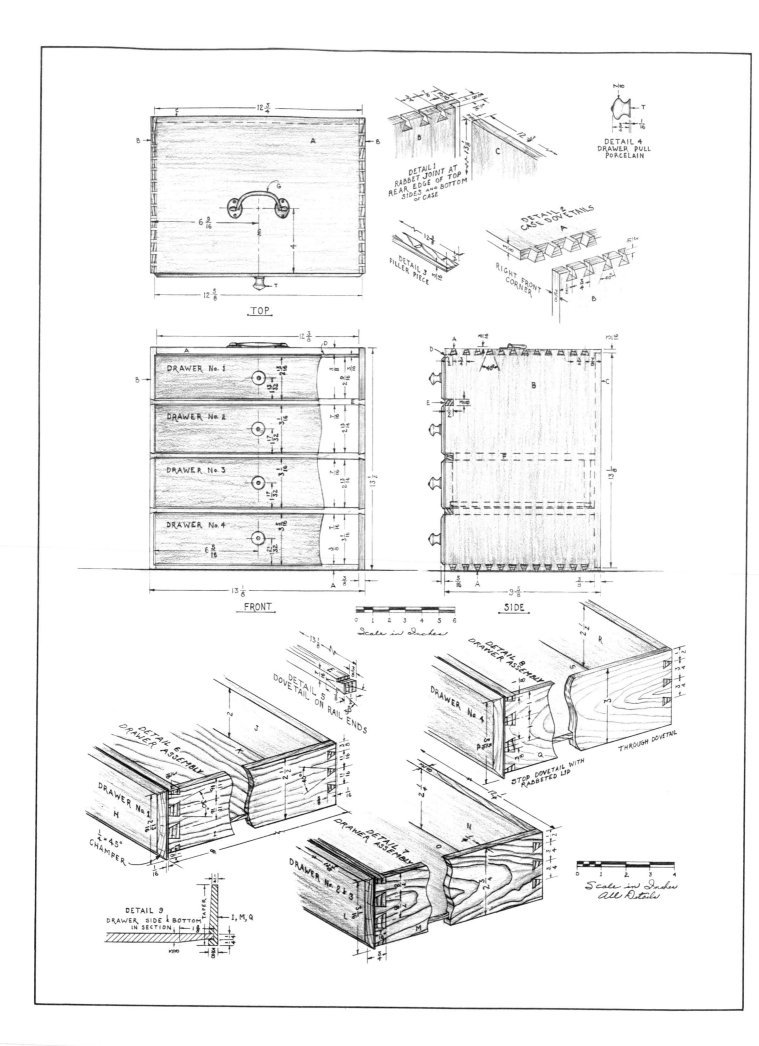

TOP

DETAIL 1
RABBET JOINT AT
REAR EDGE OF TOP
SIDES and BOTTOM
of CASE

DETAIL 3
FILLER PIECE

DETAIL 2
CASE DOVETAILS

RIGHT FRONT
CORNER

DETAIL 4
DRAWER PULL
PORCELAIN

DRAWER No. 1

DRAWER No. 2

DRAWER No. 3

DRAWER No. 4

FRONT

0 1 2 3 4 5 6
Scale in Inches

SIDE

DETAIL 5
DOVETAIL ON RAIL ENDS

DETAIL 6
DRAWER ASSEMBLY

DRAWER No. 1

¼ x 45°
CHAMFER

DETAIL 8
DRAWER ASSEMBLY

DRAWER No. 4

THROUGH DOVETAIL

STOP DOVETAIL WITH
RABBETED LIP

DETAIL 7
DRAWER ASSEMBLY

DRAWER No. 2 & 3

DETAIL 9
DRAWER SIDE & BOTTOM
IN SECTION

I, M, Q

0 1 2 3 4
Scale in Inches
All Details

10. This small, four-drawer sewing chest of mixed woods with porcelain drawer pulls was made in the second half of the nineteenth century at New Lebanon. The walnut drawer fronts, butternut sides, and pine back are finished in clear varnish. The interior parts are pine and the brass bail handle is positioned on the top, at the center of gravity. The drawer fronts are thicker and heavier than the pine parts at the rear of the case. One peculiarity of construction is the inside surfaces of the drawer sides which taper from 3/8 inch at the bottom to 1/4 inch at the top. While this made laying out the dovetails slightly more difficult, it probably was worth the effort in that drawer contents could be located more easily (for another example of a piece with tapered drawer sides, see Counters, fig. 5). Also uncommon are the chamfers on the edges of the drawer fronts; usually these edges were simply quarter-rounded (for a similar example, see Counters, fig. 6). The upper drawer should have been made the same height as the second and third, thereby eliminating the need

Letter	No.	Name	Material	T	W	L
A	2	top and bottom	butternut	3/8	9-5/8	13-1/8
B	2	sides	butternut	3/8	9-5/8	13-1/2
C	1	back	pine	3/8	12-3/4	13-1/8
D	1	filler piece	walnut	3/16	1/2	12-3/8
E	3	rails	walnut	7/16	1/2	13-1/8
F	6	drawer runners	pine	7/16	7/16	8-3/4
Hardware						
G	1	handle	brass			
Drawer 1						
H	1	front	walnut	3/4	2-13/16	12-5/8
I	2	sides (tapered)	pine	1/4 to 3/8	2-1/2	9
J	1	back	pine	3/8	2	12-1/4
K	1	bottom	pine	3/8	8-3/4	11-7/8
Drawers 2, 3						
L	2	fronts	walnut	3/4	3-1/16	12-5/8
M	4	sides (tapered)	pine	1/4 to 3/8	2-3/4	9
N	2	backs	pine	3/8	2-1/4	12-1/4
O	2	bottoms	pine	3/8	8-3/4	11-7/8
Drawer 4						
P	1	front	walnut	3/4	3-5/16	12-5/8
Q	2	sides (tapered)	pine	1/4 to 3/8	3	9
R	1	back	pine	3/8	2-1/2	12-1/4
S	1	bottom	pine	3/8	8-3/4	11-7/8
T	4	drawer pulls	porcelain			

to add a gap-filling piece under the front edge of the top. Twelve carefully made dovetails at each corner, the dovetails on the ends of the rails, and a rabbeted, nailed-in back hold the case permanently together. Private collection.

H. 13-1/2, W. 13-1/8, D. 9-5/8.

11. The plain lines and multiple drawer arrangement of this nicely made seven-drawer case of walnut and pine are typical of eastern pieces; however, this example (c. 1808) was made by Richard McNemar (1770–1839) of the Union Village society for his son Benjamin's "little tools." McNemar was a man of many talents; he was a farmer, weaver, teacher, preacher, missionary to the Indians, pharmacist, writer, singer, composer, editor, printer, bookbinder, and cabinetmaker. It was largely through his efforts that the Ohio, Kentucky, and Indiana Shaker communites were established. The flush ends on the case suggest it may have been designed or later modified to fit within a given space. Collection of Warren County Historical Society Museum, Lebanon, Ohio.

H. 7-3/4, W. 36-1/8, D. 8.

12. This two-drawer case in pine, stained light brown with a clear varnish finish, was made at Hancock during the first half of the nineteenth century. The top and bottom have a pleasing half-round molding; however, the walnut drawer pulls seem too large for the drawer fronts. The upper drawer is divided into fifteen small sections. Tools and larger items were housed in the lower, undivided drawer. Collection of Shaker Community, Inc., Hancock, Mass.

H. 6-1/4, W. 20-1/4, D. 11-1/4.

13. Brother George Wilcox (1820–1910), cabinetmaker and elder at the Enfield, Connecticut, community, made this multi-drawer, small parts chest. It dates from the second half of the nineteenth century and is pine painted red. The drawers are assembled with dovetails and let-in bottoms. The horizontal division pieces separating the drawers extend from the front to the rabbeted back and are dadoed into the sides. The vertical dividers are dadoed into the horizontal division pieces. Wear marks on the drawer fronts show that the brass pulls are replacements. Collection of Mr. and Mrs. Charles R. Muller.

H. 31-1/2, W. 29-1/2, D. 7-3/4.

14. Vegetable seeds were kept in this storage chest that was made during the first half of the nineteenth century in the Hancock community. It is of pine, with cherry drawer fronts and pulls. The contents of the dove-tailed drawers are labeled and read, from left to right and top to bottom: "French Turnip," "Early Cucumber Selected," "Variety Seeds," "Loose He'd Lettuce," "[undecipherable] Bay," "Cabbage [undecipherable]," "York Cabbage," "Frankfort He'd Lettuce," "Savory Cabbage," and "[undecipherable]." The chest has been refinished, but fortunately the labels were not removed in the process. The right side of the chest is paneled and the left is covered with solid boards; this suggests that originally the chest may have been a built-in piece—possibly the base portion of a cupboard. The Stokes Collection.

H. 35, W. 29-1/2, D. 21-3/8.

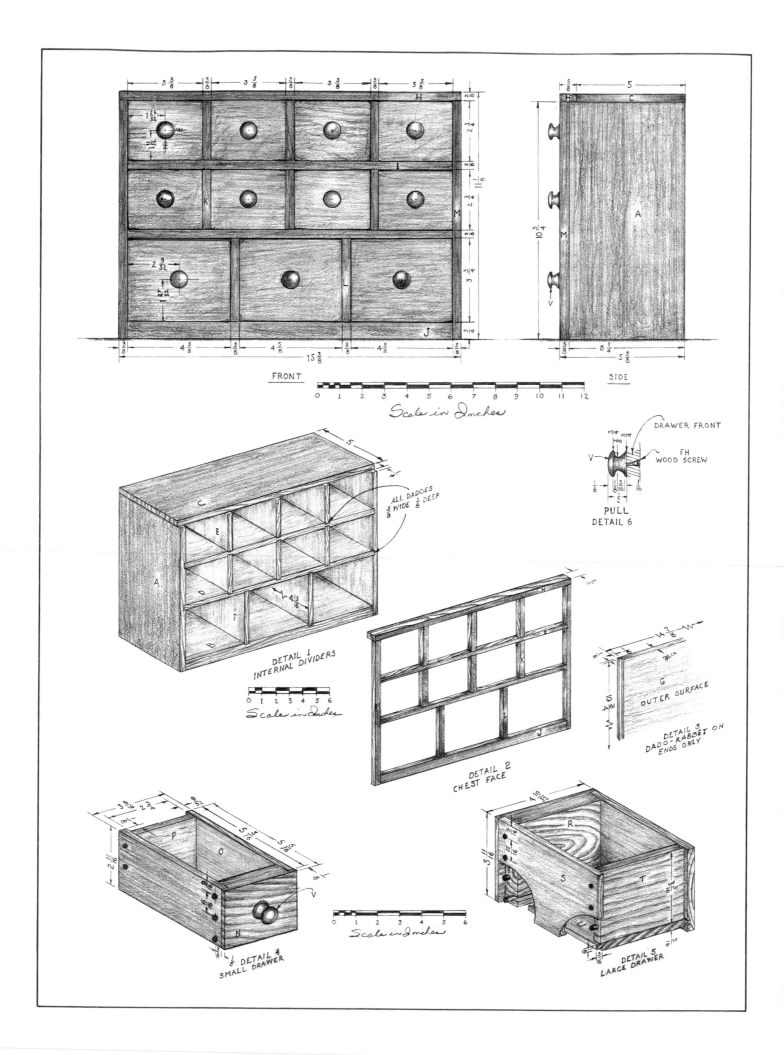

FRONT

SIDE

Scale in Inches

ALL DADOES
3/8 WIDE 1/8 DEEP

DRAWER FRONT

FH
WOOD SCREW

PULL
DETAIL 6

DETAIL 1
INTERNAL DIVIDERS

Scale in Inches

DETAIL 2
CHEST FACE

OUTER SURFACE

DETAIL 3
DADO-RABBET ON
ENDS ONLY

DETAIL 4
SMALL DRAWER

Scale in Inches

DETAIL 5
LARGE DRAWER

15. Brother Thomas Fisher (1823–1902), cabinetmaker in the Enfield, New Hampshire, society, made this spice chest. His signature "T. Fisher 1887" is written in ink on the left side of the upper left-hand drawer. Also written on the left side of the adjacent drawer are the words: "Enfield Shakers 1887." Components of the chest are pine except the walnut drawer fronts and pulls and the chestnut facing. The chest is assembled with glue and nailed dado joints. The facing hides the dado joints. A variation of the machine-made, scalloped dovetail joint holds the drawer parts together. A walnut varnish-stain covers the sides and top; the drawer fronts are clear varnished. Collection of Mr. and Mrs. Charles R. Muller.

H. 11-1/8, W. 15-3/8, D. 5-5/8.

Letter	No.	Name	Material	T	W	L
A	2	sides	pine	3/8	5-1/4	10-3/4
B	1	bottom	pine	3/4	4-15/16	14-5/8
C	1	top	pine	3/8	5	15-3/8
D	2	horizontal dividers	pine	3/8	4-15/16	14-7/8
E	6	vertical dividers	pine	3/8	4-15/16	3
F	2	vertical dividers	pine	3/8	4-15/16	4
G	1	back	pine	5/16	10-3/4	14-7/8
H	1	horizontal face piece	chestnut	3/8	5/8	15-3/8
I	2	horizontal face piece	chestnut	3/8	3/8	14-5/8
J	1	horizontal face piece	chestnut	3/8	3/4	14-5/8
K	6	vertical face pieces	chestnut	3/8	3/8	2-3/4
L	2	vertical face pieces	chestnut	3/8	3/8	3-3/4
M	2	vertical face pieces	chestnut	3/8	3/8	10-3/4
Small drawers						
N	8	fronts	walnut	11/16	2-11/16	3-5/16
O	16	sides	pine	9/32	2-11/16	5-3/16
P	8	backs	pine	3/8	2-3/16	3-5/16
Q	8	bottoms	pine	5/16	3	4-5/8
Large drawers						
R	3	fronts	walnut	11/16	3-11/16	4-19/32
S	6	sides	pine	9/32	3-11/16	5-3/16
T	3	backs	pine	3/8	3-3/16	4-19/32
U	3	bottoms	pine	5/16	4-1/4	4-3/4
V	11	pulls	walnut	3/4 dia		8/16

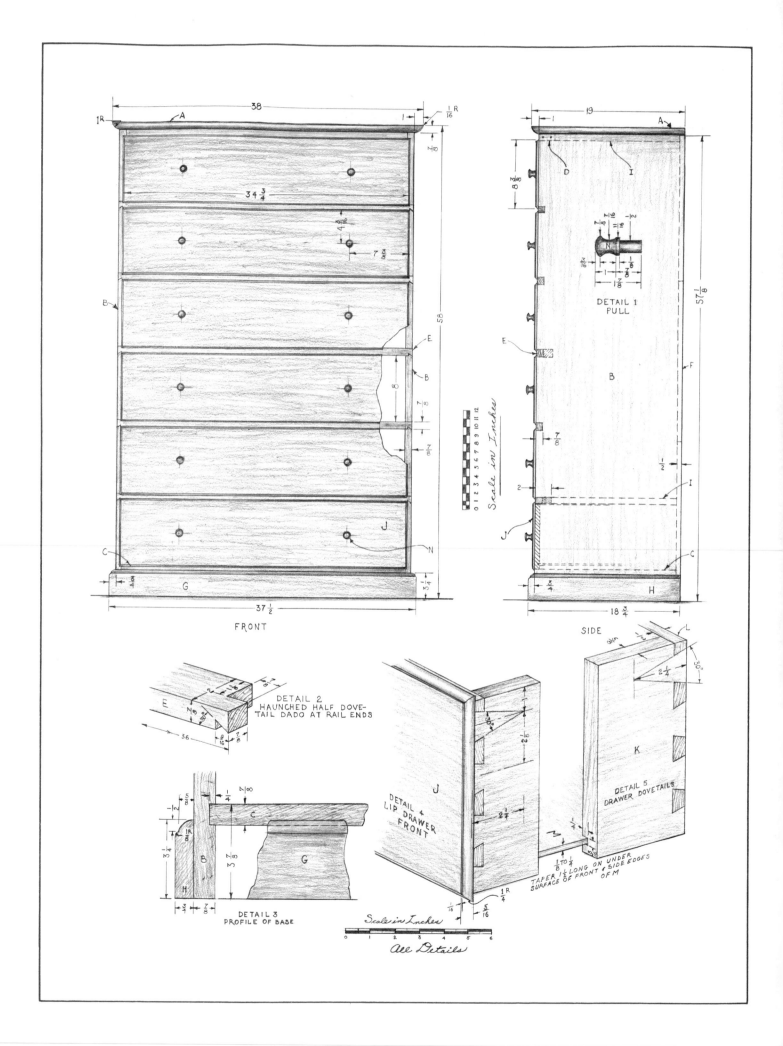

38

1R

$34\frac{3}{4}$

A

$4\frac{3}{16}$

7

B

E

8

$7\frac{8}{}$

$7\frac{}{10}$

J

N

C

G

$37\frac{1}{2}$

FRONT

$\frac{1}{16}$R

1

$7\frac{8}{}$

58

$3\frac{1}{4}$

0 1 2 3 4 5 6 7 8 9 10 11 12

Scale in Inches

19

1

A

$8\frac{3}{16}$

D

I

$\frac{7}{8}$ $\frac{11}{16}$ $\frac{1}{2}$

N

$\frac{3}{16}$ $\frac{1}{8}$

1

$1\frac{7}{8}$

DETAIL 1
PULL

E

B

F

$\frac{7}{8}$

2

J

$57\frac{1}{8}$

$\frac{1}{2}$

I

$\frac{3}{4}$

C

H

$18\frac{3}{4}$

SIDE

DETAIL 2
HAUNCHED HALF DOVE-
TAIL DADO AT RAIL ENDS

E

36

$\frac{9}{16}$ $\frac{7}{8}$

$5\frac{5}{8}$

$\frac{1}{2}$

$\frac{7}{8}$

$4\frac{1}{}$

C

$3\frac{7}{8}$

B

G

1R
$\frac{1}{8}$

$3\frac{1}{4}$

H

$\frac{3}{4}$ $\frac{7}{8}$

DETAIL 3
PROFILE OF BASE

$2\frac{9}{16}$

J

DETAIL 4
LIP DRAWER
FRONT

$2\frac{1}{2}$

$1\frac{1}{16}$ $\frac{5}{16}$

$1\frac{1}{4}$

$2\frac{1}{4}$

30°

L

K

DETAIL 5
DRAWER DOVETAILS

$\frac{1}{8}$ TO $\frac{1}{4}$

TAPER $1\frac{1}{2}$ LONG ON UNDER
SURFACE OF FRONT & SIDE EDGES
OF M

0 1 2 3 4 5 6

Scale in Inches

All Details

16. The nongraduated drawers in this New Lebanon six-drawer chest have molded edges and delightfully small pulls. The chest is pine painted red and dates from the first half of the nineteenth century. The sides are held with dovetailed front rails, and a three-board back is rabbeted into the sides and nailed. Each drawer is assembled with typical joinery. Private collection.

H. 58, W. 38, D. 19.

Letter	No.	Name	Material	T	W	L
A	1	top	pine	7/8	19	38
B	2	sides	pine	7/8	18	57-1/8
C	1	bottom	pine	7/8	17-1/2	34-3/4
D	1	top rail	pine	7/8	2	34-1/4
E	5	rails	pine	7/8	2	36
F	1	back	pine	1/2	57	34-3/4
G	1	front plinth member	pine	3/4	3-1/4	37-1/2
H	2	side plinth members	pine	3/4	3-1/4	18-3/4
I	12	drawer runners	pine	7/8	1	15-1/2
Drawers						
J	6	fronts	pine	7/8	8-3/8	34-3/4
K	12	sides	pine	5/8	7-7/8	17-1/4
L	6	backs	pine	1/2	7-1/4	34-1/8
M	6	bottoms	pine	3/8	17-1/4	33-5/8
N	12	pulls	maple	7/8 dia		1-7/8

17. The side-by-side drawer configuration of this nongraduated eight-drawer chest is aesthetically delightful and atypical in form. The piece is pine finished in orange shellac and was made in the New Lebanon community during the first half of the nineteenth century. A rabbeted, nailed-in back and locking dovetail ends on the front rails hold the chest sides in place. The sides are cut on an angle at the floor line and separate pieces, also cut on an angle, were let into the front corners; all of which form bracket feet—a foot style often used on case pieces made in this community. The drawers are dovetailed, have let-in bottoms, and small cherry pulls turned in a style typical of this community. Collection of Clifford A. Josephson.

H. 42-1/2, W. 49, D. 19-5/8.

18. This New Lebanon two-drawer pine chest is elegantly simple in form. Made during the second half of the nineteenth century, the chest is stained a light orange-brown. Dadoes in the sides hold the drawer rails and runners. The case is assembled with nails, and the drawers have ever-present dovetails and let-in bottoms. Four boards, tongue-and-grooved, make up the back. The walnut pulls may be commercial products purchased by the Shakers. In later years the practice of buying pulls, hinges, locks, and other hardware was not uncommon in the order. Private collection.

H. 29-3/4, W. 29, D. 18.

19. One of the finest examples of Shaker craftsmanship is this six-drawer chest of butternut and poplar from Union Village. Except for the fancy cyma scrolls at the base, the chest has a characteristic Shaker plainness. The drawers have molded lip edges and small, precisely turned pulls. The piece is signed and dated on the back of two drawers, "Daniel Sering, November 9, 1827." Brother Daniel (1792–1870) was converted to Shakerism at the age of thirteen, signed the covenant at twenty-one, and remained in the order until his death. He was a competent carpenter and joiner and served as a church elder. Collection of Warren County Historical Society Museum, Lebanon, Ohio.

H. 51-3/4, W. 43-5/8, D. 22.

20. From the mid-nineteenth century, this six-drawer chest in pine stained red-brown was probably made at the Hancock community. The drawer fronts and edges are quarter-round molded and are assembled with dovetails. The upper drawer is slightly more shallow than those below, which are all equal in depth. The plinth has simple convex cutouts and is assembled with corner dovetails. Collection of Greenfield Village and the Henry Ford Museum, Dearborn, Mich. Photograph courtesy of the museum.

H. 73, W. 37, D. 18.

21. This classic, tall chest of drawers is a New Lebanon piece and was made during the first half of the nineteenth century. It is of pine, has conventionally assembled drawers with cherry pulls, and is painted an orange-red wash. The drawer rails are fastened to the chest sides with shouldered dadoes instead of the more secure locking dovetails. The bracket feet are a style often found on Shaker case pieces. Collection of Darrow School, New Lebanon, N. Y.

H. 74-1/2, W. 48, D. 23-1/2.

Clocks

Most Shaker clocks were produced at the Watervliet, New York, community, some as early as 1790. Although the number of known Shaker clockmakers and their extant pieces is small, clocks were a real necessity in Shaker communities where everything went by time. Used sparingly, usually in halls, what Shaker clockmakers could not supply were purchased from the world. Shaker-made clockworks were the same as those made outside the communities, yet the design of the plain and relatively unembellished cases reflects a direct religious influence. Unnecessary superficial decoration was removed from purchased pieces. Clock types produced within the communities were wag-on-the-wall, wall, shelf, miniature-tall, and tall.

1. This early nineteenth-century tall clock of pine painted dark red is unsigned and undated but it may be the work of Benjamin Youngs (1736–1818) of the Watervliet, New York, colony. The case has severely plain, vertical lines broken only by a simple quarter-round molding at the floor line and at the hood top. An equally plain, concave molding at the upper end of the body unifies the piece visually and supports the hood. The clockworks are strike-weight driven. Private collection.

H. 81-1/2, W. 15-3/8, D. 8-3/4.

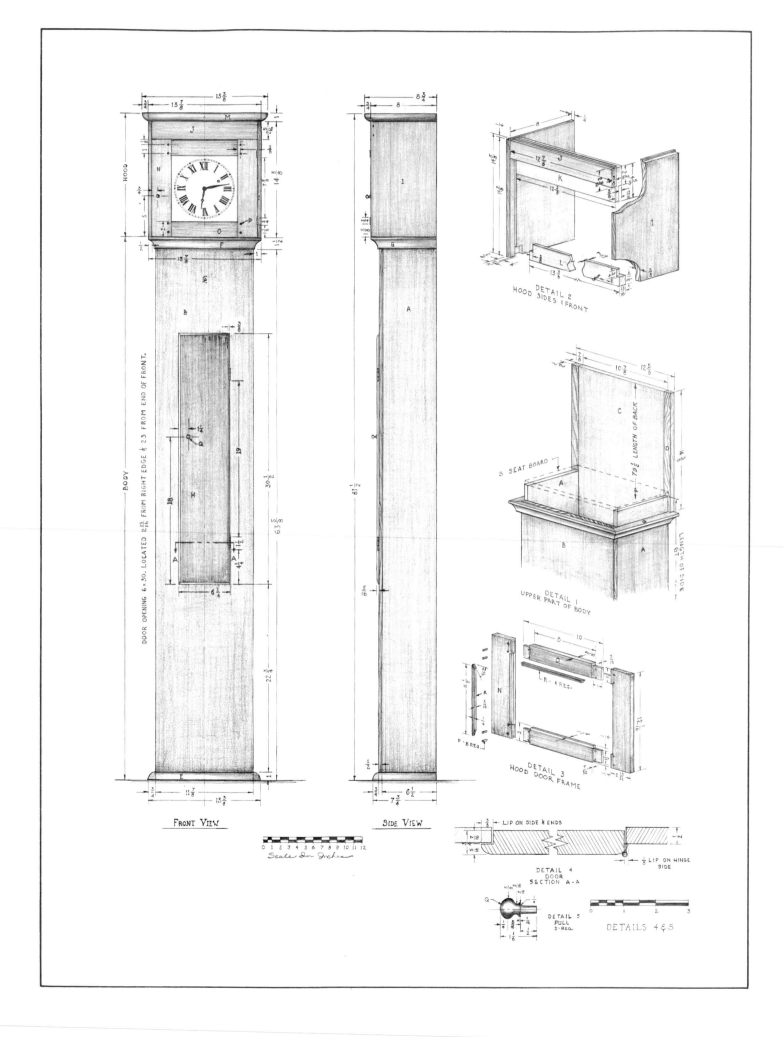

FRONT VIEW

SIDE VIEW

0 1 2 3 4 5 6 7 8 9 10 11 12
Scale In Inches

DETAIL 2
HOOD SIDES & FRONT

DETAIL 1
UPPER PART OF BODY

DETAIL 3
HOOD DOOR FRAME

LIP ON SIDE & ENDS

LIP ON HINGE SIDE

DETAIL 4
DOOR
SECTION A-A

DETAIL 5
PULL
2-REQ.

DETAILS 4 & 5

0 1 2 3

Figure 1

Letter	No.	Name	Material	T	W	L
Body						
A	2	sides	pine	1/2	6-1/2	67
B	1	front	pine	1/2	11-7/8	65-1/8
C	1	back	pine	1/2	10-7/8	79-1/2
D	2	filler pieces	pine	1/2	7/8	14-3/8
E	1	bottom	pine	1	7-3/4	13-3/8
F	1	front molding	pine	1	1-1/2	13-7/8
G	2	side moldings	pine	1	1-1/2	8
H	1	door	pine	3/4	6-1/4	30-1/2
Hood						
I	2	sides	pine	5/8	8	14-5/8
J	1	front rail	pine	5/8	2-9/16	12-7/8
K	1	upper rail (behind door)	pine	13/16	4-5/16	12-5/8
L	1	lower rail (behind door)	pine	13/16	2	13-3/8
M	1	top	pine	1	8-3/4	15-3/8
Door						
N	2	stiles	pine	5/8	2-13/32	12-1/16
O	2	rails	pine	5/8	2	10
P	8	pins	pine	3/16 dia		5/8
Q	2	pulls	cherry	5/8 dia		1-1/8
R	4	stops	pine	1/4	5/16	8-1/2
S	1	seat board	pine	9/16	6	11-7/8
Hardware	2	hinges	brass		1/2	3/4
	2	hinges	brass		1	1-1/2

2. The following data is written on the back of the face of this tall clock from Watervliet, New York:

      B. Y. Fecit
        1809
      B. Y. age 72
      Oct. 4, 1809

B. Y. is Benjamin Youngs and "Fecit" stands for creator or erector. Brother Benjamin continued to worship, work, and live another ten years after making this clock. Like figure 1, it also is pine painted red but is more worldly in style. Private collection.

H. 81, W. 20, D. 9-7/8.

3. The worldly style of this tall clock, also made by Benjamin Youngs, reflects his early clockmaking training, which was taken in Connecticut years prior to becoming a Shaker. The clock was probably made in Watervliet, New York, on special order for use by the trustees or ministry in New Lebanon where it has remained ever since. The case was fabricated in three units—base, body, and hood—and is cherry trimmed in rosewood and mahogany (both are imported woods and are a bit showy for Shakers). The interior parts are pine. Collection of Darrow School, New Lebanon, N. Y.

H. 82-15/16, W. 19-1/4, D. 9-1/4.

4. Brother Benjamin Youngs of Watervliet, New York, made this alarm wall clock (c. 1805). It has a cherry case stained red and a pine back. The lower section of the case tapers inward slightly from base to hook. Collection of the Western Reserve Historical Society, Cleveland, Ohio. Photograph by Elroy Sanford.

H. 41-1/2, W. 10, D. 5-1/2.

5. Another example of an alarm wall clock by Benjamin Youngs is shown here. It was made in 1810–1812, at Watervliet, New York, and has a pine case with a cherry door stained brown. The Arabic numerals on the clock face were not used as often as Roman numerals. Collection of Greenfield Village and the Henry Ford Museum, Dearborn, Mich. Photograph courtesy of the museum.

H. 36-1/8, W. 10-1/2, D. 9-1/2.

6. This wall clock from New Lebanon is numbered, signed, and dated on the back as follows:

No 21, Made by Isaac N. Youngs
May 12th 1840

The following verse also appears:

O' Time! how swift that solemn day
rolls on
when from these mortal scenes we
shall be gone!!

Issac Newton Youngs (1793–1865) was Benjamin's nephew and chief clockmaker at New Lebanon. The case is walnut stained red and has a pine backboard (backplate), painted chrome-yellow. The top and bottom are nailed to the sides of the case and the back is rabbeted into the sides. The door frames are mortised-and-tenoned and the stops are nailed from the outer, rather than the customary inner, surface. Using glass for the panel in the lower door is showy and therefore unusual Shaker practice. Suspended from a peg on a pegrail, the clock was kept level with string tied to two screw eyes at the top and anchored to adjacent pegs. Clock adjustments were made by removing the inspection-window keepers and the glass. Collection of Shaker Community, Inc., Hancock, Mass.

H. 33-3/4, W. 11-1/8, D. 4-1/4.

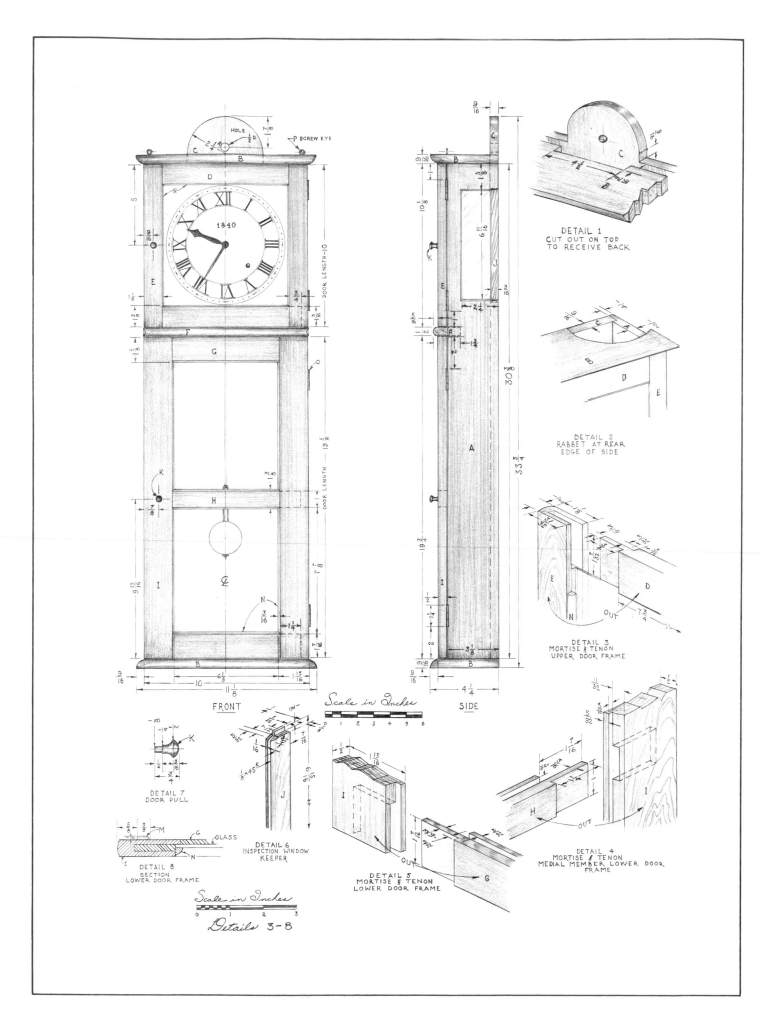

HOLE

2¼φ ½φ

P SCREW EYE

1840

N

D

B

C

5

9/16

E

1⅛

3/16

¾

DOOR LENGTH—10

F

1⅝

G

K

3/8

H

7/8

19⅝

DOOR LENGTH—19¾

7⅞

9 13/16

I

N

3/16

1⅛

7/16

B

9/16

10

6⅛

1 15/16

11⅛

FRONT

Scale in Inches
0 1 2 3 4 5 6

9/16

9/16

B

10⅛

5⅝

K

E

2

1¼

A

I

1¼

2

3⅝

9/16

SIDE

4¼

6 11/16

J

9/16

2¼

30⅜

33¾

19¾

DETAIL 1
CUT OUT ON TOP
TO RECEIVE BACK

C

1½

B

A

D

E

DETAIL 2
RABBET AT REAR
EDGE OF SIDE

E

N

OUT

D

DETAIL 3
MORTISE & TENON
UPPER DOOR FRAME

K

DETAIL 7
DOOR PULL

J

R

⅛ x 45°

1/16

DETAIL 6
INSPECTION WINDOW
KEEPER

M

G

GLASS

I

N

DETAIL 8
SECTION
LOWER DOOR FRAME

1½

1 15/16

I

OUT

G

DETAIL 5
MORTISE & TENON
LOWER DOOR FRAME

11/32

H

OUT

I

DETAIL 4
MORTISE & TENON
MEDIAL MEMBER LOWER DOOR
FRAME

Scale in Inches
0 1 2 3

Details 3-8

Figure 6

Letter	No.	Name	Material	T	W	L
A	2	sides	walnut	1/2	3-1/8	30-3/8
B	2	top–bottom	wlanut	9/16	4-1/4	11-1/8
C	1	back	pine	9/16	9-1/2	33-3/16
D	2	rails (upper door)	walnut	1/2	1-3/8	9-1/4
E	2	stiles (upper door)	walnut	1/2	1-1/8	10
F	1	division rail	walnut	1/2	1-3/4	10-1/8
G	2	rails (lower door)	walnut	1/2	1-5/8	9
H	1	medial rail	walnut	1/2	1-3/8	9
I	2	stiles (lower door)	walnut	1/2	1-15/16	19-5/8
J	2	inspection window keeper	walnut	1/4	9/16	6-15/16
K	2	door pulls	walnut	1/2 dia		3/4
L	1	dust strip (upper door)	walnut	1/8	3/8	10
M	1	dust strip (lower door)	walnut	1/8	3/8	19-5/8
N	1	molding	walnut	3/16	3/16	90
Hardware						
O	4	butt hinges	brass		3/8	1-1/4
P	2	screw eyes	steel			11/16
Q	1	upper door	glass	single strength		cut to fit
R	2	lower doors	glass	"		cut to fit
S	2	inspection windows	glass	"		cut to fit

Commodes

Prior to the installation of indoor plumbing, the sanitary needs of society members were provided through the use of washhouses and privys. Privys were located behind dwellings, out of view, and, to be less obvious, were painted a dark color. Indoor facilities were limited to chamber pots, commodes, and washstands located in closets (washrooms) which connected directly to retiring-rooms.

1. This commode in unfinished pine with a walnut drawer front and cherry pull is similar to commodes used in the Hancock Church family brick dwelling. The open space located at the left side of the unit most likely held a supply of toilet paper. The chest handles, one at each end, may be a late application, and indicate that commodes of this style were moved about and used where needed in rooms occupied by ill or infirm Believers. An explanation of the function of the drawer is unnecessary. The two large holes on the right end have metal tubes which were vented directly into a chimney to help expel odors. Collection of Shakertown, Pleasant Hill, Inc., Harrodsburg, Ky.

H. 16-1/4, W. 25, D. 15-3/4.

2. The commode shown here is pine in original red wash paint and was made during the first half of the nineteenth century, probably in Pleasant Hill. The carrying arms on the extended sides and the backrest suggest that it was designed for bedside use. The toilet paper drawer located at the left side is missing its knob. Collection of Shakertown, Inc., Pleasant Hill, Ky.

H. 24, W. 20, D. 16.

Counters

The Shakers, in their desire for self-sufficiency, in their early years raised their own flax and wool, wove their own cloth, and made their own clothes. The nature and extent of these activities created a need for shop furniture more functional than conventional tables. Therefore, a combination worktable and chest of drawers, referred to as a weave or tailoring counter, was designed and produced in a variety of sizes and drawer configurations. The chest portion of what is probably the earliest type rests directly on the floor; later forms have corner posts with short, turned legs and represent a higher level of Shaker furniture making.

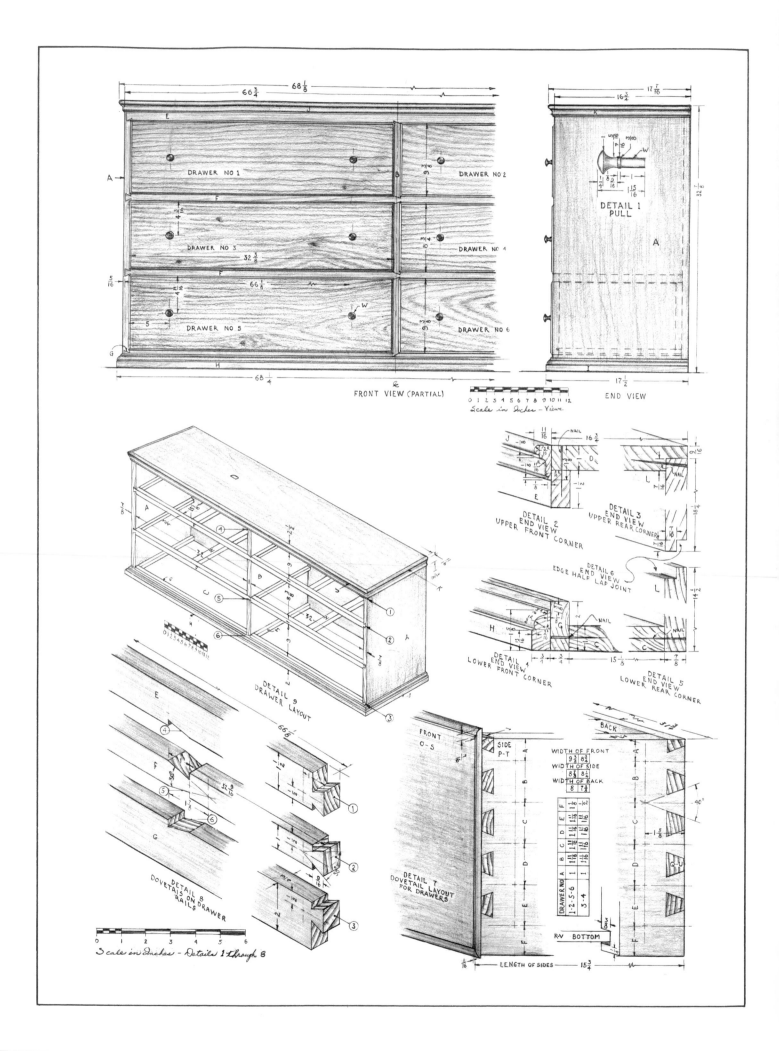

FRONT VIEW (PARTIAL)

Scale in Inches – Views

END VIEW

DETAIL 1
PULL

DETAIL 2
END VIEW
UPPER FRONT CORNER

DETAIL 3
END VIEW
UPPER REAR CORNER

DETAIL 6
END VIEW
EDGE HALF LAP JOINT

DETAIL 4
END VIEW
LOWER FRONT CORNER

DETAIL 5
END VIEW
LOWER REAR CORNER

DETAIL 9
DRAWER LAYOUT

DETAIL 8
DOVETAILS ON DRAWER
RAILS

DETAIL 7
DOVETAIL LAYOUT
FOR DRAWERS

Scale in Inches – Details 1 through 8

DRAWER NO 1
DRAWER NO 2
DRAWER NO 3
DRAWER NO 4
DRAWER NO 5
DRAWER NO 6

DRAWER NO	A	B	C	D	E	F
1-2-5-6	1	1 11/16	1 11/16	1 11/16	1 11/16	1-16/2
3-4		1 1/16	1 11/16	1 1/16		

WIDTH OF FRONT
9 3/8 | 8 1/2

WIDTH OF SIDE
8 3/8 | 8 1/2

WIDTH OF BACK
8 | 7 1/2

1. This weaver's counter in pine with pulls of apple or pear was made in the first half of the nineteenth century at New Lebanon. Originally painted red, it is now natural with clear varnish. The base, top, and drawers have molded edges. Those on the case were applied after the case was assembled. The top and bottom have rabbet joints into which the sides fit, and the middle partition seats into a dado; all are nailed in place. The dovetailed drawer rails and the rabbeted, two-piece back hold the sides in place. The two middle drawers are more shallow than the others. Collection of the Metropolitan Museum of Art, Purchase, 1966, Friends of the American Wing Fund. Photograph courtesy of the museum.

H. 32-7/8, W. 68-1/8, D. 17-1/2.

Letter	No.	Name	Material	T	W	L
A	2	sides	pine	7/8	16-3/4	31-3/4
B	1	middle partition	pine	1	15-7/8	31-3/4
C	1	bottom	pine	1	15-1/8	66-3/4
D	1	top	pine	1	16-3/4	66-3/4
E	1	drawer upper rail	pine	3/4	1-1/2	66-1/8
F	2	drawer middle rails	pine	3/4	1	66-1/8
G	1	drawer lower rail	pine	3/4	2	66-1/8
H	1	base molding (front)	pine	3/4	1-5/8	68-1/4
I	2	base moldings (sides)	pine	3/4	1-5/8	17-1/2
J	1	top molding (front)	pine	11/16	1-3/8	17-7/16
K	2	top moldings (sides)	pine	11/16	1-3/8	68-1/8
L	1	back	pine	7/8	32-5/16	65-7/8
M	12	drawer runners	pine	1	1	15-1/8
N	4	kick rails	pine	1	1-1/2	15-1/8
Drawers 1, 2, 5, 6						
O	4	fronts	pine	1	9-3/8	32-3/8
P	8	sides	pine	3/4	8-7/8	15-3/4
Q	4	backs	pine	3/4	8	31-3/4
R	4	bottoms	pine	5/8	15-5/16	31
Drawers 3, 4						
S	2	fronts	pine	1	8-3/4	32-3/8
T	4	sides	pine	3/4	8-1/4	15-3/4
U	2	backs	pine	3/4	7-3/8	31-3/4
V	2	bottoms	pine	5/8	15-5/16	31
W	12	pulls	apple/ pear?	1 dia		1-15/16

2. The maxim "form follows function" is very well expressed in this six-drawer tailor's counter. It was made at New Lebanon in mid-nineteenth century and is of pine with butternut drawer fronts all stained light orange-brown. The generous over-hanging top increased the work surface, the deep drawers afforded ample storage space for textiles, and the base which sets flush on the floor eliminated dust accumulation. The severely plain lines and balanced form are features that make the counter a classic Shaker piece. Collection of Darrow School, New Lebanon, N. Y.

H. 33-1/2, W. 79-1/4, D. 35-3/4.

3. This twelve-drawer double counter from
New Lebanon was made during the second
half of the nineteenth century and is of pine
painted a light orange-red wash. The counter has four rows of drawers which are graduated from top to bottom, with six along the
upper row, all equal in width. All the drawer
fronts have slightly rounded edges and are
set flush with the front of the case. The
drawer parts are assembled with dovetails.
The unnecessarily large, uniformly shaped
drawer pulls of butternut are a style found
on many late Shaker pieces. The counter has
been recoated with orange shellac. Collection of Darrow School, New Lebanon, N. Y.

H. 34, W. 68, D. 30-1/2.

4. Made of figured maple and pine, this double tailor's or weaver's counter was made during the first half of the nineteenth century in Hancock. The graduated drawers are dovetailed and have molded lip fronts, pine sides and bottoms, and walnut pulls. Counter sides, particularly those of hard wood, were usually of frame and panel construction. In this example, the sides are of solid maple set flush with the corner post. Wooden casters fixed under each corner facilitated relocation of the piece. The top has cleated ends and a drop-leaf to increase the working surface. Collection of New York State Historical Association, Cooperstown, N. Y. Photograph by Rollins.

H. 33, W. 72, D. with leaf down, 32.

5. One of the most beautiful tailoring counters is this one from Watervliet, New York. It was made in the first half of the nineteenth century and is of mixed woods. It has a maple frame, figured maple top and drawer fronts, and pine sides, back panels, and interior components. The panels were set into pinned mortise-and-tenon frame members without glue. The frame members have exposed molded inner edges. Although the drawers are assembled with conventional joinery they are exceptional in that the inside surface of the sides and back taper from 11/16 inch at the bottom edge to 5/16 inch at the top. This was probably done to facilitate locating specific pieces of material and is probably not a Shaker innovation. (The Winterthur Museum owns a double chest, c. 1800, signed by Reuben Beman, Jr., a cabinetmaker working in Kent, Connecticut, that also has drawers with sides similarly tapered.) The working surface of the counter top was increased by

raising the drop-leaf at the back. The leaf is walnut and possibly was added later. Collection of the American Museum in Britain, Bath, England.

H. 31-5/16, W. 45-3/16, D. 24, D. with leaf up, 30-3/4.

5

6. Although the origin of this second-half nineteenth-century counter is unknown, it is very similar in style to case pieces made by Elder Henry Green (1844–1931) of the Alfred society. (Similar case pieces were also made in the Canterbury and Sabbathday Lake communities.) The mixed woods in original clear varnish give a pleasing contrast in color and grain figure. The frame is of bird's-eye and curly maple, the panels are butternut, the drawer fronts and pulls are walnut, and the interior parts and back are pine. Bevels were planed on the inside surface of the panels which then fit into grooves in the frame members. Frame members were assembled with typical pinned, mortise-and-tenon joints. A cleat, nailed to the back, supports the rear end of the drawer runner guide, which in turn supports the two small drawers. The dovetailed drawers have chamfered lipped edges, a molding form rarely used. End cleats on the top were nailed in place. Collection of Jean Sladek Popelka.

H. 31-7/8, W. 44-1/2, D. 24-1/8.

7. The practice of using mixed woods in Shaker case pieces was common throughout all the communities; however, the custom of staining drawer fronts red and finishing other parts in clear shellac or varnish seems to be limited to furniture made in the Maine societies and has since become a distinguishing feature. This six-drawer counter dates from mid-nineteenth century and was made in the Sabbathday Lake society. The case is maple in a clear finish and the drawers are pine with fronts stained red. They have quarter-round molded lip fronts and original pulls. Collection of The United Society of Shakers at Sabbathday Lake, Maine. Photograph by David W. Serette.

H. 32, W. 52, D. 26.

8. This tailor's counter with a drop-leaf and added casters is from Enfield, Connecticut, and was made in the first half of the nineteenth century. The casters made it easier to move the counter, and thus made it possible to raise the drop-leaf and work at the counter from all sides. The seven drawers, three of which could be locked, are of three different depths. All have quarter-round, molded lip front edges. The door frames have mortise-and-tenon joints, double-pinned. The location of the two pins is ninety degrees from the generally accepted corner positioning. The counter is pine and the condition of the original finish justified stripping and refinishing. Private collection.

H. 32-1/4, W. 101, D. 28-5/8, D. with leaf up, 38-5/8.

9. A good example of utility in a Victorian Shaker form is this counter from Canterbury. It was made in the second half of the nineteenth century and is fitted with drawers, cupboards, and sliding shelves. The exterior wood is cherry with a clear varnish finish and the interior parts are poplar. Collection of Shaker Village, Inc., Canterbury, N. H. Photograph by Bill Finney.

H. 38-3/4, W. 41, D. 27-1/2.

8

9

143 Counters

Cradles

In a celibate religious society, cradles may seem to be an unnecessary kind of furniture. However, Believers took in infant foundlings, orphans, entire families, and unwed mothers and caring for babies was an accepted humane church duty.

1. Community origin of this cradle in pine painted red is unknown; however, it dates from the first half of the nineteenth century. Its style is not uniquely Shaker for many cradles that are similar to this were made by the world's people. The ends and sides were cut on the same angle, thereby forming a compound angle of equal degrees at the corners. For no explainable reason, the curve on the headboard is different from that on the footboard. The wavelike curves on the upper edge of the sides are particularly graceful. Carefully fitted dovetails hold the corners together and the bottom is let into the sides and ends and nailed in place. Rockers are fastened to the bottom with wood screws and given added support with a keyed stretcher. It is interesting to note that the keys were installed incorrectly; the wide part should be nearest the top of the rocker. Collection of the Shaker Museum, Old Chatham, N. Y.

H. 21-3/8, W. 22-7/8, L. 39-1/4.

Letter	No.	Name	Material	T	W	L
A	2	sides	pine	3/4	16	39-1/4
B	1	headboard	pine	3/4	17-1/2	17
C	1	footboard	pine	3/4	14-1/4	15-1/2
D	1	bottom	pine	3/4	9-7/8	31-7/8
E	2	rockers	pine	7/8	4-5/8	22-7/8
F	1	stretcher	oak	3/4	1-1/4	25-3/8
G	2	keys	oak	5/16	5/16	2
Hardware	4	wood screws	steel	FH 2-8		

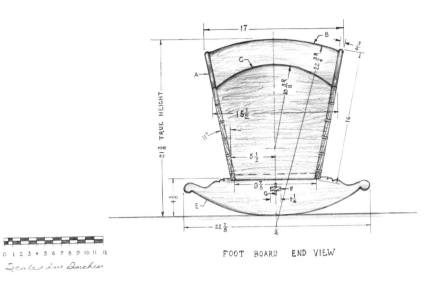

17

B

22 3/4

3/4

C

A

10 3/8 R

21 3/8 TRUE HEIGHT

15 1/2

16

11°

5 1/2

9 7/8

G   F

1 1/4

E

4 5/8

22 7/8

FOOT BOARD   END VIEW

0 1 2 3 4 5 6 7 8 9 10 11 12
Scale in Inches

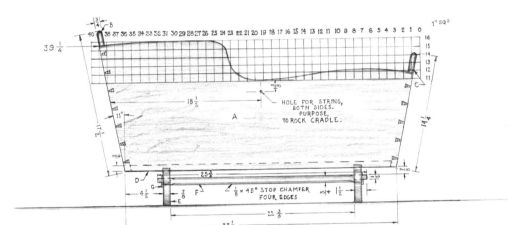

1" SQ S

3/4

B

40 39 38 37 36 35 34 33 32 31 30 29 28 27 26 25 24 23 22 21 20 19 18 17 16 15 14 13 12 11 10 9 8 7 6 5 4 3 2 1 0

18
15
14
13
12
11

39 1/4

18 1/2

HOLE FOR STRING,
BOTH SIDES.
PURPOSE,
TO ROCK CRADLE.

A

11°

7 11/16

14 1/4

C

D

25 3/4

1/8 × 45° STOP CHAMFER
FOUR EDGES

4 1/8

7/8

F

1 1/2

E

22 3/8

33 1/8

SIDE VIEW

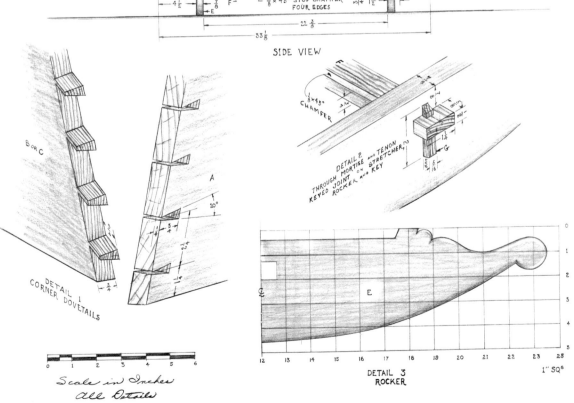

DETAIL 2
THROUGH MORTISE and TENON
KEYED JOINT on STRETCHER,
ROCKER and KEY

1/8 × 45°
CHAMFER

G

B or C

A

20°

3/4
5/4

2 1/4

1 1/4

DETAIL 1
CORNER DOVETAILS

0 1 2 3 4 5 6
Scale in Inches
All Details

DETAIL 3
ROCKER

E

0
1
2
3
4
5

12 13 14 15 16 17 18 19 20 21 22 23 25

1" SQ S

2. This cradle for two infants dates from the first half of the nineteenth century and was made in Pleasant Hill. It has maple sides and rockers, and pine ends, all finished in clear varnish. There is nothing distinctively Shaker about the rockers—non-Shaker cradle-makers used the same form—but the curved sides which are let into the ends are most unusual. The curve of the ends continues uninterrupted through the sides. The sides were either hot-water soaked or steamed, then bent while still pliable and nailed in place. The cutouts on the sides were used to move or rock the cradle. Collection of Shakertown at Pleasant Hill, Inc., Harrodsburg, Ky.

H. 22-3/8, W. 22-1/4, L. 60.

Desks

Included in this category are writing desks, table- (lap-) desks, teachers' and students' desks, trustees' desks, and sisters' sewing desks. Production of writing desks was never large because their use was reserved for those assigned the spiritual and temporal responsibilities of the community. Early records show that table-desks as shown here were made for a number of years in the New Lebanon society. They were probably made for sale to the world's people rather than for Believers' use. Multi-drawer sewing desks are very similar in appearance to sewing cabinets but incorporated in their design are additional, pull out work surfaces, and for this reason they are referred to as desks. The wood used and the designs of these pieces varied greatly, as did the writing units.

1. The slant of the writing surface on this desk is slightly greater than the one shown in figure 2, but otherwise its features are very similar. It also was made in New Lebanon during the first half of the nineteenth century and is pine stained light red-brown. The top has bread-board ends and the case contains an ink drawer, a pencil till, and a drawer for writing paper. The case is assembled with well-made corner dovetails, which seem to be standard joinery for such pieces. Private collection.

H. 5, W. 18-5/8, D. 13-1/4.

2. The details of construction and craftsmanship that went into these small writing conveniences were equal to those put into the finest Shaker furniture pieces. This table-desk was made in the New Lebanon community early in the nineteenth century and, except for the maple bread-board ends on the top, is of pine finished in a light red-orange wash. The writing surfaces on some desks were flat; however, in this example the surface is slanted. A simple but ingenious keeper on the ink drawer was designed to prevent the drawer from being pulled out all the way. Writing implements were stored in the inside till and the shallow drawer on the left side held stationery. Collection of the Shaker Museum, Old Chatham, N. Y.

H. 6-1/8, W. 19-3/8, D. 13.

Letter	No.	Name	Material	T	W	L
A	1	front	pine	3/8	3-7/8	18-3/4
B	1	back	pine	3/8	5-5/8	18-3/4
C	2	ends	pine	3/8	5-5/8	12-3/4
D	1	inner bottom	pine	3/16	18-1/4	12-1/4
E	1	bottom	pine	3/16	13	19
F	1	top	pine	5/16	13	19
G	2	bread-board ends	maple	5/16	1	13
H	2	pencil till supports	pine	1/16	1-3/16	2-7/16
I	1	pencil till bottom	pine	1/8	2-5/16	12
J	1	pencil till side	pine	1/8	3/4	12
K	2	molding—paper-drawer opening	pine	1/8	1/2	2-1/8
L	1	molding—paper-drawer opening	pine	1/8	1/2	12-3/16
Paper drawer						
M	1	front	pine	3/8	1-7/8	11-15/16
N	2	sides	pine	1/4	1-7/8	18-1/8
O	1	back	pine	1/4	1-7/8	11-7/8
P	1	bottom	pine	1/4	11-5/8	17-7/8
Ink drawer						
Q	1	front	pine	3/8	2	2-5/8
R	1	left side	pine	1/8	1-13/16	2-5/8
S	1	right side	pine	1/8	1-13/16	5-5/8
T	1	back	pine	1/8	1-13/16	2-3/16
U	1	bottom	pine	1/8	2-1/2	2-5/8
V	1	keeper	pine	5/16	5/16	1-1/2
Hardware	1 pr	butt hinges	brass		3/8	1-1/4
	1	lock	brass			
	2	pulls	brass	1/2 dia		13/16

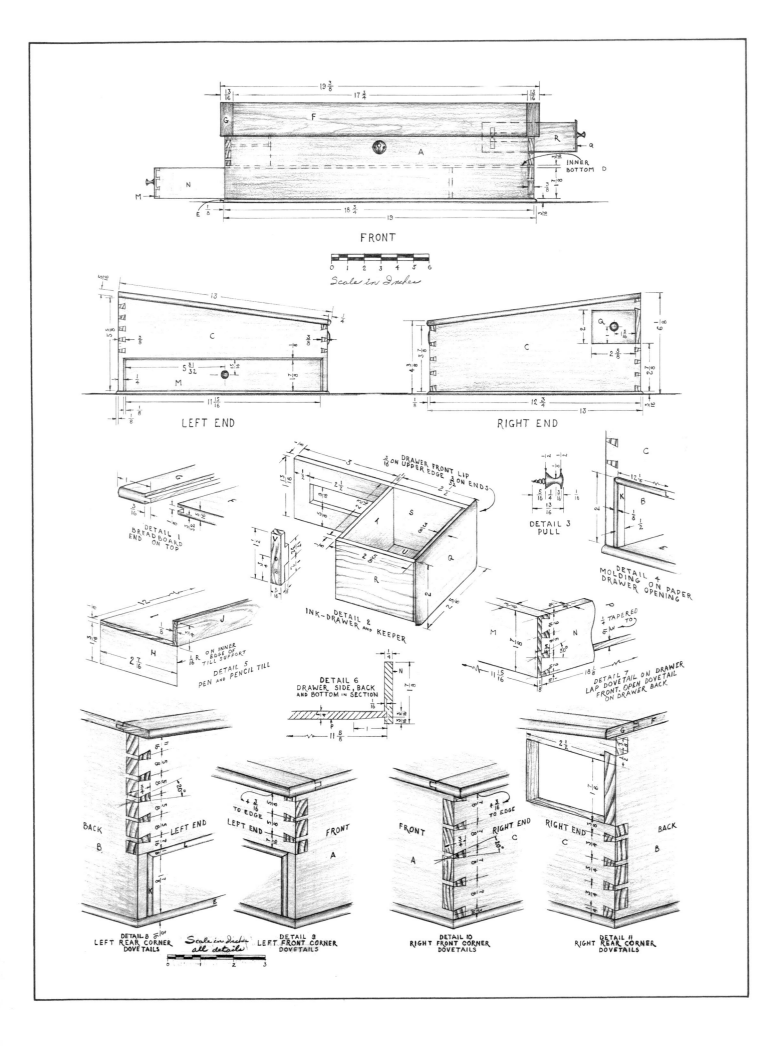

FRONT

Scale in Inches

LEFT END

RIGHT END

DETAIL 1
BREADBOARD
END ON TOP

DETAIL 2
INK-DRAWER AND KEEPER

DETAIL 3
PULL

DETAIL 4
MOLDING ON PAPER
DRAWER OPENING

DETAIL 5
PEN AND PENCIL TILL

DETAIL 6
DRAWER SIDE, BACK
AND BOTTOM IN SECTION

DETAIL 7
LAP DOVETAIL ON DRAWER
FRONT. OPEN DOVETAIL
ON DRAWER BACK

DETAIL 8
LEFT REAR CORNER
DOVETAILS

Scale in Inches
all details

DETAIL 9
LEFT FRONT CORNER
DOVETAILS

DETAIL 10
RIGHT FRONT CORNER
DOVETAILS

DETAIL 11
RIGHT REAR CORNER
DOVETAILS

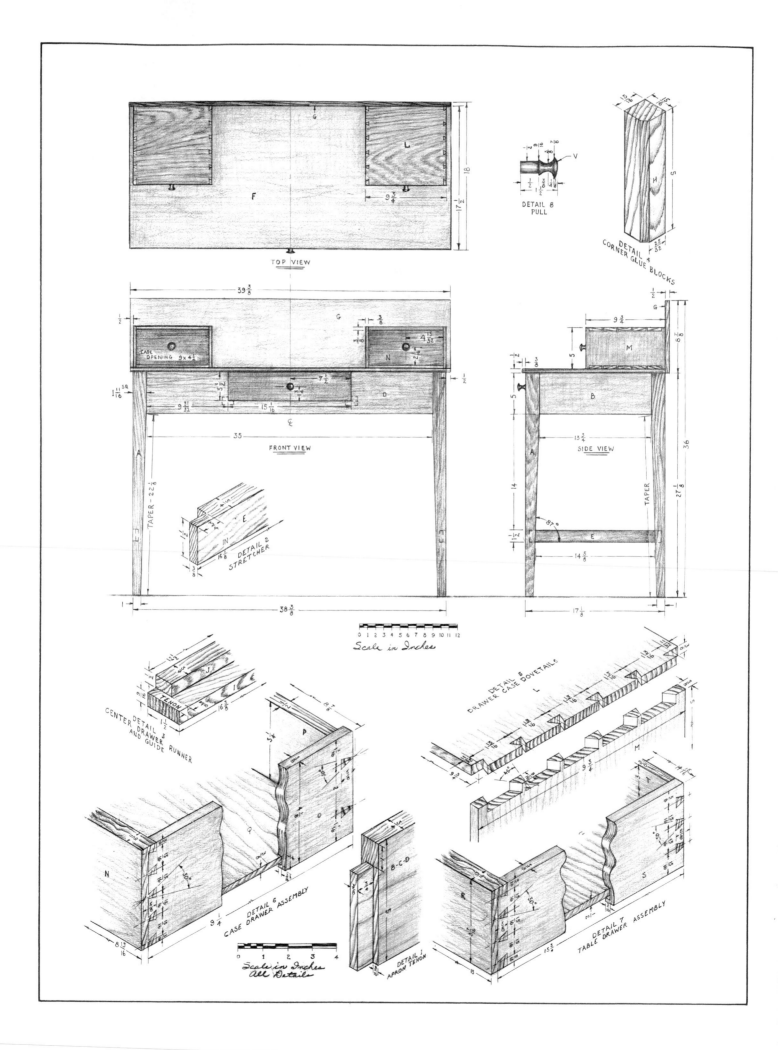

TOP VIEW

DETAIL 8
PULL

DETAIL 4
CORNER GLUE BLOCKS

FRONT VIEW

SIDE VIEW

DETAIL 2
STRETCHER

Scale in Inches

DETAIL 3
CENTER DRAWER RUNNER
AND GUIDE

DETAIL 5
DRAWER CASE DOVETAILS

DETAIL 6
CASE DRAWER ASSEMBLY

DETAIL 1
APRON TENON

DETAIL 7
TABLE DRAWER ASSEMBLY

Scale in Inches
All Details

3. The nailed-on additions of a backboard and two drawer boxes make a desk of what is essentially a rectangular table. This writing desk was made in an unknown eastern community during the first half of the nineteenth century. In pine with maple legs, the desk was originally painted a yellow wash but is now stained light maple and clear varnished. The stretchers and aprons are tenoned into the square, tapered legs and the center drawer was let into the front apron. The boxes are assembled with open-corner dovetails and are nailed to the table top. The drawer pulls are not original but are a style appropriate for the piece. Collection of Jean Sladek Popelka.

H. to backboard, 36, H. of table, 27-5/8, W. 39-3/8, D. 18.

Letter	No.	Name	Material	T	W	L
A	4	legs	maple	1-11/16 sq		27-1/8
B	2	side aprons	pine	3/4	5	15-1/4
C	1	back apron	pine	3/4	5	36-1/2
D	1	front apron	pine	3/4	5	36-1/2
E	2	stretchers	pine	3/4	1-1/2	16-1/8
F	1	top	pine	1/2	17-1/2	39-3/8
G	1	back	pine	1/2	8-7/8	39-3/8
H	8	corner glue blocks	pine	15/16 sq		5
I	2	drawer runners	pine	9/16	1-1/2	16-3/8
J	2	drawer guides	pine	1/2	3/4	12-1/2
K	2	drawer stops	pine	1/4	13/16	1-1/4
Drawer cases						
L	4	tops and bottoms	pine	3/8	9-3/4	9-3/4
M	4	sides	pine	3/8	9-3/4	5
Case drawers						
N	2	fronts	pine	11/16	4-1/8	8-15/16
O	4	sides	pine	3/8	4-1/8	9-1/4
P	2	backs	pine	1/2	3-1/4	8-7/8
Q	2	bottoms	pine	3/8	9-1/16	8-3/8
Table drawer						
R	1	front	pine	13/16	3-7/16	15
S	2	sides	pine	3/8	3-7/16	15-3/4
T	1	back	pine	3/8	3	14-15/16
U	1	bottom	pine	1/2	14-5/8	15-1/2
V	3	pulls	maple	7/8 dia		1-1/2

4. What at first appears to be a box on long legs is actually a writing desk that contains four drawers plus a row of pigeonholes, and a storage compartment. The lower portion of the desk contains a single full drawer and the upper front part is hinged to open and is supported by two pullout brackets. When so positioned, three drawers and a writing surface are made accessible. The writing surface is hinged and covered with an overlay of cotton fabric. When these hinged sections are raised the pigeonholes and storage compartment are exposed. The desk was made during the first half of the nineteenth century in an unidentified eastern community and is pine painted apricot-orange. Although the desk is an unusual Shaker form, the plain turned legs and total utilization of interior space express the unmistakable Shaker concept of functionalism.

A lady's desk made for the world about 1800 in Massachusetts is part of the Winterthur Collection of Federal furniture and, except for the mahogany and rosewood ve-neers and reeded legs, it is remarkably similar in its exterior form to this piece. Did the Shaker cabinetmaker see that desk and was it his inspiration? Private collection.

H. 35-3/8, W. 26-1/2, D. 18-1/2.

5. Even though this slant-top writing desk on a stand has features similar to those found on table-desks, its large size, particularly its width and depth, belies the assumption that it was designed for table or lap use. The stand in all probability was designed for the desk and made at the same time during the first half of the nineteenth century in the Watervliet, New York, colony. It is pine stained brown. The writing surface is hinged and has bread-board ends. The desk corners are dovetailed; a pencil till is located inside, and a drawer for stationery is located at the left end. The ink bottle is housed like those in the desks shown in figures 1 and 2. The stand has square legs, tapered on the inside surfaces and mortised to accept the tenoned aprons. To provide leg room the front and end aprons have a long arc cutout on their lower edges. The Stokes Collection.

H. 28-1/2, W. 23-1/8, D. 15-1/2.

6. This slant-top writing desk on a tripod base was used for many years by a deaconess at Hancock, but probably was made at the Enfield, Connecticut, colony in the first half of the nineteenth century, for it is similar to schoolroom desks made in that community. The desk is in mixed woods; the legs and pedestal are curly maple, the desk box is butternut, and the hinged top is pine. All parts are finished in a light red varnish-stain. Three plain-styled Queen Anne cabriole legs with snake feet are dovetailed to the pedestal and a substantial cleat holds the pedestal to the desk box. Collection of Shaker Community, Inc., Hancock, Mass.

H. 28, W. 24-3/4, D. 20-5/8.

7. This double trustees' desk, from New Lebanon, was made in the first half of the nineteenth century and possibly was used by two trustees or deacons. The two sill doors drop down and make writing surfaces. (Thin boards were installed over the recessed panels on the inner surfaces to form a level writing surface.) The doors rest on a narrow sill which separates the double bank of drawers below from the double cupboards above. The writing table doors and cupboard doors hide double rows of pigeonholes and shelves. The desk is pine stained a rose-brown and, though large, is a well-proportioned piece. A similar desk is in the Pleasant Hill collection. Collection of Shaker Community, Inc., Hancock, Mass.

H. 84-3/4, W. 48-3/8, D. 18.

8. The architectural details and fine craftsmanship suggest this Victorian-style writing desk from the second half of the nineteenth century was made by a competent cabinetmaker for an important member of the society. Record has it that the desk was used by Eldress Emma J. Neal (1847–1943) of the New Lebanon community. The desk is of mixed woods: it rests on a platform of pine, has frame members and moldings of walnut, panels and drawer fronts of bird's-eye maple, and interior parts of poplar. The cupboard part contains a single shelf in the outer cupboards and twelve pigeonholes in the small center cupboard. The lift-up writing surface is covered with green simulated leather. The decorative brass pulls have a blue floral design in their centers and were purchased from the world. Collection of Shaker Village, Inc., Canterbury, N. H.

H. 56-3/8, H. writing surface at front edge, 29-1/2, W. 47-3/4, D. 29-7/8, D. cupboard top, 11-1/4.

9. Eldress Josephine Wilson (1866–1946) of Canterbury used this four-drawer sewing desk. It dates from the first half of the nineteenth century and all parts are pine except the birch corner posts and walnut pulls. The side and back panels are held in grooves milled into the frame members and the frame members are assembled with pinned mortise-and-tenon joints. In the base section, the two upper drawers are locked with metal pins that are inserted into holes bored through the drawer bottoms located immediately behind the rails. When the bottom drawer is locked the contents of all the drawers are secured. Collection of the Philadelphia Museum of Art. Photograph by A. J. Wyatt.

H. 34, W. 27-5/16, D. 21.

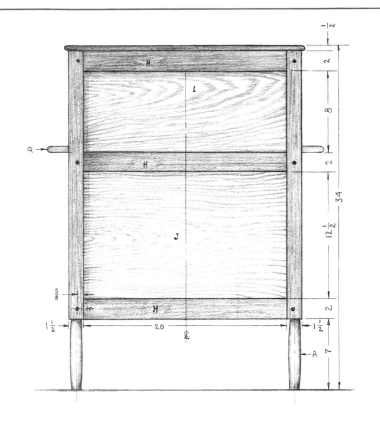

BACK VIEW

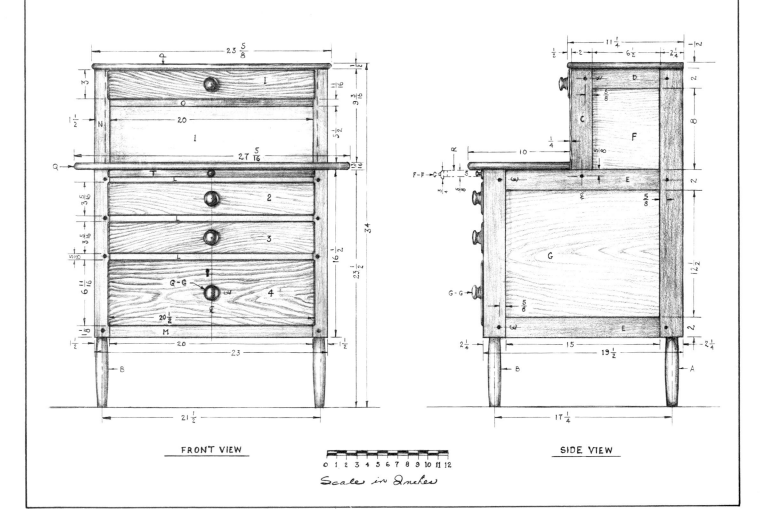

FRONT VIEW

Scale in Inches

SIDE VIEW

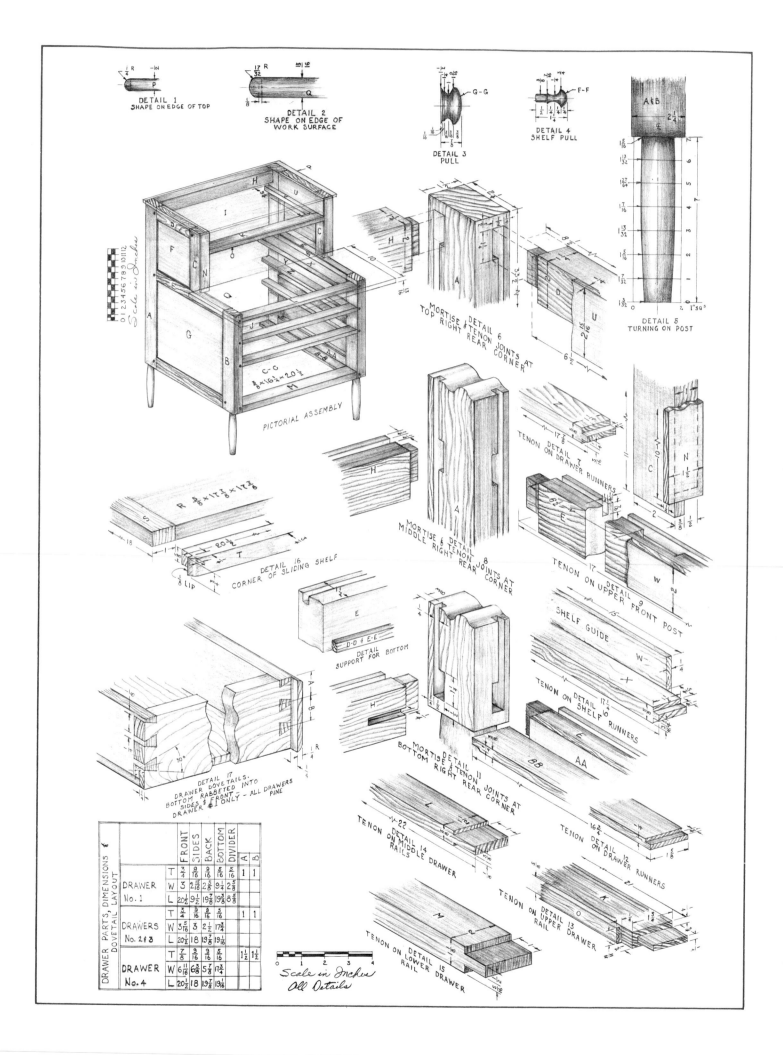

DETAIL 1
SHAPE ON EDGE OF TOP

DETAIL 2
SHAPE ON EDGE OF WORK SURFACE

DETAIL 3
PULL

DETAIL 4
SHELF PULL

DETAIL 5
TURNING ON POST

PICTORIAL ASSEMBLY

DETAIL 6
MORTISE & TENON JOINTS AT TOP RIGHT REAR CORNER

DETAIL 7
TENON ON DRAWER RUNNERS

DETAIL 8
MORTISE & TENON JOINTS AT MIDDLE RIGHT REAR CORNER

DETAIL 9
TENON ON UPPER FRONT POST

DETAIL 10
TENON ON SHELF RUNNERS

SHELF GUIDE

DETAIL 11
MORTISE & TENON JOINTS AT BOTTOM RIGHT REAR CORNER

DETAIL 12
TENON ON DRAWER RUNNERS

DETAIL 13
TENON ON UPPER DRAWER RAIL

DETAIL 14
TENON ON MIDDLE DRAWER RAILS

DETAIL 15
TENON ON LOWER DRAWER RAIL

DETAIL 16
CORNER OF SLIDING SHELF

DETAIL
SUPPORT FOR BOTTOM

DETAIL 17
DRAWER DOVETAILS.
BOTTOM RABBETED INTO SIDES & FRONT - ALL DRAWERS
DRAWER #1 ONLY PINE

Scale in Inches
All Details

DRAWER PARTS, DIMENSIONS & DOVETAIL LAYOUT		FRONT	SIDES	BACK	BOTTOM	DIVIDER	A	B
DRAWER No. 1	T	$\frac{3}{4}$	$\frac{5}{16}$	$\frac{5}{16}$	$\frac{5}{16}$	$\frac{3}{16}$	1	1
	W	3	$2\frac{15}{16}$	$2\frac{5}{8}$	$9\frac{1}{4}$			
	L	$20\frac{1}{2}$	$9\frac{1}{2}$	$19\frac{7}{8}$	$19\frac{3}{8}$	$8\frac{5}{8}$		
DRAWERS No. 2 & 3	T	$\frac{3}{4}$	$\frac{5}{16}$	$\frac{5}{16}$	$\frac{5}{16}$		1	1
	W	$3\frac{5}{16}$	3	$2\frac{1}{2}$	$17\frac{3}{4}$			
	L	$20\frac{1}{2}$	18	$19\frac{7}{8}$	$19\frac{1}{16}$			
DRAWER No. 4	T	$\frac{7}{8}$	$\frac{3}{8}$	$\frac{3}{8}$	$\frac{5}{16}$		$1\frac{1}{2}$	$1\frac{1}{2}$
	W	$6\frac{11}{16}$	$5\frac{3}{8}$	$5\frac{7}{8}$	$17\frac{3}{4}$			
	L	$20\frac{1}{2}$	18	$19\frac{7}{8}$	$19\frac{1}{16}$			

Figure 9

Letter	No	Name	Material	T	W	L
A	2	rear posts	birch	1-1/2	2-1/4	33-1/2
B	2	front posts	birch	1-1/2	2-1/4	23-1/2
C	2	upper front posts	pine	1	2	11
D	2	upper side frames	pine	1-1/4	2	8-1/2
E	4	side frames	pine	1-1/4	2	17
F	2	upper side panels	pine	1/4	8-3/4	7-1/4
G	2	lower side panels	pine	3/8	13-1/4	15-3/4
H	3	rear frame members	pine	1-1/4	2	22
I	1	upper rear panel	pine	1/4	8-3/4	20-3/4
J	1	lower rear panel	pine	3/8	13-1/4	20-3/4
K	1	upper drawer rail	pine	5/8	1-3/4	22-1/2
L	3	middle drawer rails	pine	5/8	1-1/2	22
M	1	lower drawer rail	pine	1-1/8	2	22
N	2	facings for C	pine	1/4	1-1/2	10
O	1	facing for K	pine	1/4	11/16	20
P	1	top	pine	1/2	11-1/4	23-5/8
Q	1	work surface	pine	13/16	20-1/2	27-5/16
R	1	sliding shelf	pine	5/8	17-7/8	17-7/8
S	2	shelf ends	pine	5/8	1	18
T	1	shelf front	pine	3/4	3/4	20-1/2
U	2	guides—drawer 1	pine	1/4	2-15/16	8-1/2
V	2	runners—drawer 1	pine	5/8	1-1/4	9-1/4
W	2	guides—sliding shelf	pine	1/4	2	15
X	2	runners—sliding shelf	pine	5/8	1-1/2	17-1/4
Y	4	guides—drawers 2 and 3	pine	7/8	2	15
Z	4	runners—drawers 2 and 3	pine	5/8	1-1/4	17-7/8
AA	2	guides—drawer 4	pine	1/4	2	15
BB	2	runners—drawer 4	pine	3/8	1-5/8	16-3/4
CC	1	bottom	pine	3/8	16-1/4	20-1/2
DD	2	supports for bottom	pine	1/4	3/8	16-1/4
EE	2	supports for bottom	pine	1/4	3/8	20-1/2
FF	1	sliding shelf pull	walnut		3/4 dia	1-1/4
GG	4	drawer pulls	walnut		1-9/16 dia	7/8

10. The origin and date of this five-drawer sewing desk is undetermined. Nevertheless, it obviously was made in an eastern community and most probably very early in the nineteenth century. It is pine stained red and has a rimmed working top, an upper drawer fitted with a lock, and a pullout work shelf located on the right side. Collection of Greenfield Village and the Henry Ford Museum, Dearborn, Mich. Photograph courtesy of the museum.

H. 35-1/2, W. 24-3/4, D. 24-3/4.

11. The straight lines and rectangular patterns produced by the frame, side panels, and drawer fronts on this sewing desk belie its late date of manufacture (c. 1880). It shows that the Sabbathday Lake Shaker cabinetmaker responsible for this beautiful desk did not succumb to worldly Victorian styles. The desk has a maple frame, pine panels, and walnut drawer fronts and pulls, all protected with clear varnish. The interior parts are pine. All drawers have hand-cut dovetails and molded lip-fronts. Collection of The United Society of Shakers at Sabbathday Lake, Maine. Photograph by David W. Serette.

H. 38-5/8, W. 31-3/16, D. 23-3/4.

12. This twelve-drawer sewing desk with a pullout work shelf and small cupboard was made during the second half of the nineteenth century, at the Enfield, New Hampshire, society. The desk is transitional in style—part classic, part Victorian. Its overall size and shape, drawer configuration, working surfaces, corner-post turnings, and drawer pulls are classic forms, while the contrasting mixed woods, applied moldings, and mirrored cupboard-door panels are most worldly. Nevertheless, the desk is a beautiful example of a well-made piece of Shaker cabinetry. Collection of Philadelphia Museum of Art. Photograph by A. J. Wyatt.

H. 39-1/2, W. 33-3/16, D. 25-1/4.

13. Of mixed woods is this late nineteenth-century eleven-drawer, two-cupboard sewing desk from Canterbury. The desk is attributed to Elder William Briggs (1851–?). Elder William was brought to Canterbury when only an infant and stayed nearly fifty years. Records show he was a competent joiner and also held many responsible positions in the society before leaving in 1899. This desk is also a beautiful piece of Victorian Shaker work and is an exceptionally fine example of the cabinetmaker's art. Private collection. Photograph by Bill Finney.

H. 40, W. 34-3/4, D. 23-1/2.

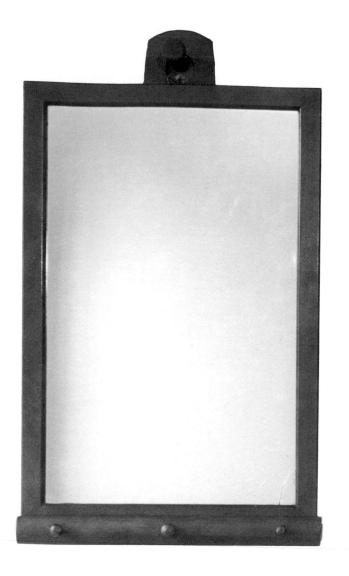

Looking Glasses

In the Society's early years, looking glasses were considered instruments of vanity and unnecessary worldly luxuries. However, in their desire to promote cleanliness, neatness, and uniformity, the leaders gradually recognized their need of them and in 1845 lifted the prohibition against their use. They prescribed their size (not to exceed twelve inches in width and eighteen inches in length), the shape of the frame molding (a plain frame), where they could be hung, and the number allowed. Very small framed looking glasses were also allowed but were kept out of sight in closets or cupboards.

1. Although the origin and date of this framed looking glass and hanging shelf is unknown it also is probably eastern and dates from mid-nineteenth century. It is pine finished in a red-orange wash and has cherry pegs. Inscribed in pencil on the backboard are the following words: "Belongs to the caretaker at the girls shop. If ever usurped again for the [sic] purpose. Borrowed for the Hat Shop, 1874 in March." The frame is fastened together with glued slip-feather splines and holds a replacement glass. The hanger blade is tapered in thickness and width, and is nailed to the back of the shelf. A peg similar in size to those of the shelf is in the back of the hanger at the lower end and

positions the hanger when hung from a pegboard parallel to the wall. Collection of Shaker Community, Inc., Hancock, Mass.

Frame: H. 18-1/8, W. 12, D. 1/2.
Hanging shelf: H. 21-1/8, W. 12-1/4, D. 1-3/8.

2. This small framed looking glass dates from the first quarter of the nineteenth century and was made in New Lebanon. The frame is walnut and is assembled with slip-feather splines. A thin, solid pine back protects the glass. Collection of the Shaker Museum, Old Chatham, N. Y.

H. 6-1/2, W. 5-1/2, D. 9/16.

Letter	No.	Name	Material	T	W	L
A	2	side frame members	walnut	3/8	13/16	6-1/2
B	2	end frame members	walnut	3/8	13/16	5-1/2
C	4	slip feathers	walnut	1/16	3/4	1-1/2
D	1	back	pine	3/16	5-1/4	6-1/4

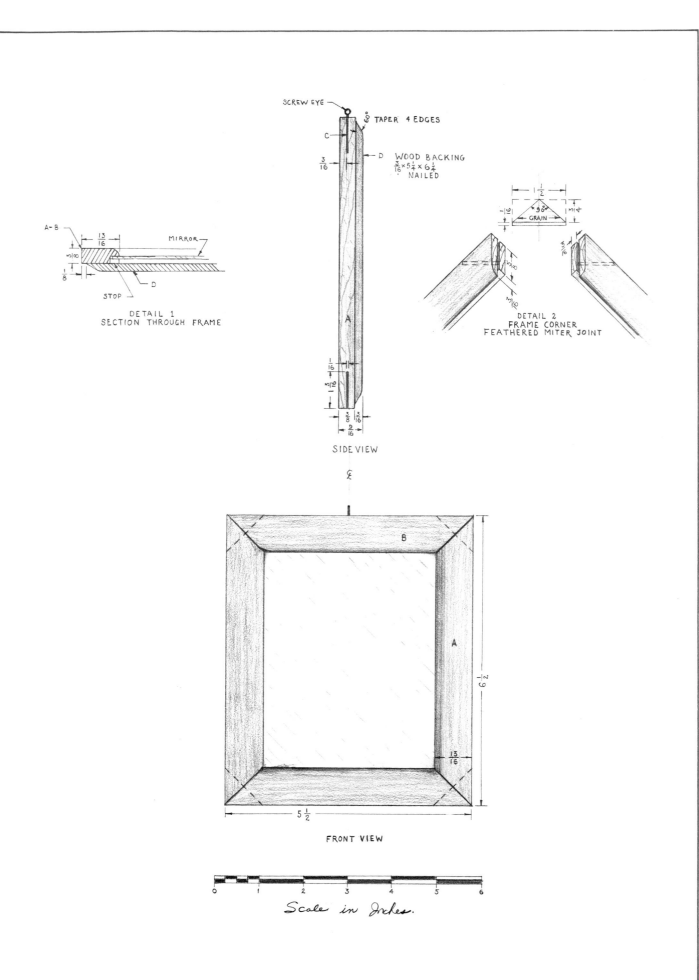

SCREW EYE

60° TAPER 4 EDGES

C

3/16

D WOOD BACKING
3/16 × 5 1/4 × 6 1/4
NAILED

A-B

13/16

MIRROR

3/8

1/8

D

STOP

DETAIL 1
SECTION THROUGH FRAME

1/2

90°

1/16

GRAIN

3/4

5/8

3/16

DETAIL 2
FRAME CORNER
FEATHERED MITER JOINT

1/16

3/16

A

3/8   3/16

9/16

SIDE VIEW

B

A

6 1/2

13/16

5 1/2

FRONT VIEW

Scale in Inches.

3. The community origin of this mid-nine-teenth-century looking glass and hanging shelf (rack) is unknown. The frame and shelf are cherry and the hanger blade is pine; all are in clear varnish. Frame corners are mit-ered and assembled with glued slip-feather splines. The hanger blade is let into the back of the shelf and glued. Particularly pleasing is the shape of the upper portion of the blade. A comb and brush hung from the miniature pegs. The outer ones are of cherry but the center one is brass and is possibly a replacement. Wooden wedges hold the glass in place and the back is covered with pressed paperboard nailed to the frame. Collection of the Golden Lamb Inn, Lebanon, Ohio.

Frame: H. 19-1/2, W. 13-1/8, D. 5/8.
Hanging shelf: H. 24-7/8, W. 12-7/8, D. 1-7/16.

Letter	No.	Name	Material	T	W	L
Mirror frame						
A	2	top and bottom frame members	cherry	1/2	7/8	13-1/8
B	2	side frame members	cherry	1/2	7/8	19-1/2
C	4	splines or feathers	cherry	1/16	15/16	1-13/16
D	1	back	paper-board	1/16	13	19-3/8
Hanging rack						
E	1	blade	pine	1/4	2-15/16	23-7/8
F	1	shelf	cherry	7/16	2	12-7/8
G	1	front	cherry	1	1-3/16	12-7/8
H	3	pegs	cherry	5/16 dia		1/2

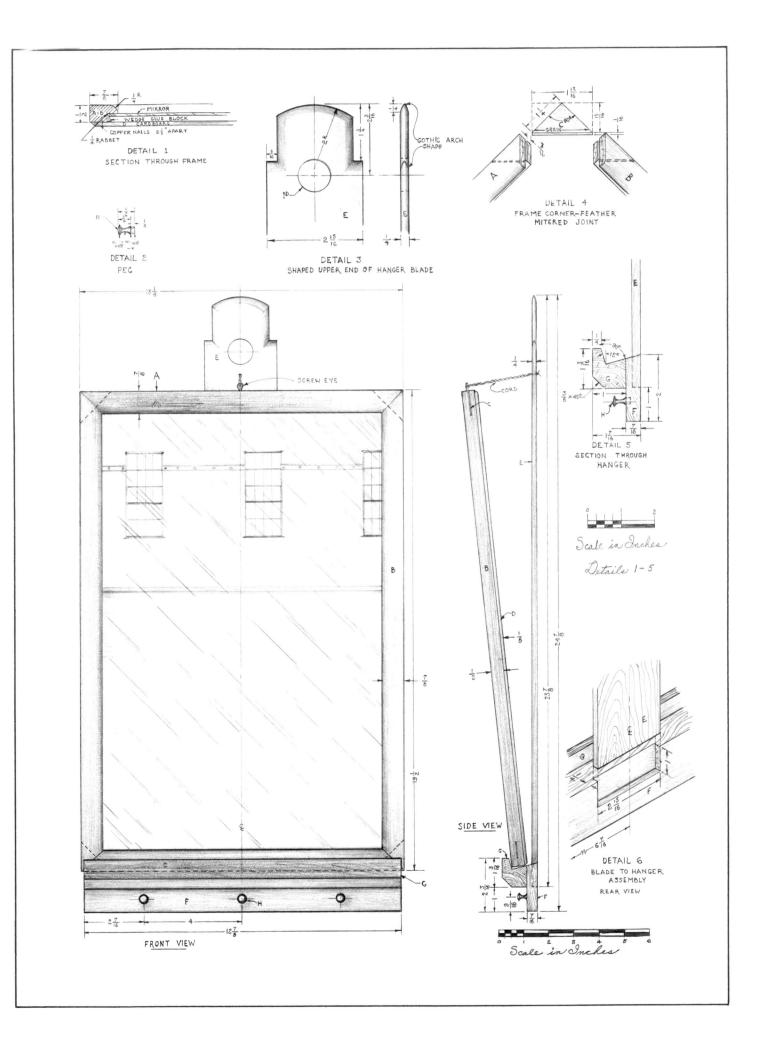

DETAIL 1
SECTION THROUGH FRAME

MIRROR
WEDGE GLUE BLOCK
CARDBOARD
COPPER NAILS 2½ APART
RABBET

DETAIL 2
PEG

DETAIL 3
SHAPED UPPER END OF HANGER BLADE

GOTHIC ARCH SHAPE

DETAIL 4
FRAME CORNER—FEATHER
MITERED JOINT

GRAIN

DETAIL 5
SECTION THROUGH
HANGER

CORD

Scale in Inches
Details 1 - 5

SCREW EYE

FRONT VIEW

SIDE VIEW

DETAIL 6
BLADE TO HANGER
ASSEMBLY
REAR VIEW

Scale in Inches

4. From New Lebanon and made during the same period as the looking glass in figure 2 is this small framed looking glass. The glass is original to the pine frame but the frame, now waxed natural wood, was originally painted red. Slip-feather splines installed on an angle hold the mitered corners together. A thin wood backing is let into rabbet joints cut into the frame. Private collection.

H. 5-3/4, W. 5-3/4, D. 1/2.

5. The frame of this small looking glass is painted dark green and is made of an unidentified wood. It dates from the first half of the nineteenth century and was made at Union Village. The glass is original to the frame. Collection of Warren County Historical Society Museum, Lebanon, Ohio.

H. 15, W. 8-5/8, D. 1.

Pegs, Pegboards, and Pulls

Pegs and pegboards, while not furniture, were an important accessory of almost every Shaker building for they lined the walls of rooms and hallways, from cellar to attic. Chairs, wall clocks, looking glasses, wall racks and shelves, clothes hangers, kitchen utensils and house-cleaning articles, school-room and teaching aids, shop equipment and accessories—all were hung on these ubiquitous pegboards, and Shaker orderliness and cleanliness were thus facilitated. These graceful, individually made, lathe-turned pegs which were threaded or simply doweled into the pegboards at regularly spaced intervals had gradually tapered shanks and mushroom-shaped domed ends. The shortest pegs were about two inches, the average were about three (the approximate pegboard width), and the longest were five to seven inches, with some even longer. The length of the pegboards and the spacing of the pegs were determined by their purpose. Pegs and pegboards were made from dry wood. Pegboards were usually made of pine. After they were installed, both even-

tually shrunk—mostly across the annual rings—causing the pegs to be permanently fastened in the pegboard holes. In some cases pegboards were installed before walls were plastered and were used as a plaster gauge line; at other times the boards were installed over preplastered walls.

Shaker-made pulls were also individually lathe-turned, and most are as graceful as pegs but considerably smaller. The smallest measure a little over 1/4 inch in diameter and 1/2 inch in length; others are as large as 1-3/8 inches in diameter and 1-3/4 inches long. Some were even longer, depending on their purpose. Clock doors, chest, table, and desk drawers, sides of washstands, beneath window sills and looking-glass shelves: all had pulls. Indeed, pulls were installed wherever needed. Because of their strength, hardwood species such as cherry, maple, and walnut were commonly used; however, examples of apple and pear are found on a few pieces of furniture.

1. This sampler of nineteenth-century pegs, pegboards, and pulls is the product of different communities and gives some idea of the many forms that were produced. Public and private collections.

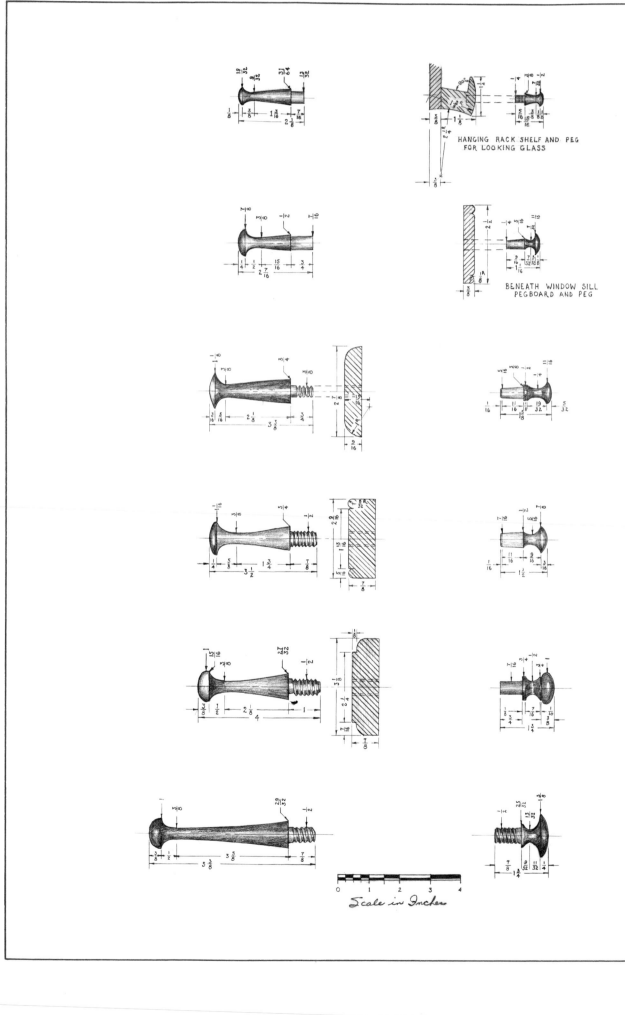

HANGING RACK SHELF AND PEG
FOR LOOKING GLASS

BENEATH WINDOW SILL
PEGBOARD AND PEG

Scale in Inches

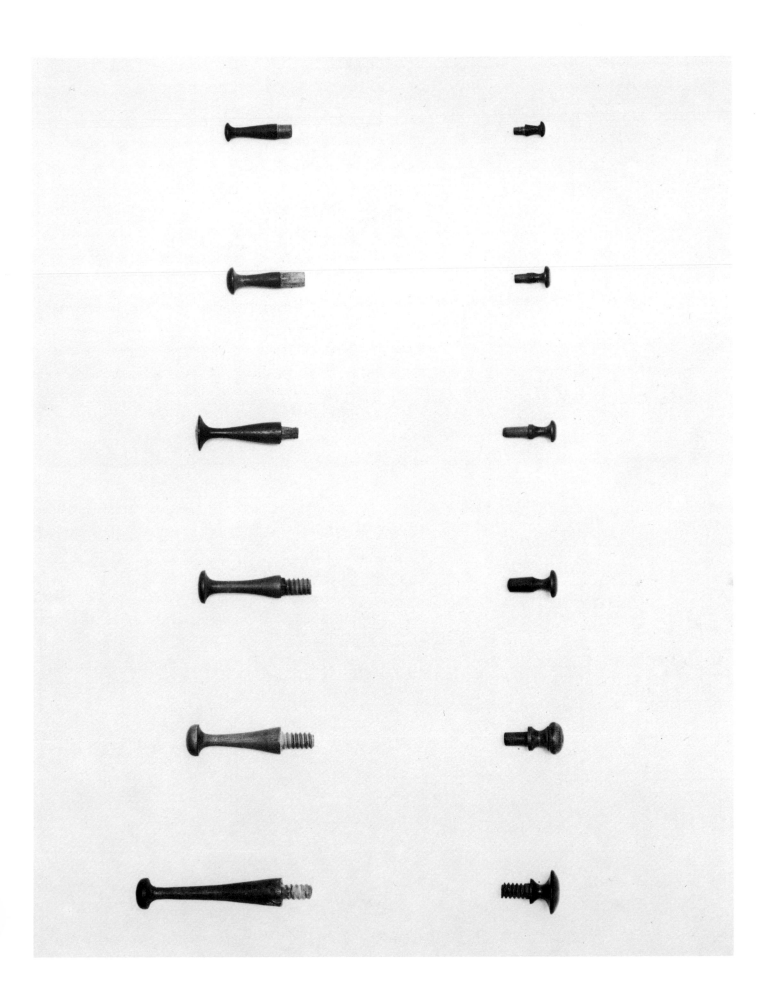

169 Pegs, Pegboards, and Pulls

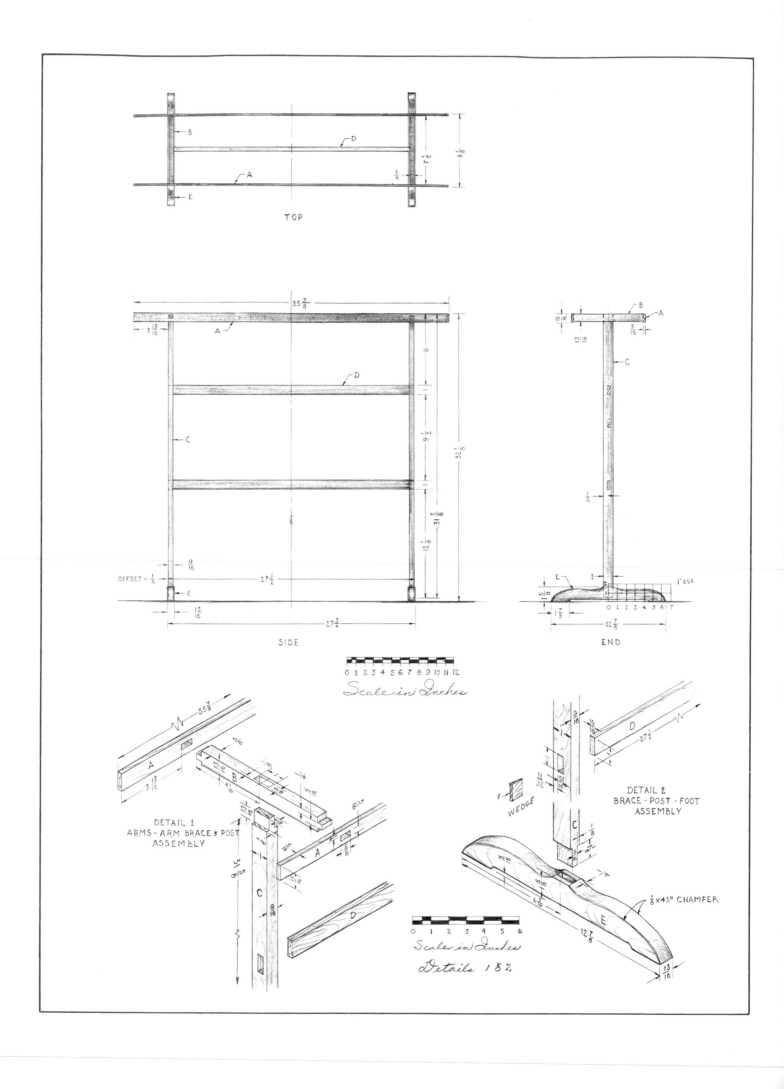

TOP

SIDE

END

Scale in Inches
0 1 2 3 4 5 6 7 8 9 10 11 12

DETAIL 1
ARMS - ARM BRACE & POST
ASSEMBLY

WEDGE

DETAIL 2
BRACE - POST - FOOT
ASSEMBLY

⅛ x 45° CHAMFER

Scale in Inches
0 1 2 3 4 5 6

Details 1 & 2

Racks

The term "racks" as used in this section describes a variety of free-standing floor stands used to dry towels and laundry and to air bedding. The smallest were used to hold Believers' towels and were placed in retiring-rooms or in connecting washrooms. Somewhat larger racks were used in kitchens, canning rooms, and similar work areas, and still larger, folding types served to air mattresses and blankets and were used in washhouses to dry laundry. Pine was the wood most often used.

1. Records show that Eldress Emma Neale of the New Lebanon society used this towel rack. It was made in the second half of the nineteenth century in that community and is pine stained light orange. The rack has twelve wedged mortise-and-tenon joints. Collection of Philadelphia Museum of Art. Photograph by A. J. Wyatt.

H. 32-1/8, W. 35-3/8, D. 12-7/8.

Letter	No.	Name	Material	T	W	L
A	2	arms	pine	5/16	15/16	35-3/8
B	2	arm braces	pine	5/8	13/16	8-1/8
C	2	posts	pine	9/16	1	31-5/8
D	2	post braces	pine	5/16	1	27-1/2
E	2	feet	pine	13/16	1-5/8	12-7/8
F	12	wedges	pine	1/8	5/8 to 1	1/4 to 3/8

2. This early nineteenth-century pine towel rack stained red-brown is from the New Lebanon community. It has eight through-tenons, each pinned for security. The uppermost crossbar has curved ends. Its upper edge is also curved and changes to a taper on the sides, which matches the taper at the top of the post. The upper edges of the other crossbars are chamfered. Private collection.

H. 31, W. 25-1/4, D. 9-1/8.

3. Also of pine, this towel rack was made during the first half of the nineteenth century in the Canterbury society. It has double-pinned through-tenons at the crossbars and a single pin through the unusually high arc feet. The standards (uprights) are tapered on the three outer edges. When made, the rack was left in its natural wood color and was so used for many years; later it was painted green. The Stokes Collection.

H. 31-1/4, W. 26, D. 10-1/4.

4. The crossbars on this drying rack of ash and basswood are tenoned and pinned into the lathe-turned ash posts. The upper bar of basswood is double-pinned and the shoe feet (also of basswood) hold the posts. The rack was made during the nineteenth century in the Sabbathday Lake community. The intermediate size of the rack suggests that possibly it was designed to be used in a kitchen or canning room. Collection of the Henry Francis du Pont Winterthur Museum. Photograph courtesy of the museum.

H. 47-3/8, W. 34-7/8, D. 16-5/8.

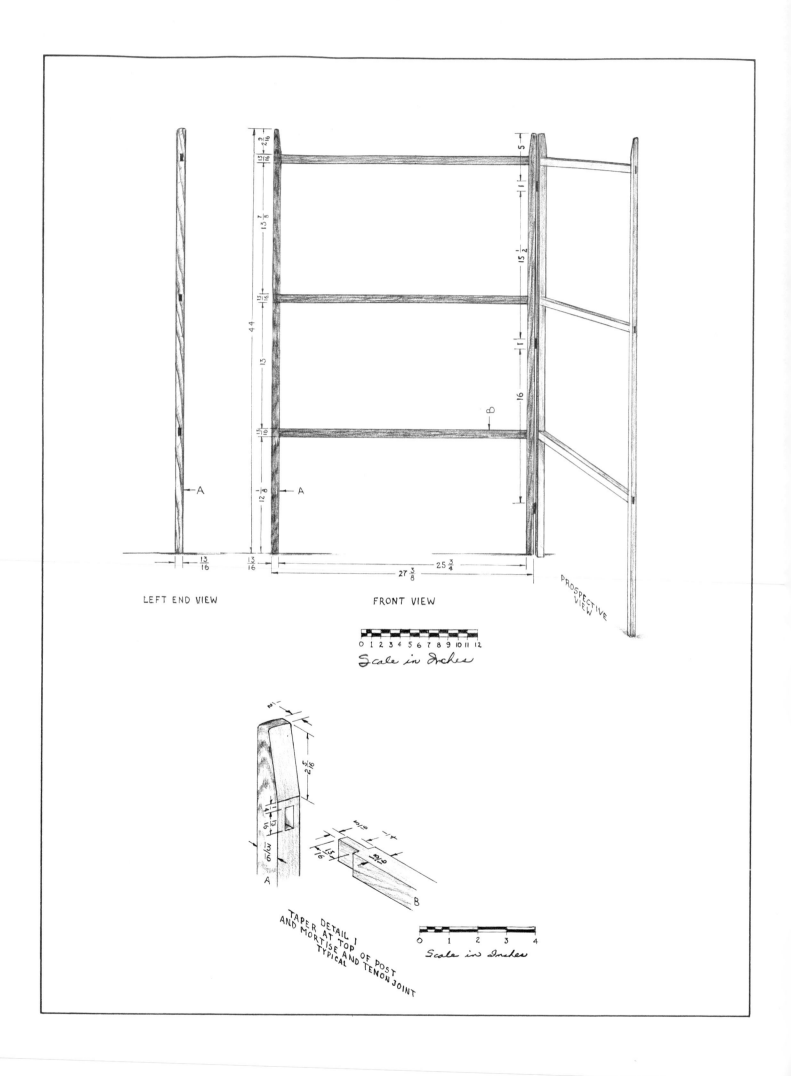

LEFT END VIEW

FRONT VIEW

PROSPECTIVE VIEW

Scale in Inches

DETAIL 1
TAPER AT TOP OF POST
AND MORTISE AND TENON JOINT
TYPICAL

Scale in Inches

5. This folding drying rack of pine in yellow wash paint was made in the first half of the nineteenth century at New Lebanon. Without wedges or pins, the sixteen through-tenons are held together with glue. Collection of the Shaker Museum, Old Chatham, N. Y.

H. 44, W. per section, 27-3/8, D. 13/16.

Letter	No.	Name	Material	T	W	L
A	4	legs	pine	13/16	13/16	44
B	6	cross bars	pine	13/16	13/16	27-3/8
Hardware						
		hinges	steel		1/2	1

6. The three sections of this drying rack are assembled with pinned mortise-and-tenon joints and fold together with leather hinges. The rack was made at the Sabbathday Lake community during the first half of the nineteenth century and is painted a yellow wash. Collection of the Shaker Museum, Old Chatham, N. Y.

H. 45, W. per section, 28-5/8, D. 5/8.

Screen

Concerned care for ill, infirm, and aged Shakers was an accepted communal responsibility. Located in family dwellings were nurse-shops that, given the health standards of the time, were well-equipped and adequately staffed. Communities that had large memberships built centrally located infirmaries. These facilities required special furnishings and equipment. Elevating beds, bed backrests, adult cradles for the severely feeble, commodes, washstands, towel racks, wheelchairs, walkers, canes, and isolating screens were made by Shaker cabinetmakers. Through expediency, existing furniture forms were modified to meet special needs: large wooden cam devices were attached to specially designed beds to make raising and lowering mattresses possible; wheelchairs were made by installing wheels on armchairs; and walkers were fabricated from turned parts similar to those used in chair manufacturing. In all probability, infirmary screens were never produced in great numbers or to any prescribed pattern.

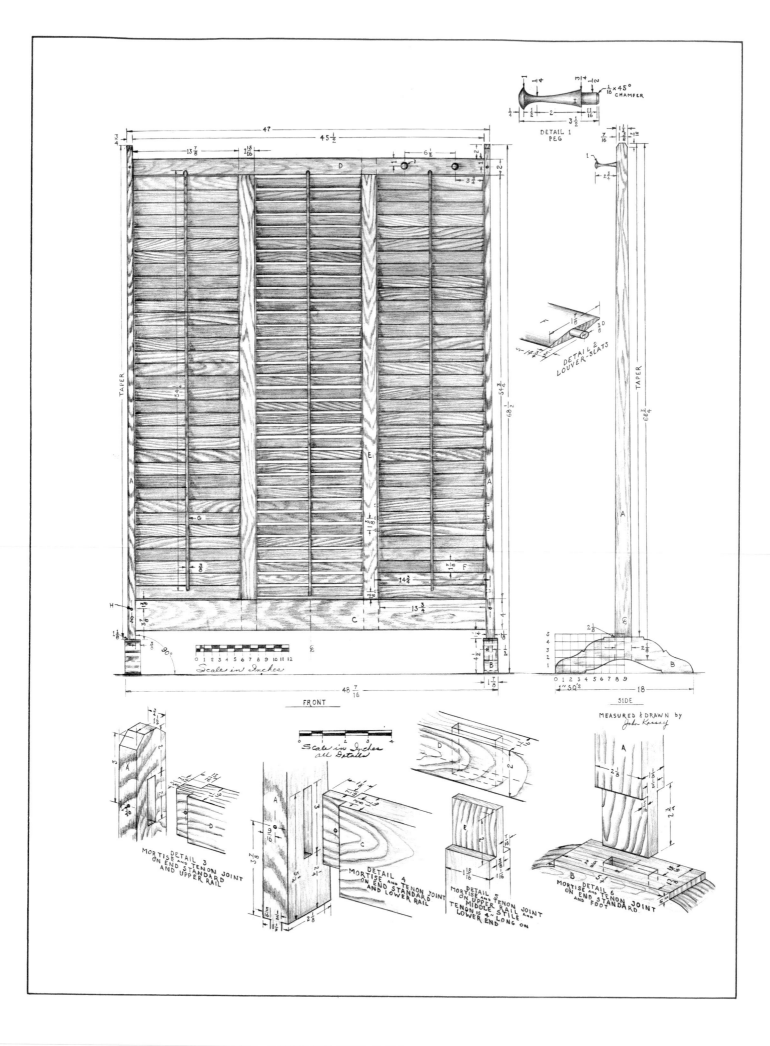

DETAIL 1
PEG

1/16 × 45° CHAMFER

DETAIL 2
LOUVER SLATS

TAPER

TAPER

FRONT

Scale in Inches

SIDE

1" SQ's

Scale in Inches
all Details

MEASURED & DRAWN by
John Kassay

DETAIL 3
MORTISE and TENON JOINT
ON END STANDARD
AND UPPER RAIL

DETAIL 4
MORTISE and TENON JOINT
ON END STANDARD
AND LOWER RAIL

DETAIL 5
MORTISE and TENON JOINT
ON UPPER RAIL and
ON MIDDLE STILE
TENON 4" LONG ON
LOWER END

DETAIL 6
MORTISE and TENON JOINT
ON END STANDARD
AND FOOT

1. This louvered infirmary screen was made during the first half of the nineteenth century, and was used in the nurse-shop or infirmary at New Lebanon. It is made of chestnut. Because of its strength and durability, chestnut was generally used for heavy frame members in Shaker buildings and only occasionally for furniture. The wood has turned an attractive dark brown color. The louvers have dowel ends that pivot in holes bored into the stiles and end standards. The standards are unusual in that they are tapered on the edges and outer surfaces. Pins through the upper and lower rail tenons lock the frame together. Shoe feet, here a clumsy form, are incompatible with the rest of the screen. Two pegs at the top of the screen held towels. Collection of Mrs. Edward Deming Andrews. Photograph courtesy of the Smithsonian Institution.

H. 68-1/2, W. 48-7/16, D. 18.

Letter	No.	Name	Material	T	W	L
A	2	end standards	chestnut	1-1/8	2-1/8	66-3/4
B	2	feet	chestnut	1-7/8	4-1/2	18
C	1	lower rail	chestnut	1-1/16	4	47-3/4
D	1	upper rail	chestnut	1-1/16	2	47
E	2	stiles	chestnut	1-1/16	1-15/16	60-3/4
F	102	louver-slats	chestnut	3/8	1-7/8	14-3/4
G	3	adjusting bars	chestnut	3/8	9/16	54-1/4
H	4	pins	maple	1/4 dia		2-1/8
I	2	pegs	maple	1 dia		3-1/2
Hardware	208	staples	iron			

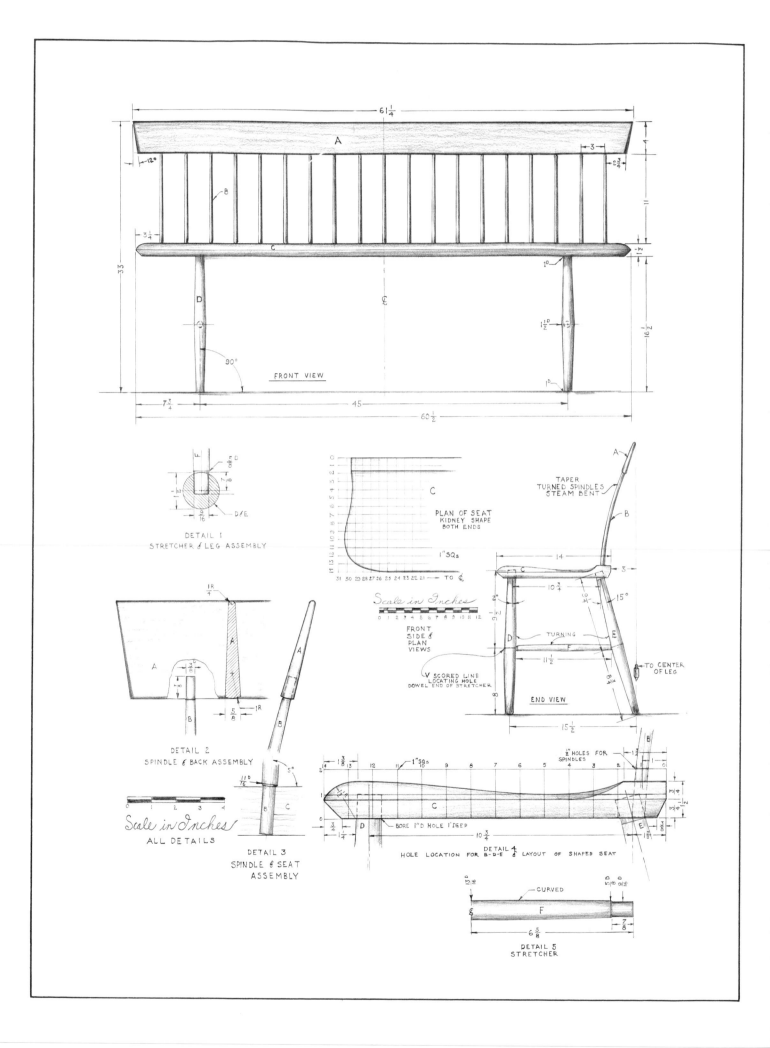

FRONT VIEW

61¼
3
2¾
4
12°
11
3¼
1½
1ᴰ
33
90°
16½
7¾
45
60½

DETAIL 1
STRETCHER & LEG ASSEMBLY

C
PLAN OF SEAT
KIDNEY SHAPE
BOTH ENDS
1" SQs
TO ℄

Scale in Inches
0 1 2 3 4 5 6 7 8 9 10 11 12
FRONT SIDE & PLAN VIEWS

V SCORED LINE
LOCATING HOLE
DOWEL END OF STRETCHER

TAPER
TURNED SPINDLES
STEAM BENT

14
3
10¾
2°
15°
TURNING
11½
8
8¾

END VIEW

15½

TO CENTER OF LEG

1R
A
A
5°
11ᴰ
16
B
C

DETAIL 2
SPINDLE & BACK ASSEMBLY

Scale in Inches
0 1 2 3 4
ALL DETAILS

DETAIL 3
SPINDLE & SEAT ASSEMBLY

1" SQs
½" HOLES FOR SPINDLES
C
BORE 1"D HOLE 1"DEEP
10¾
DETAIL 4
HOLE LOCATION FOR B-D-E & LAYOUT OF SHAPED SEAT

13ᴰ
16
CURVED
F
6⅝
7
8

DETAIL 5
STRETCHER

Settees

The typical Shaker spindle-back settee is American Windsor in style, although Shaker cabinetmakers modified the form by omitting the armrests and the medial stretcher. Maple and pine were the woods most generally used. The area where the legs are joined (doweled) into the plank seat is structurally the weakest part because the soft-wood fibers of the pine seat compressed quite readily when coupled with the denser, hardwood maple legs. The delicate spindle back stood up quite well, probably because Shakers respected their furniture, which was community property, and certainly did not slouch while sitting. No doubt the settee was used in many different rooms; however, early photographs from the Enfield, New Hampshire, community show several used in their music room.

1. This settee has a spindle back of maple, a pine-plank seat, and maple legs, all finished in clear varnish. From the Enfield, New Hampshire, community, it was made very early in the second half of the nineteenth century. The nineteen delicately tapered, steam-bent spindles were clamped in a bending mold and allowed to dry in place. The form of the back rail is interesting; its thickness is tapered, the ends are cut on an angle, and all

the edges are rounded. The kidney- or horse-shoe-shaped ends of the contoured plank seat is a beautiful form. The front edge and ends are convexly curved on the upper surface and tapered on the underside. Collection of the Philadelphia Museum of Art. Photograph by A. J. Wyatt.

H. 33, W. 61-1/4, D. 17-1/2.

Letter	No.	Name	Material	T	W	L
A	1	back rail	maple	5/8	4	61-1/4
B	19	spindles	maple	11/16 dia		13-7/8
C	1	seat	pine	1-1/2	14	60-1/2
D	2	front legs	maple	1-1/2 dia		17-1/2
E	2	back legs	maple	1-1/2 dia		18
F	2	stretchers	maple	13/16 dia		13-1/4

2. The community origin of this settee has been assigned to Canterbury, however, it is a style believed to have originated at the Enfield, New Hampshire, society. It may have been made on order for the Canterbury group or moved over when the Enfield community closed in 1928. It is made of maple and has a pine seat. Very similar to the settee shown in figure 1, it dates from the same period. However, it is shorter in width and the back has tapered, straight spindles. The finish, which may not be original, is probably clear shellac. Collection of the Shaker Museum, Old Chatham, N. Y.

H. 31, W. 49-3/4, D. 16-3/4.

3. From the second half of the nineteenth century, this settee from New Lebanon is also in maple and pine, and is stained a red-orange wash. The pine, two-sectioned seat probably held cushions. The form of the plainly turned legs is characteristically Shaker. Collection of the Shaker Museum, Old Chatham, N. Y.

H. 27, W. 68, D. 15.

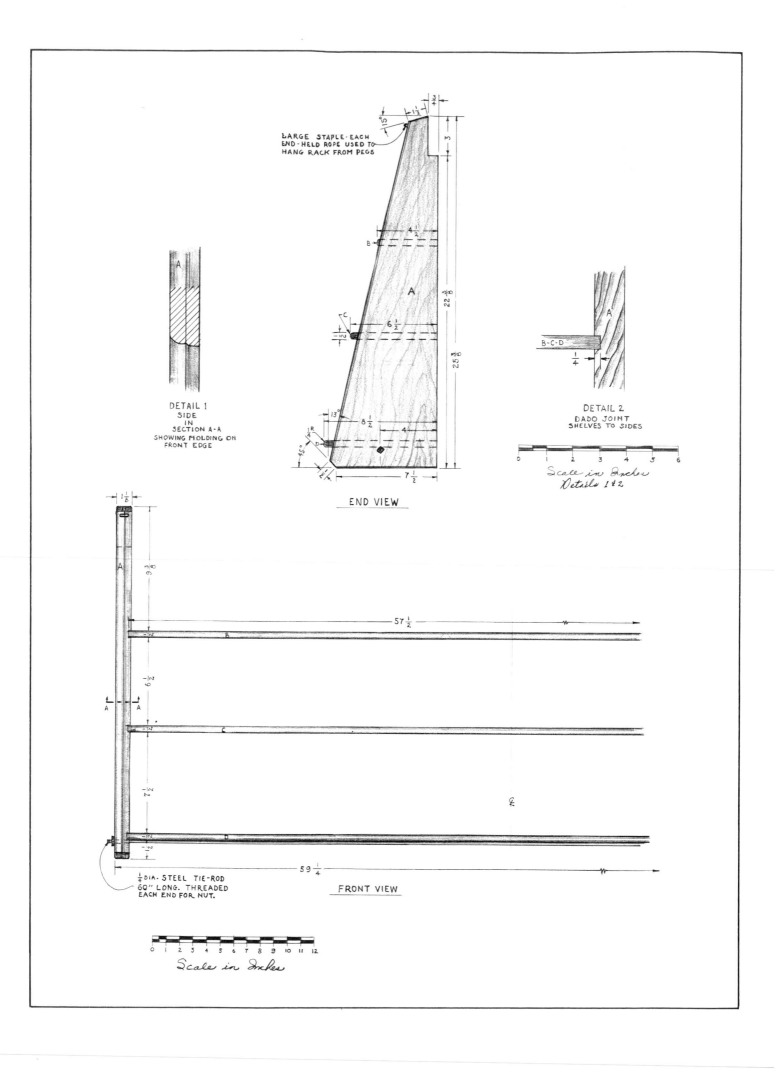

LARGE STAPLE·EACH
END·HELD ROPE USED TO
HANG RACK FROM PEGS

DETAIL 1
SIDE
IN
SECTION A·A
SHOWING MOLDING ON
FRONT EDGE

END VIEW

DETAIL 2
DADO JOINT
SHELVES TO SIDES

B·C·D

Scale in Inches
Details 1 & 2

0   1   2   3   4   5   6

¼ DIA· STEEL TIE-ROD
60" LONG. THREADED
EACH END FOR NUT.

FRONT VIEW

Scale in Inches
0 1 2 3 4 5 6 7 8 9 10 11 12

Shelves

The Shaker Society was a complex communal organization, one that required Believers to divide their time between worship and work. Therefore, in order to promote an ordered look and contribute to the efficient operation of a community, furniture designed for specific functions was most necessary.

Numerous meetinghouse benches, long communal dining tables, large tailor's counters, built-ins and cupboards of all sizes, step-stools, and shelves, all represent special furniture forms found in every Shaker community.

Specially designed shelves, freestanding and wall, short to long, and low to tall, held books, tools, textiles, sale merchandise, and candle holders.

1. These hanging bookshelves of maple in natural brown patina were made in the first half of the nineteenth century. They were suspended from a peg rail in a schoolroom in the New Lebanon community. The shelves are dadoed into the sides and a steel rod under the bottom shelf holds the sides together. Collection of Shaker Community, Inc., Hancock, Mass.

H. 25-3/8, W. 59-1/4, D. 8-1/2.

Letter	No.	Name	Material	T	W	L
A	2	sides	maple	1-1/8	8	25-3/8
B	1	upper shelf	maple	1/2	4-1/2	57-1/2
C	1	middle shelf	maple	1/2	6-1/2	57-1/2
D	1	lower shelf	maple	1/2	8-1/2	57-1/2
Hardware						
	2	staples	steel		9/16	
	1	rod	steel	1/4 dia		60
	2	nuts	steel	1/4		

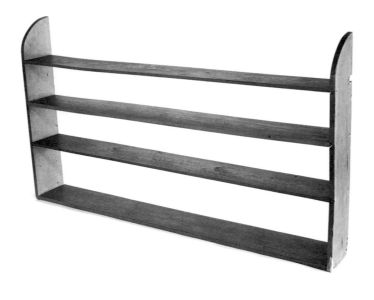

2. This hanging wall shelf in pine has a natural brown patina. Made in the first half of the nineteenth century, it was used for displaying Shaker-made items in the Hancock sisters' shop. Private collection.

H. 36-3/8, W. 63-1/2, D. 7-1/2.

3. Also from New Lebanon and made in the same period as the shelves in figure 1 are these bookshelves in unfinished pine. Assembled with nailed joinery, the bottom and shelves are dadoed into the sides and the sides have arc cutouts at the floor line forming feet. The quarter-round molded edges on the top are a form that was often used on boxes, chests, and cupboards. Private collection.

H. 40, W. 49, D. 15.

4. The piece of sheet metal attached to the upper end of the hanger was used to suspend this candle sconce. The sconce, made in New Lebanon during the first quarter of the nineteenth century, is pine stained light brown, finished with orange shellac. The undersurface of the shelf is interestingly curved through its width; that is, the front edge is much thinner than the rear. Private collection.

H. 25-1/8, W. 10-7/16, D. 4-3/8.

5. The series of holes in the hanger of this candle sconce, from Pleasant Hill, made it possible to adjust the light to a convenient angle. The sconce dates from the first half of the nineteenth century and is made of walnut that has turned an attractive golden brown. A dado cut into the round bottom holds the hanger, and the bent one-piece rim is joined at the back. Collection of Shakertown at Pleasant Hill, Inc., Harrodsburg, Ky.

H. 28-3/4, Dia. 9.

6. Liberal use of curved edges makes this candle sconce atypical. The sconce dates from the first half of the nineteenth century and was made in the Hancock community. The bracket supporting the shelf is dadoed into the underside of the shelf and the sconce is fastened to the wall with three small screws. It is made of maple stained light brown and covered with a light coat of shellac or varnish. Private collection.

H. 5-1/32, W. 8, D. 5-7/8.

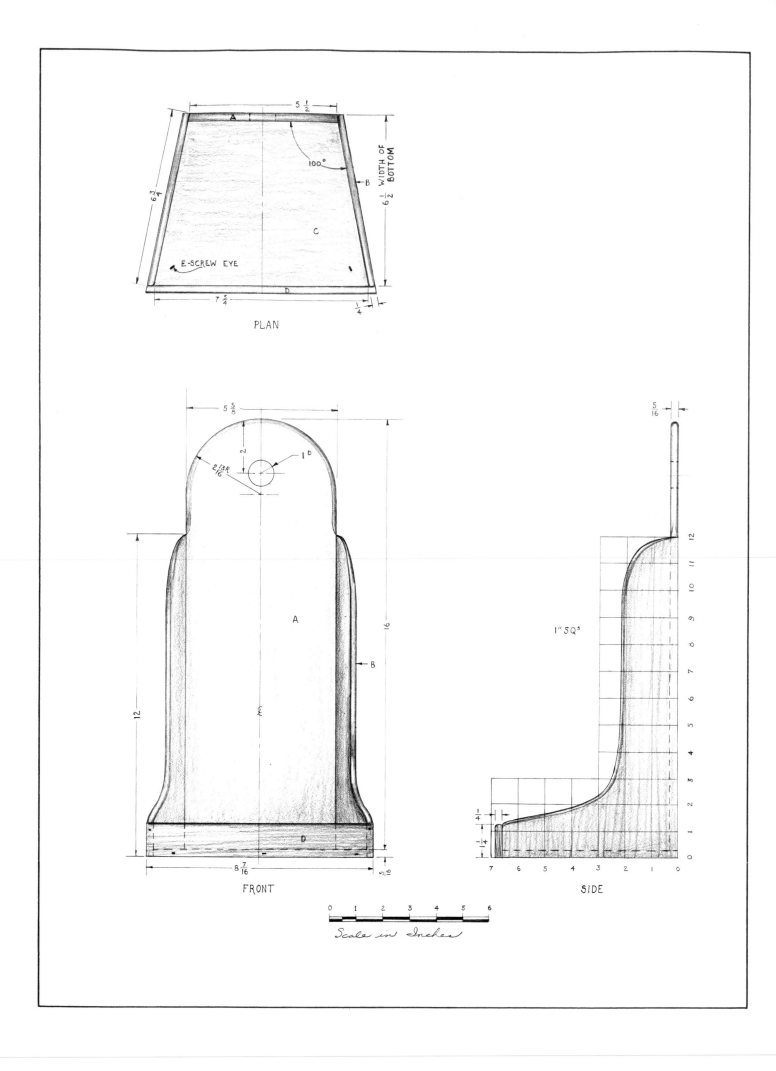

PLAN

FRONT

SIDE

5 5/8

2

1 D

2 13R
2 16

16

B

12

A

C

D

8 7/16

5 16

5 16

1" SQ⁵

12
11
10
9
8
7
6
5
4
3
2
1
0

7 6 5 4 3 2 1 0

1/4

1/4

5 1/2

6 3/4

WIDTH OF BOTTOM

6 1/2

100°

A

B

C

D

E-SCREW EYE

7 3/4

1/4

0 1 2 3 4 5 6

Scale in Inches

7. This New Lebanon candle sconce dates from the first quarter of the nineteenth century. It is made of butternut stained orange-brown, and has developed a lovely satin finish. The crudely enlarged hole in the back may have been done hastily to fit the sconce over a large peg. To stabilize the sconce, strings were tied to the screw-eyes at the bottom and to adjacent pegs. The steel candle holder called a "hog-scraper" is typical of those made in Shaker metalworking shops. Collection of the American Museum in Britain, Bath, England. Photograph by Derek Balmer.

H. 16-5/16, W. 8-7/16, D. 6-3/4.

Letter	No.	Name	Material	T	W	L
A	1	back	butternut	5/16	5-5/8	16
B	2	sides	butternut	1/4	6-3/4	12
C	1	bottom	butternut	5/16	6-1/2	7-3/4 front
						5-1/2 back
D	1	front	butternut	1/4	1-1/4	8-7/16
Hardware						
E	2	screw eyes	steel			11/16

Stands

This section includes several types of stands, classified by their purpose. Candle stands (referred to by the Shakers as round stands), sewing stands with single or double drawers, and washstands were produced in considerable quantity within the various communities for family use. The earliest Shaker stands date from about 1805. When communities began to close in the last quarter of the nineteenth century and into the first half of the twentieth, the stands were sold or given to friends. Today they are eagerly sought by museums and private collectors.

Typically, stands (except washstands, which are dealt with last) have round, square, or rectangular tops. Oval, octagonal, and clover-leaf shapes seem not to have been used, possibly because the forms were considered too worldly. Some stands are rimmed for sewing occupations, others have openings in the rims for sorting, counting, and packaging garden seeds. A few round stands have tilt-tops, a form no doubt borrowed from the world's furniture makers. Stand tops made in eastern communities are quite thin, as slight as 7/16 inch and rarely ever more than 3/4 inch; those made in the western communities are much thicker, some exceeding an inch. The edges of candle-stand tops are plain, unmolded, and conform to no uniform pattern. Some are square with slightly rounded edges, some are slightly rounded throughout; still others have an upper edge slightly rounded, joined by a long taper or convex radius cut on the underside.

Almost without exception, tripod bases were assembled to the pedestals with glued dovetail joints. A thin metal plate was generally fastened to the underside of the pedestal to secure the legs to the base. Addition of this plate served to strengthen stands and prevent the legs from breaking out of their dovetail socket. On peg-leg stands, the plain rodlike legs were simply let into holes bored into the sides of the pedestal and then glued. Other leg shapes were borrowed from the Queen Anne cabriole style or from Sheraton convex umbrella forms. The average height of stands is twenty-six inches. The usefulness of stands was greatly increased when rectangular tops with rims were installed and one or two drawers added, to accommodate sewing activities. This innovation seems to be an exclusively Shaker one, for the equivalent is not found in other eighteenth- or nineteenth-century American furniture.

Quite different from tripod stands are those articles of furniture known as washstands which, depending on their size, are also referred to as wash-benches or infirmary counters. They were usually placed in anterooms off the retiring-rooms. With their doors, drawers, and shelves, they resemble counters but are considerably less deep. Their purpose and importance prior to indoor plumbing is obvious. Like shop furniture, washstands were service pieces and were generally nail assembled. Complicated joinery was not required, however, some

few examples do exhibit fine dovetailing and a high level of the cabinetmaker's art. Though varieties of woods were used, most were made of pine which was painted, left unfinished, or lightly stained and protected with varnish.

1. This rimmed top peg-leg stand from New Lebanon dates from the same time period as the stand illustrated in figure 3. It has a maple base and an adjustable pine top. The legs are widely raked for stability. A threaded peg in the turned pedestal supports the top at a given height. A light red wash finish protects the piece. Collection of the Metropolitan Museum of Art, Purchase, 1966, Friends of the American Wing Fund.

H. 25-1/2, W. 19-1/2, D. 12-3/4.

2. Although the rectangular rimmed top and single drawer on this sewing stand are similar to those shown in figure 3, the fancier Queen Anne leg indicates that it was made at a slightly later date. The shape of the pedestal is like that used on later round stands (see figs. 4, 9, and 10). The stand is from New Lebanon and is of mixed woods. The top, drawer case, and drawer are pine, the pedestal is birch, and the legs are cherry. Dovetail joints hold the leg to the pedestal and a dowel, turned on the end of the pedestal, holds the drawer case. The top is fastened to the drawer case with flat-head wood screws. Collection of the Metropolitan Museum of Art, Purchase, 1966, Friends of the American Wing Fund.

H. 26, W. 18-3/4, D. 12-5/8.

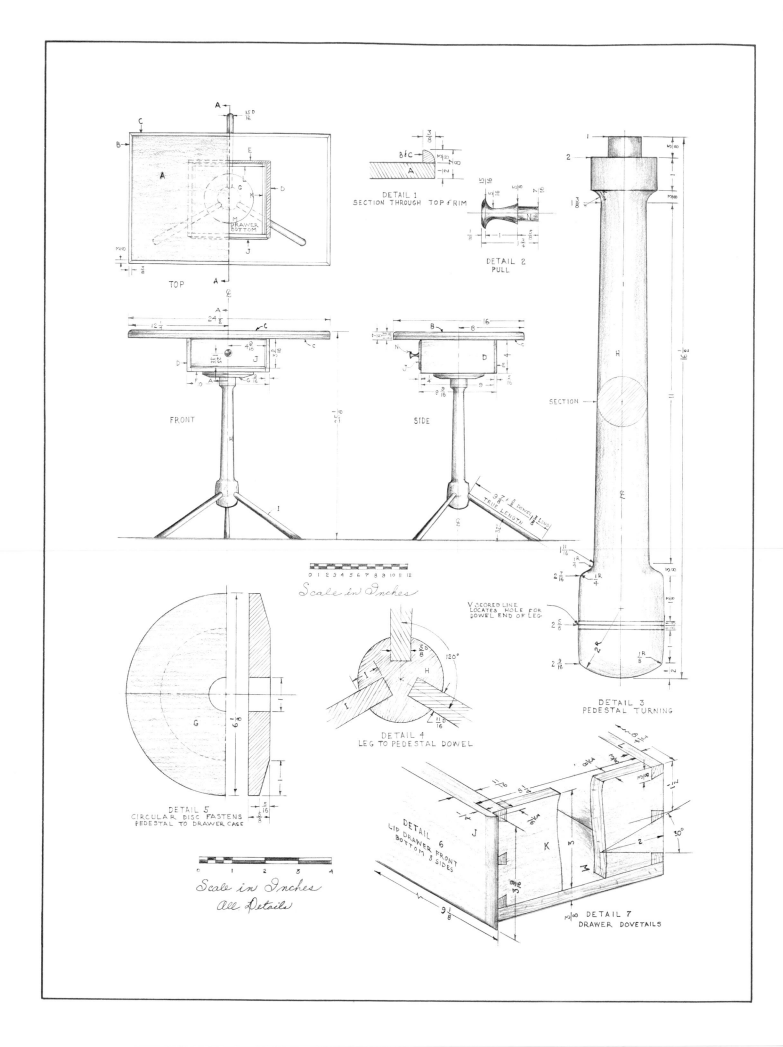

TOP

DETAIL 1
SECTION THROUGH TOP & RIM

DETAIL 2
PULL

FRONT

SIDE

SECTION

9 7/8 + 5/8 DOWEL 3 1/8 LONG
TRUE LENGTH

DETAIL 3
PEDESTAL TURNING

V SCORED LINE
LOCATES HOLE FOR
DOWEL END OF LEG

Scale in Inches

DETAIL 5
CIRCULAR DISC FASTENS
PEDESTAL TO DRAWER CASE

120°

DETAIL 4
LEG TO PEDESTAL DOWEL

DRAWER
BOTTOM

DETAIL 6
LIP DRAWER FRONT
BOTTOM & SIDES

DETAIL 7
DRAWER DOVETAILS

Scale in Inches
All Details

3. This peg-leg stand may date from the earliest days of the New Lebanon society, which would place it from the fourth quarter of the eighteenth century. In design the piece is related to peg- or stick-leg stands made during the early colonial period. It is fabricated of mixed woods; the maple legs are doweled into the cherry pedestal and the remaining parts are pine. The drawer case is fastened to the pedestal with an interconnecting small circular disc fastened with wood screws driven through the top. The stand has a natural brown patina. Private collection.

H. 25-1/8, W. 24-1/2, D. 16.

Letter	No.	Name	Material	T	W	L
A	1	top	pine	1/2	16	24-1/2
B	2	short rims	pine	3/8	3/8	16
C	2	long rims	pine	3/8	3/8	24-1/2
D	2	drawer case sides	pine	9/16	4	9
E	1	drawer case back	pine	5/16	4	10
F	1	drawer case bottom	pine	9/16	8-11/16	8-7/8
G	1	circular disc	pine	5/8	6-1/8 dia	
H	1	pedestal	cherry	2-5/8 dia		16-1/2
I	3	legs	maple	15/16 dia		11-1/4
Drawer						
J	1	front	pine	11/16	3-9/16	9-1/8
K	2	sides	pine	3/8	3	8-5/8
L	1	back	pine	3/8	3	8-3/4
M	1	bottom	pine	3/8	8-5/8	8-3/4
N	1	pull	cherry	15/16 dia		1-3/4

4. The rounded edge of the extra thin top, the slight concave line on the tapered pedestal, and the crescent shape of the legs harmonize beautifully and lend visual delicacy to this round stand. It was made in New Lebanon very early in the nineteenth century. Both edges on the legs are rounded, although the underedge is only slightly so. The legs are fastened to the pedestal with dovetails; a thin metal plate, cut to profile, is nailed over the dovetails for added strength. A small circular disc is glued to the dowel end of the pedestal and the disc is fastened to the top with wood screws. Collection of the American Museum of Britain, Bath, England. Photograph by Derek Balmer.

H. 25-5/16, Dia. of top, 16-1/8.

Letter	No.	Name	Material	T	W	L
A	1	top	cherry	1/2	16-1/8 dia	
B	1	disc	cherry	3/4	7 dia	
C	1	pedestal	cherry	2 dia		19-3/8
D	3	legs	cherry	5/8	4	11-3/16
Hardware						
E	1	sheet-metal plate	20 GA	3-1/4 dia		
F	4	wood screws	steel	FH 3/4-7		

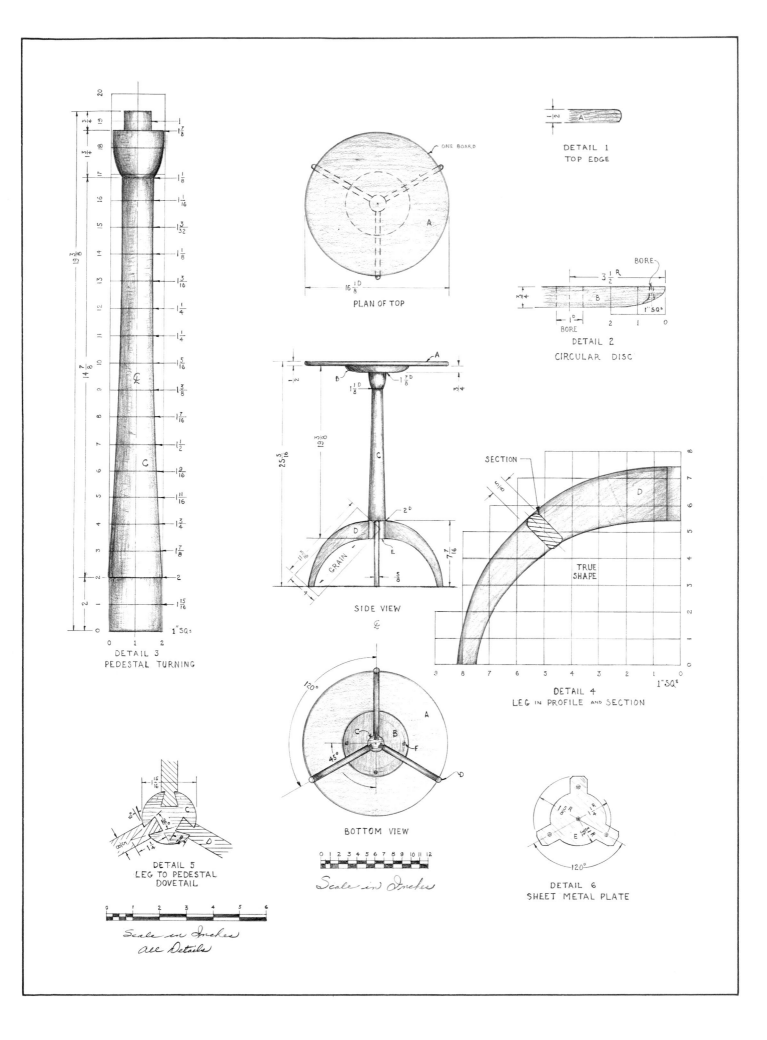

ONE BOARD

PLAN OF TOP

$16\frac{1}{8}$ D

DETAIL 1
TOP EDGE

$3\frac{1}{2}$ R

BORE

B

$1"$ SQ^s

BORE

DETAIL 2
CIRCULAR DISC

DETAIL 3
PEDESTAL TURNING

$1"$ SQ^s

SIDE VIEW

$25\frac{5}{16}$

$19\frac{3}{8}$

2^D

GRAIN

$7\frac{7}{16}$

SECTION

TRUE
SHAPE

D

$1"$ SQ^s

DETAIL 4
LEG IN PROFILE AND SECTION

DETAIL 5
LEG TO PEDESTAL
DOVETAIL

C

D

BOTTOM VIEW

$120°$

$45°$

A

B

C

F

D

0 1 2 3 4 5 6 7 8 9 10 11 12
Scale in Inches

DETAIL 6
SHEET METAL PLATE

$120°$

E

0 1 2 3 4 5 6
Scale in Inches
All Details

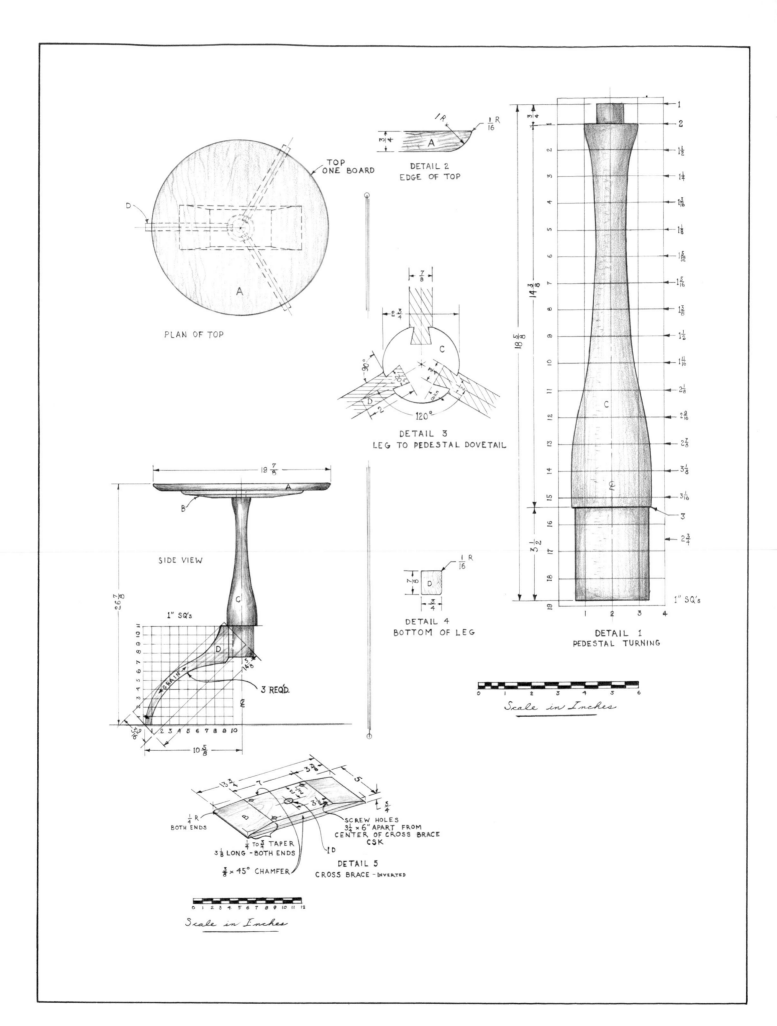

TOP
ONE BOARD

DETAIL 2
EDGE OF TOP

PLAN OF TOP

DETAIL 3
LEG TO PEDESTAL DOVETAIL

SIDE VIEW

1" SQ's

GRAIN

3 REQD.

DETAIL 4
BOTTOM OF LEG

DETAIL 1
PEDESTAL TURNING

1" SQ's

Scale in Inches

SCREW HOLES
3¼ × 6" APART FROM
CENTER OF CROSS BRACE
CSK

¼ R
BOTH ENDS

⅛ to ⅝ TAPER
3⅛ LONG - BOTH ENDS

⅜ × 45° CHAMFER

DETAIL 5
CROSS BRACE - INVERTED

Scale in Inches

5. This round stand of cherry was made at the New Lebanon community in the first half of the nineteenth century. The legs are a derivation of a Sheraton form and were referred to by the Shakers as umbrella or spider feet. It is a leg style that seems not to have been used by Shaker cabinetmakers in the western communities. The legs are fastened to the pedestal with dovetails whose shoulders seat against flats previously cut to the pedestal. The location of the first leg is at a right angle to the pedestal's broad-grained figure. A rectangular cleat, tapered and chamfered for concealment, holds the top to the pedestal. The cleat, pedestal, and legs are very similar to the stands shown in figures 6 and 8. The J. J. G. McCue Collection, The Museum of Fine Arts, Boston, Mass.

H. 26-7/8, Dia. of top, 19-7/8.

Letter	No.	Name	Material	T	W	L
A	1	top	cherry	3/4	19-7/8 dia	
B	1	cross brace	cherry	3/4	5	13-3/4
C	1	pedestal	cherry	3-1/8 dia		18-5/8
D	3	legs	cherry	7/8	3-9/16	14-5/8
Hardware						
E	4	wood screws	steel	FH 1-1/4-9		

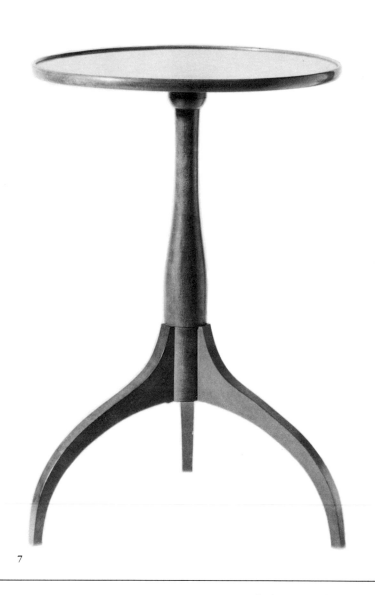

7

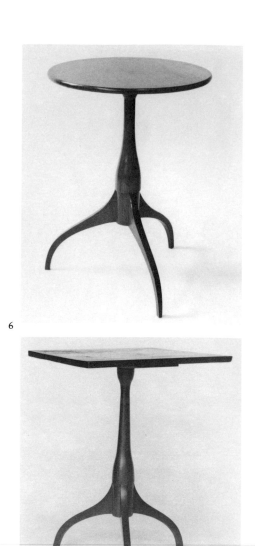

6

8

6. Made during the first half of the nineteenth century, this round stand of cherry is an example of Shaker furniture at its finest. If, as proposed, good art has a beginning, a middle, and an end, then this stand from the New Lebanon community qualifies as a work of art. A visual, nearly unbroken line can be traced from the underside of the top, down the pedestal, to the bottom of the leg. The tapered, umbrella-shaped legs are dovetailed into the urn-shaped pedestal. The top is fastened to the pedestal with a rectangular cleat that has been tapered and chamfered to hide it as much as possible. The finish is clear varnish. Collection of the Metropolitan Museum of Art, Purchase, 1966, Friends of the American Wing Fund.

H. 25-1/2, Dia. of top, 18-1/16.

7. Examples of Shaker round stands with dish tops are very rare. The community origin of this early nineteenth-century classic stand of cherry is unknown, but probably it was made in New Lebanon. The legs have the same physical elements as those on the stand shown in figure 6. Conventional dovetails hold the legs to the pedestal and a small interconnecting disc fastens the pedestal to the top. Collection of the Smithsonian Institution. Photograph courtesty of the institution.

H. 25-3/4, Dia. of top, 17-3/16.

8. Although not nearly so common as the round form, square-shaped tops were also used on the typically plain tripod bases. This stand is cherry and has an orange-red wash. The stand is from New Lebanon and was made in the early nineteenth century. The Stokes Collection.

H. 25-5/8, W. 16-13/16, D. 16-11/16.

9

10

11

9. Judging from the number in existence, this stand is in a style that was produced in quantity at New Lebanon during the first half of the nineteenth century. The stand is made of cherry and has a clear varnish finish. The Queen Anne cabriole leg with snake foot was a popular leg style and it was often used by Shaker cabinetmakers in the simplified form shown here. The legs are fastened to the pedestal with dovetails. A circular disc is fixed to the underside of the top with wood screws and the pedestal has wood threads on the end which screw into threads in the disc. Collection of the Shaker Museum, Old Chatham, N.Y.

H. 26, Dia. of top, 19.

10. What was originally a plain round stand (see fig. 9) was transformed into a tiered stand through the addition of a shelf. The stand is from New Lebanon and is made of cherry that has been stained red-brown and varnished. The turned hub separating the

top from the shelf, the shelf, and the large platelike disc beneath the shelf are late nineteenth-century Shaker additions. Their incorporation has Victorianized the stand. The legs are dovetailed to the pedestal and a metal plate is attached to the bottom of the pedestal. Modifying a piece of furniture to meet changing needs was common Shaker practice. Typical examples are shelves added to tops of sewing tables, towel racks attached to wood-boxes, and drawers suspended beneath chests, chairs, and tables. Stokes Collection.

H. 30-3/4, Dia. of top, 17-1/4, Dia. of shelf, 15.

11. Round stands made in the Kentucky societies, as was this example from Pleasant Hill, have an overall heavier form and generally more elaborately turned pedestals than their eastern counterparts. This stand is made of cherry, has a rubbed varnish finish, and dates from the first half of the nineteenth century. The plain-styled Queen Anne legs are joined to the pedestal with dovetails. A small circular disc connects the pedestal to the top. Collection of Shakertown at Pleasant Hill, Inc., Harrodsburg, Ky.

H. 26, Dia. of top, 17.

12. Except for the bead on the upper portion of the pedestal and the unmolded edge of the top, the stand shown here is quite similar to the one in figure 11. Stands with similar tops (figs. 13 and 14) seem to be a typical form made in the western societies, especially Kentucky. This stand was made at South Union for Eldress Jane Cowan (1818–1909) and is made of cherry with a varnish finish. The upper edges of the dovetailed legs are slightly rounded. A rectangular cleat, tapered and chamfered, holds the pedestal to the top. Collection of the Kentucky Library and Museum, Western Kentucky University, Bowling Green, Ky.

H. 29-1/4, Dia. of top, 17-5/8.

13. Designed as a lectern, this unusually tall round stand was used by the South Union Church family ministry. The words "Meeting Room Stand" are written in old script on the underside of the top. The square-edged top, the large collar, the accentuated, urn-shaped turning on the pedestal, and the Queen Anne legs are forms preferred by western Shaker cabinetmakers and are features useful in determining regional origin. The legs are dovetailed to the pedestal and a tapered cross cleat holds the top to the pedestal. Made in the first half of the nineteenth century, the stand is finished in clear varnish. Collection of Shaker Museum, South Union, Ky.

H. 33-1/2, Dia. of top, 17-9/16.

14. Also from the South Union community and made during the early part of the nineteenth century is this round stand in walnut and ash. The three short peg legs are doweled into a heavy, round, ash base; this in turn holds a rather ornate pedestal which seems a contradiction of form to the severe plainness of the other parts. A thin, small disc is used to fasten the pedestal to the top. Collection of Shaker Museum at South Union, Ky.

H. 24, Dia. of top, 11-7/8.

15. The concave profile on the plainly shaped pedestal suggests this sewing stand, also from Hancock, was produced slightly earlier than the one in figure 17. The spread of the Queen Anne legs is exceptionally great but necessary to support the large drawer. Two incised lines on the pedestal (probably layout lines) suggest the legs were either double-doweled or tenoned, rather than dovetailed. The upper end of the pedestal has a reduced dowel end which supports the U-shaped frame, which in turn holds the dual purpose cleat-hangers. All parts are maple except the top and drawer. The top is grained and simulates figured maple. Graining was a violation of Shaker principles regarding unnecessary ornamentation and therefore was rarely practiced. The natural brown patina of the wood is protected with clear shellac. Collection of Shaker Community, Inc., Hancock, Mass.

H. 26, W. 21, D. 17-5/8.

16. Although similar in form to figure 18, this two-drawer sewing stand has quite different details. The legs are Sheraton, the pedestal has a more pronounced bit of excess turning, and the drawers are assembled with open dovetails. Non-Shaker brass pulls are installed on the drawer fronts and the stand has a light brown stain protected with clear varnish. Collection of Mrs. Edward Deming Andrews.

H. 26, W. 20-1/2, D. 17-1/2.

17. This classic one-drawer sewing stand from Hancock was made during the first half of the nineteenth century. All parts are cherry except the top and drawer, which are pine. The umbrella-shaped legs are fastened to the pedestal with tenons rather than the customary dovetails. The three U-shaped frame members are joined with open dovetails and the dual-purpose cleat-drawer-hangers are fastened to the frame with pinned mortise-and-tenons. The horizontal member of this assembly is glued to the dowel end of the pedestal. Flat-head wood screws driven through the cleat-drawer-hangers hold the top in place. Drawer runners, formed separately, are applied to the drawer sides and allow it to be pulled from either side. The open dovetails at the drawer corners, the thinness of the top, and the undercurve of its edge are interesting features. Small, commercially made brass pulls were installed on each end of the drawer and a varnish finish protects the table's warm brown patina. Private collection.

H. 25-5/16, W. 19-5/8, D. 16-7/8,
D. at floor line, 19-1/4.

Letter	No.	Name	Material	T	W	L
A	1	top	pine	7/16	16-7/8	19-5/8
B	2	cleat-drawer-hangers	cherry	3/4	1-1/4	15-1/2
C	2	vertical frame members	cherry	3/4	2-1/4	5-3/8
D	1	horizontal frame member	cherry	7/8	2-1/4	8-5/8
E	1	pedestal	cherry	2-7/8 dia		13-3/4
F	3	legs	cherry	5/8	4-1/4	14-1/8
G	2	pegs	cherry	1/8 dia		1-1/8
Drawer						
H	2	fronts	pine	9/16	4-11/16	7
I	2	sides (upper part)	pine	11/16	1	15-5/8
J	2	sides (lower part)	pine	7/16	3-11/16	15-5/8
K	1	bottom	pine	3/8	6-1/8	14-1/2
Hardware						
L	4	wood screws	brass	FH 1–8		
M	2	pulls	brass	1/2 dia		7/8

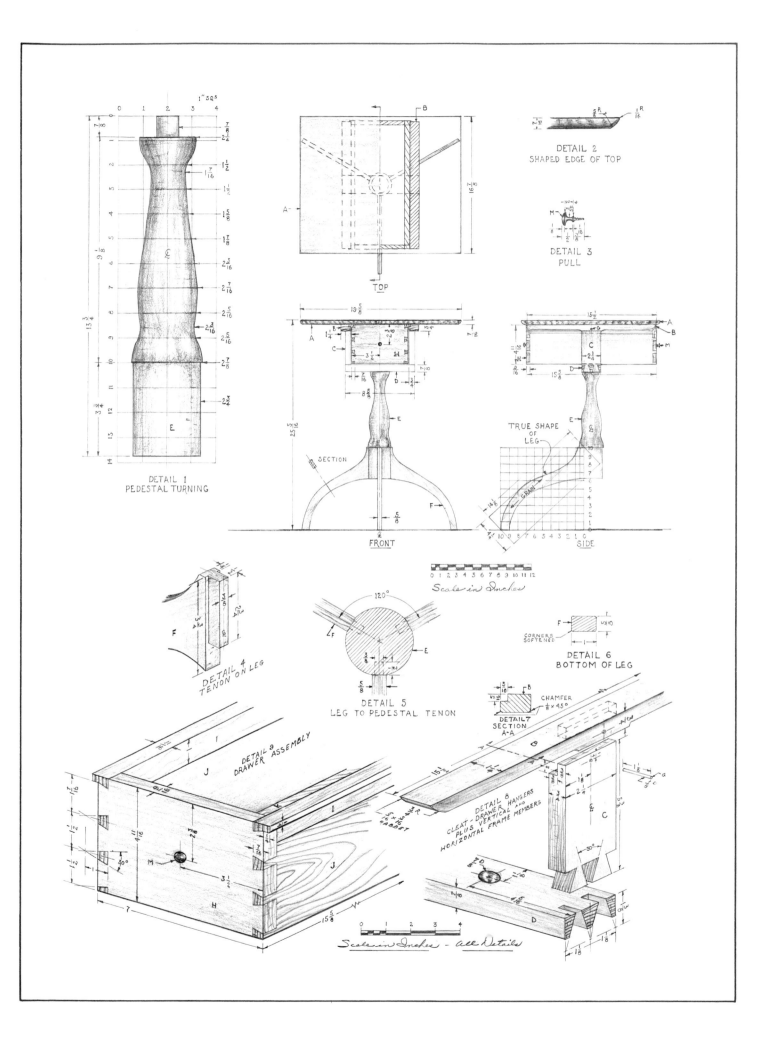

DETAIL 1
PEDESTAL TURNING

DETAIL 2
SHAPED EDGE OF TOP

DETAIL 3
PULL

TOP

FRONT

SIDE

TRUE SHAPE
OF
LEG

GRAIN

SECTION

Scale in Inches

DETAIL 4
TENON ON LEG

DETAIL 5
LEG TO PEDESTAL TENON

DETAIL 6
BOTTOM OF LEG

CORNERS
SOFTENED

DETAIL 7
SECTION
A-A

CHAMFER

DETAIL 8
CLEAT - DRAWER HANGERS
PLUS VERTICAL AND
HORIZONTAL FRAME MEMBERS

DETAIL 9
DRAWER ASSEMBLY

RABBET

Scale in Inches - All Details

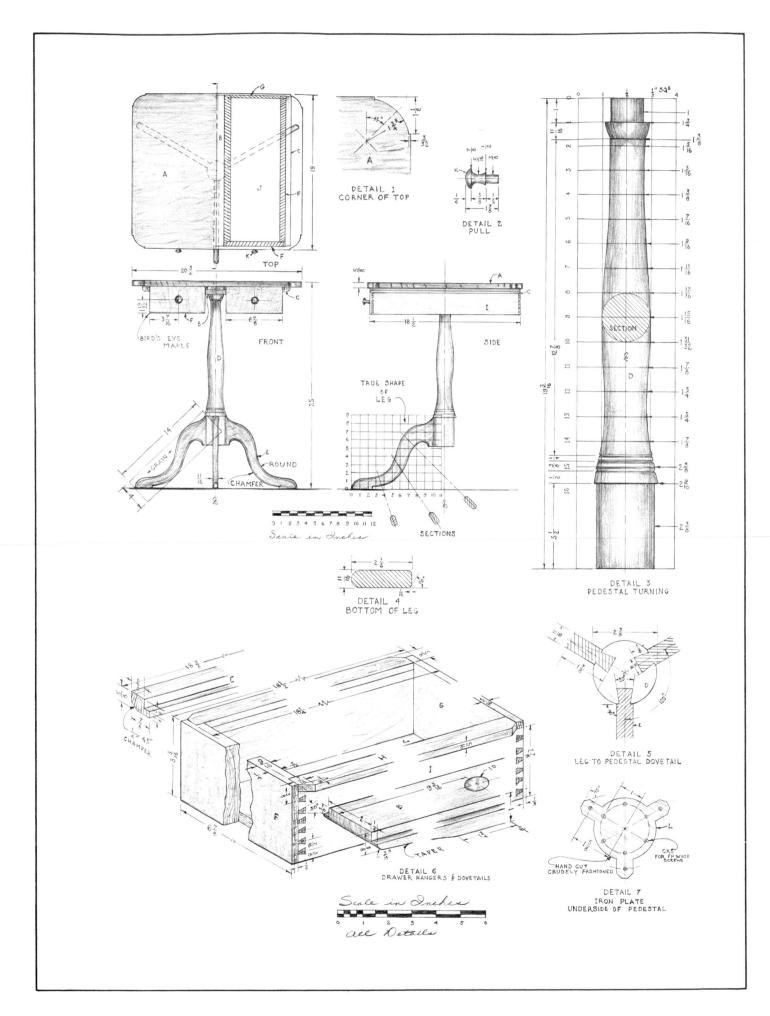

DETAIL 1
CORNER OF TOP

DETAIL 2
PULL

DETAIL 3
PEDESTAL TURNING

FRONT

BIRD'S EYE MAPLE

SIDE

TRUE SHAPE
OF
LEG

ROUND

CHAMFER

GRAIN

SECTIONS

Scale in Inches

DETAIL 4
BOTTOM OF LEG

DETAIL 5
LEG TO PEDESTAL DOVETAIL

DETAIL 6
DRAWER HANGERS & DOVETAILS

CHAMFER

TAPER

DETAIL 7
IRON PLATE
UNDERSIDE OF PEDESTAL

HAND CUT
CRUDELY FASHIONED

CKS
FOR FH WOOD
SCREWS

Scale in Inches

all Details

18. Also from Hancock, and made during the early part of the nineteenth century, is this two-drawer sewing stand of pine and maple. All parts are maple except the top and the drawer sides and bottoms, which are pine. Dovetail joints hold the legs to the pedestal and a center cleat-drawer-hanger holds the top to the pedestal and supports the suspended drawers. Two outer cleat-drawer-hangers also support the drawers and restrict the top from warping. The drawers can be opened from either side and are assembled with dovetails. Tiger-stripe, curly maple is used for the legs and drawer fronts. The top has ovolo corners and the cleat-drawer-hangers have chamfered edges. The edges of the legs are rounded and the drawer runners are separate pieces of wood attched to the drawer sides. A thin metal plate is fastened to the underside of the pedestal. A coat of clear varnish has been applied over a red wash. The J. J. G. McCue Collection, The Museum of Fine Arts, Boston, Mass.

H. 25, W. 20-3/4, D. 19.

Letter	No.	Name	Material	T	W	L
A	1	top	pine	5/8	19	20-3/4
B	1	center cross cleat-drawer-hanger	maple	1	2-1/2	18-3/8
C	2	outer cross cleat-drawer-hangers	maple	5/8	7/8	18-3/8
D	1	pedestal	maple	2-9/16 dia		19-3/16
E	3	legs	maple	11/16	4	14
Drawers						
F	2	fronts	maple	9/16	3-3/16	6-7/8
G	2	backs	maple	5/16	3-3/16	6-7/8
H	4	sides (upper part)	pine	5/16	5/8	17-15/16
I	4	sides (lower part)	pine	7/16	2-7/8	18-1/4
J	2	bottoms	pine	5/16	6	17-15/16
K	2	pulls	maple	7/8 dia		1-3/8
Hardware						
L	1	sheet-metal plate	iron	18 GA-4 dia		

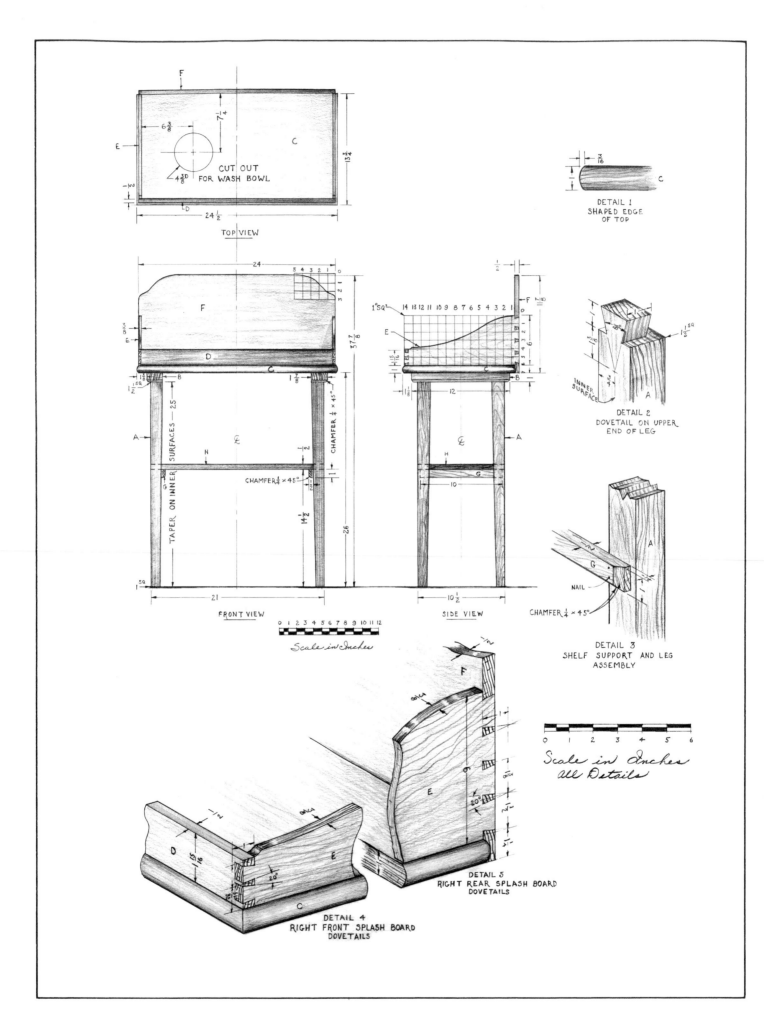

F

7 1/4

6 3/8

C

E

4 3/8 D

13 3/4

1/2

D

24 1/2

CUT OUT
FOR WASH BOWL

TOP VIEW

3/4
1/16

C

DETAIL 1
SHAPED EDGE
OF TOP

24

5 4 3 2 1 0

3 2 1

F

3/8

E

D

C

37 7/8

1/2

1 7/8

1 1/4
SQ

1 5/8

B

1 7/8

CHAMFER 1/4 × 45°

A

E

TAPER ON INNER SURFACES — 25

H

1/2

G

CHAMFER 1/4 × 45°

1

1/2

14 1/2

26

21

FRONT VIEW

0 1 2 3 4 5 6 7 8 9 10 11 12
Scale in Inches

1" SQ

14 13 12 11 10 9 8 7 6 5 4 3 2 1 0

F

7 1/2

E

15/16

6

5 4 3 2 1

7 5 3 1

C

B

1 1/8

12

A

H

G

10

10 1/2

SIDE VIEW

1/2

28°

3/16

INNER SURFACE

3/4

1 5/8 SQ

A

DETAIL 2
DOVETAIL ON UPPER
END OF LEG

3/4

G

A

NAIL

CHAMFER 1/4 × 45°

DETAIL 3
SHELF SUPPORT AND LEG
ASSEMBLY

1/2

F

13/16

1/2

15/16

D

1/16

20°

E

C

DETAIL 4
RIGHT FRONT SPLASH BOARD
DOVETAILS

1/2

13/16

9

13/16

1

20°

2 1/2

1 1/4

E

DETAIL 5
RIGHT REAR SPLASH BOARD
DOVETAILS

0 1 2 3 4 5 6
Scale in Inches
All Details

19. This early nineteenth-century washstand of pine painted coral-red was made in New Lebanon. The square legs are tapered on the inner surfaces and have dovetail pins cut on their upper ends that assemble to dovetailed sockets cut into the ends of the cross cleats. Dovetails hold the splashboards together and are fastened to the top with nails driven through the top from below. The back splashboard laps the back edge of the top and is nailed to the edge. This subassembly is fixed to the cross cleats with wood screws driven through the cleats into the top. Shelf cleats nailed to the inside of the legs support the shelf. Collection of Mrs. Edward Deming Andrews.

H. 37-7/8, W. 24-1/2, D. 14-1/4.

Letter	No.	Name	Material	T	W	L
A	4	legs	pine	1-1/2 sq		26
B	2	cleats	pine	1	1-7/8	12
C	1	top	pine	1	13-3/4	24-1/2
D	1	front splashboard	pine	1/2	1-15/16	24
E	2	side splashboards	pine	3/8	6	14
F	1	back splashboard	pine	1/2	11-7/8	24
G	2	shelf supports	pine	1/2	1	10
H	1	shelf	pine	1/2	10-1/2	21

20. The unique features of this beautiful washstand are the single underslung drawer, which can be pulled out from either side, and the circular shelf designed to hold a wash bowl and pitcher, which can be swung out of the way. The stand was made in New Lebanon during the first half of the nineteenth century. In mixed woods, it has tiger-stripe maple splashboards and drawer fronts, plain maple legs and stretchers, and pine shelf, drawer sides and bottom. The finish is original to the piece and is a reddish brown stain. Private collection. Photograph by Charles R. Muller.

H. to top of back splashboard, 28-3/4, W. 21-1/8, D. 17-1/4.

21. Made in New Lebanon and dating from the same period as the washstand in figure 20 is this washstand of pine stained light brown. The base contains a single shelf and the upper part has splashboards with interesting rounded and chamfered edges. The components of the stand are simply nailed together. Private collection.

H. 35-1/8, W. 30-1/4, D. 16-1/2.

22. Utilization of prominently figured hard woods for the exterior parts of this washstand make the piece exceptionally desirable. The piece was made in the second quarter of the nineteenth century at Hancock. In mixed woods, it has a cherry base, pine interior, and tiger-stripe maple splashboards. Most unusual is the rounding on the front edge of the sides, which simulates a beaded corner. A repeat of this form is found on the splashboard sides. The center location of the door, with its darker fielded panel, presents a strong focal point. The shape of the molded lip on the drawer front closely parallels that on the back splashboard. Closely spaced, well-made corner dovetails were used to assemble the splashboards. Angled as they are, they present a visual relief from the predominantly horizontal and vertical lines. In clear varnish, the stand may hve been refinished. Collection of Shaker Community, Inc., Hancock, Mass.

H. 37-3/4, W. 27, D. 21.

23. In mixed woods, this washstand dates from the first half of the nineteenth century and was made in the Pleasant Hill society. The sides, front, and top are pine; the back is chestnut; the bowl support under the top is butternut; and the door panel is walnut. Although the stand was made in Pleasant Hill, its plain form gives it an undeniably eastern look. The two especially long pegs at the right side held towels, but the purpose of the small metal peg at the left is unknown. A strip of molding at the base on each side was no doubt installed to fill unwanted open space. Collection of Shakertown at Pleasant Hill, Inc., Harrodsburg, Ky.

H. 28, W. 36-1/4, D. 16-1/4.

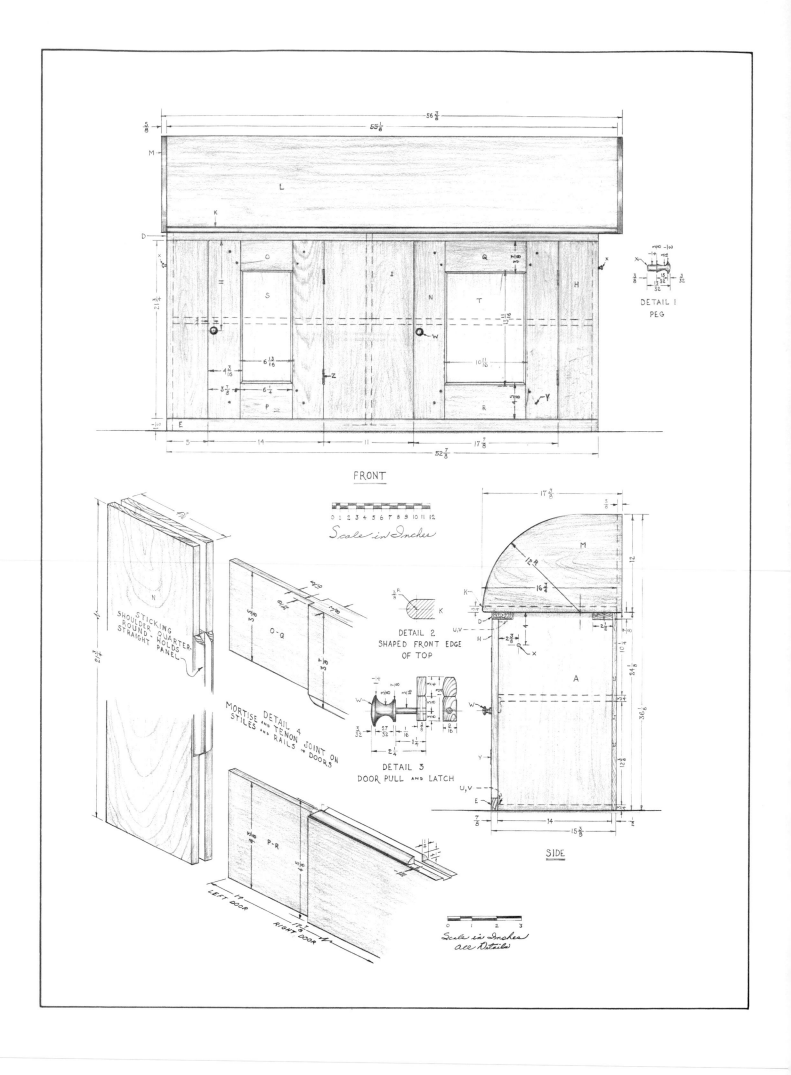

FRONT

DETAIL 1
PEG

Scale in Inches

DETAIL 4
MORTISE AND TENON JOINT ON
STILES AND RAILS OF DOORS

STICKING. QUARTER-
ROUND. HOLDS
STRAIGHT PANEL

DETAIL 2
SHAPED FRONT EDGE
OF TOP

DETAIL 3
DOOR PULL AND LATCH

SIDE

Scale in Inches
all Details

LEFT DOOR

RIGHT DOOR

24. The large size of this first-quarter nine-teenth-century washstand suggests it was used in a nurse-shop or infirmary. It was made in the New Lebanon community and is pine with a light brown varnish-stain. The stand has a single shelf, two cupboard doors of unequal size, and generously high splash-boards. Double-pinned, open mortise-and-tenon joints hold the flat panel doors together. Collection of Mrs. Edward Deming Andrews.

H. 24-7/8, H. to top of back splashboard, 36-1/8, W. 56-3/8, D. 15-3/8, D. at side splashboard, 17-3/8.

Letter	No.	Name	Material	T	W	L
A	2	sides	pine	3/4	14	24-1/8
B	1	shelf	pine	3/4	14	51-3/8
C	1	bottom	pine	3/4	14	51-3/8
D	2	upper horizontal frame members—front and back	pine	7/8	2-1/2	52-7/8
E	1	lower horizontal frame member—front	pine	7/8	1-1/2	52-7/8
F	1	lower partition member	pine	3/4	14	12-3/8
G	1	upper partition member	pine	3/4	14	10-1/4
H	2	vertical end frame members—front	pine	7/8	5	21-3/4
I	1	vertical center frame member—front	pine	7/8	11	21-3/4
J	1	back	pine	1/2	24-1/8	52-7/8
K	1	top	pine	3/4	16-3/4	55-1/8
L	1	back splashboard	pine	5/8	12	55-1/8
M	2	ends—splashboards	pine	5/8	12	17-3/8
N	4	door stiles	pine	7/8	4-3/16	21-3/4
O	1	upper rail (left door)	pine	7/8	3-7/8	14
P	1	lower rail (left door)	pine	7/8	4-5/8	14
Q	1	upper rail (right door)	pine	7/8	3-7/8	17-7/8
R	1	lower rail (right door)	pine	7/8	4-5/8	17-7/8
S	1	door panel (left door)	pine	5/16	6-13/16	13-11/16
T	1	door panel (right door)	pine	5/16	10-11/16	13-11/16
U	2	door stops (left door)	pine	1/4	1	15
V	2	door stops (right door)	pine	1/4	1	19
W	2	pulls	maple	1-1/4 dia		2-1/4
X	3	pegs	maple	1/2 dia		15/32
Y	16	pins	pine	1/8 dia		7/8
Hardware						
Z	4	butt hinges	iron		3/4	1-3/4

25. This washstand was made in the Enfield, New Hampshire, society where it was used in a washhouse. It is made of pine and maple painted orange-red and is assembled with pinned mortise-and-tenon joints. The stand is very much like another washstand still at this former Shaker community. Collection of the Golden Lamb Inn, Lebanon, Ohio.

H. 27-3/4, W. 84, D. 26-5/8.

Stools

Eight different styles of stools are treated in this section. The first three were mass produced in the New Lebanon chair factories and sold to the world's people; they are foot benches, footstools, and utility stools. The others are examples of furniture made for communal use and were produced in limited quantity and never marketed; they are footstools, milking stools, shop stools, sewing steps, and step-stools.

1. The tie cushion on this foot bench is a heavy wool plush, a material "peculiarly" Shaker that was hand-woven and available in solid colors or striped with a border, as in this example in red and olive. The bench is maple, varnish stained red mahogany and was made during the first half of the twentieth century in the New Lebanon community. Collection of Robert F. W. Meader.

H. 7-3/4, W. 13, D. 13.

2. The crudely made button-foot legs on this footstool or cricket appear to have been hand shaped rather than lathe turned. They have dowel ends which are fastened directly to the one-board plank top. The stool was made in Enfield, Connecticut, very early in the nineteenth century and is pine with a natural brown patina. Tack marks along the edge of the top indicate the piece was once upholstered. Collection of Shaker Community, Inc., Hancock, Mass.

H. 5-3/4, W. 14-5/8, D. 7-5/8.

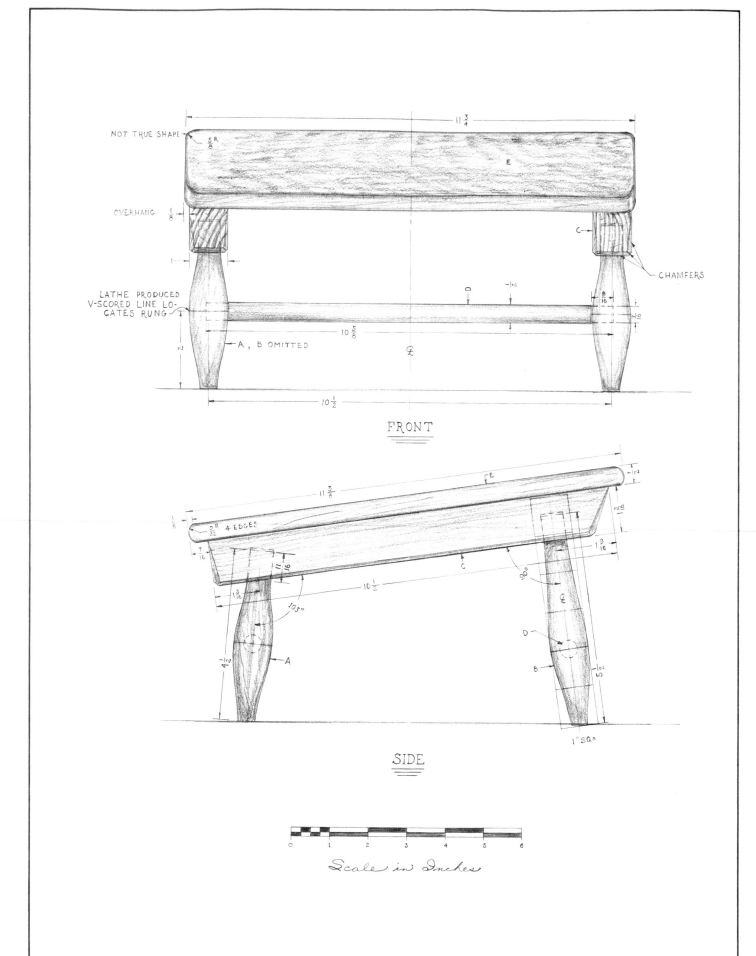

NOT TRUE SHAPE

$\frac{5}{8}$ R

11 $\frac{3}{4}$

E

OVERHANG $\frac{1}{8}$

C

CHAMFERS

LATHE PRODUCED V-SCORED LINE LO-CATES RUNG

D

$\frac{1}{2}$

$\frac{9}{16}$

$\frac{9}{16}$

10 $\frac{5}{8}$

A, B OMITTED

$\frac{2}{1}$

$\mathcal{C}$

10 $\frac{1}{2}$

FRONT

11 $\frac{3}{8}$

F E

$\frac{1}{2}$

$\frac{1}{8}$

$\frac{9}{32}$ R 4 EDGES

$\frac{9}{16}$

$\frac{7}{16}$

1 $\frac{9}{16}$

$\frac{11}{16}$

C

10 $\frac{1}{2}$

90°

1 $\frac{3}{16}$

103°

$\mathcal{C}$

4 $\frac{1}{2}$

A

D

5 $\frac{1}{2}$

B

1" SQ.

SIDE

0   1   2   3   4   5   6

Scale in Inches

3. This late-manufacture slant-top footstool from New Lebanon is identified in an illustrated catalogue (c. 1875) of Shaker chairs and is referred to as a "foot bench." Thousands were manufactured during the latter part of the nineteenth and early twentieth centuries and sold for a dollar. They were available in three varnish-stain colors: cherry, ebony, mahogany, and in white, which was the natural color of the maple wood. For an additional $2.75 a tie cushion of a coarse plush was available. The incline of the top "favored" one's feet while sitting and also lent itself for kneeling. This example is made of maple and has a mahogany stain.

During the years of manufacture, slight variations were made in the overall size of the bench and the shape of the legs. On some examples the portion of the leg above and below the point of rail intersection is more acutely concaved and terminated at the floorline in a rather petite diameter. The scribed line on each leg was made with a skew or spear-point lathe tool while the leg

was rotated in the lathe. This line located the point where the legs were bored to receive the two rungs. Tops were fastened to the cleats by one of two methods; they were simply nailed in place or, as in this example, fastened with six counter-bored and plugged flat-head wood screws. The underedges of the cleats were bored to accept the dowel

end on the legs. All the exposed edges on the cleats were lightly chamfered and a Shaker decal was applied to the underside of the top. Collection of The United Society of Shakers, Sabbathday Lake, Maine.

H. 6-3/4, W. 11-3/4, D. 11-3/4.

Letter	No.	Name	Material	T	W	L
A	2	legs	maple	1 dia		4-1/2
B	2	legs	maple	1 dia		5-1/2
C	2	rails	maple	1	1-3/16	10-1/2
D	2	rungs	maple	1/2 dia		10-5/8
E	1	top	maple	1/2	11-3/8	11-3/4
F	6	plugs	maple	9/16 dia		1/8
Hardware						
G	6	wood screws	steel	FH 1-8		

4. This utility stool was made in New Lebanon during the first quarter of the twentieth century. It is made of maple stained mahogany and has a combination tan cotton and black wool tape seat woven in a basket-weave pattern. A Shaker decal is on the inside of a leg, the customary place on such pieces. Author's collection.

H. 16, W. 14, D. 14.

5. Also from New Lebanon and made about 1926 is this utility stool of maple with a white finish. The cotton tape seat is a replacement. It was purchased by the owner from Sister Lillian Barlow. The stool is slightly taller than the one shown in figure 4. Collection of Donald Weeks.

H. 17-7/8, W. 12-5/8, D. 12-5/8.

Letter	No.	Name	Material	T	W	L
A	4	legs	maple	1-5/16 dia		17-7/8
B	4	seat rails	maple	13/16 dia		12-11/16
C	8	leg rails	maple	3/4 dia		12-11/16

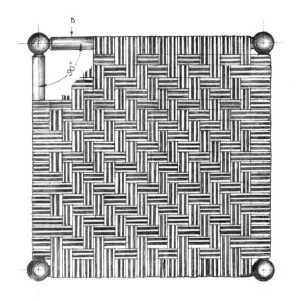

PLAN OF TAPE SEAT

B

90°

0 1 2 3 4 5 6

Scale in Inches

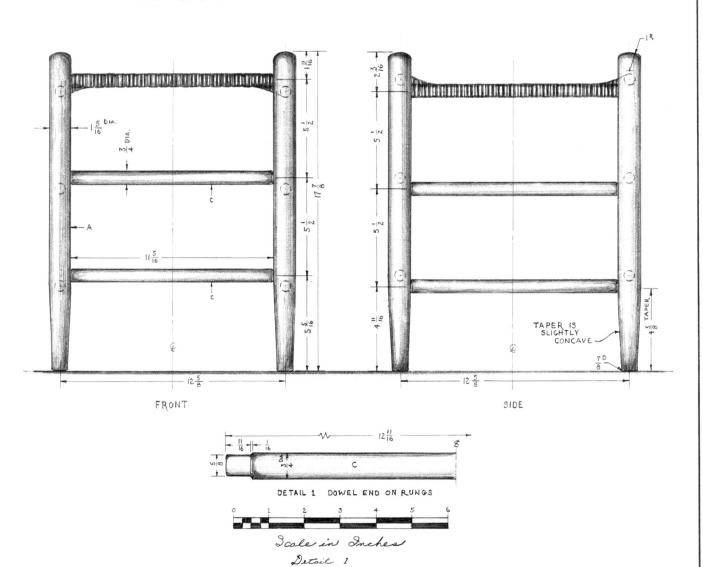

$1\frac{5}{16}$ DIA.

$\frac{3}{4}$ DIA.

A

C

C

$11\frac{5}{16}$

$12\frac{5}{8}$

FRONT

$\frac{9}{16}$

$5\frac{1}{2}$

$17\frac{7}{8}$

$5\frac{1}{2}$

$5\frac{5}{16}$

℄

$2\frac{3}{16}$

$5\frac{1}{2}$

$5\frac{1}{2}$

$4\frac{11}{16}$

TAPER IS
SLIGHTLY
CONCAVE

$12\frac{5}{8}$

℄

1 R

TAPER

$4\frac{5}{8}$

$\frac{7}{8}$ D

SIDE

$\frac{11}{16}$ $\frac{1}{16}$ $12\frac{11}{16}$

$\frac{5}{8}$

$\frac{3}{4}$ DIA.

C

DETAIL 1   DOWEL END ON RUNGS

0 1 2 3 4 5 6

Scale in Inches

Detail 1

6. This footstool was made around 1934 by Eldress Sarah Ann Collins (1855–1947) expressly for the owner. Eldress Sarah was brought to the New Lebanon Shakers as an orphan at the age of eight. She lived in the South family and came to head that family and the chair industry for over sixty years. The stool is made of maple finished in a medium walnut varnish-stain and is upholstered in a coarse rush. As a rule, stools were not sized with a decal, however, this stool has a No. 0 decal applied to the inside of one leg. The two cove cuts on each leg are pure decoration. The diameter of the rungs is constant—even at the ends where they penetrate the legs. Collection of Dr. Clara Nigg.

H. 9-1/8, W. 14-3/4, D. 10-3/4.

7. The maple pencil-post legs and hickory rungs on this utility stool with a cane seat are in the original dark green paint. This was a color often used on Shaker furniture made in the Ohio and Kentucky colonies. The stool was made during the second half of the nineteenth century at Union Village. Collection of Tim J. Bookout. Photograph by Dennis C. Darling.

H. 9-3/4, W. 12, D. 12.

8. The legs of this milking stool are maple and the seat is pine. The stool was made during the third quarter of the nineteenth century in New Lebanon. The lathe-turned legs have dowel ends, which were pinned after being inserted into holes previously bored into the underside of the seat. The large angled ends on the undersurface of the seat gave a cant to the legs and reduced the physical and visual weight of the stool. Lightly varnished, the wood has developed a rich, warm brown patina. The seven scored lines on each leg are purely decorative. Collection of the Shaker Museum, Old Chatham, N. Y.

H. 10, W. 10-5/8, D. 7-7/8.

9. This shop stool in mixed woods was made during the first half of the nineteenth century in New Lebanon. The legs are chestnut, rungs are birch, and the seat frame is pine. The exposed parts are stained brown. The seat is padded with a horsehair cushion supported by a piece of pressed paperboard and upholstered with tan-colored leather, a replacement which closely matches the original. The tapered rungs imply early manufacture and were individually lathe produced. The dowel ends on the rungs were grooved to accept a wedge after being glued in place. The wedges were added for firmness and permanency. The partially square, partially round legs are not especially pleasing, but for the Shaker craftsman were a departure from the traditional square- or round-turned legs and a greater challenge to make. To produce them, the legs were first squared, then cut to length, and mounted in a lathe. Next, holes for the rungs were located and marked. Then, those parts of the leg above, between, and below the points where the rungs were to be located were turned round. Adjacent surfaces (inside corners) were flattened with a hand plane. Finally, using the flat surfaces on the legs for added stability, holes for the rungs were bored. Private collection.

H. 25-3/4, W. 15-1/2, D. 15-1/2.

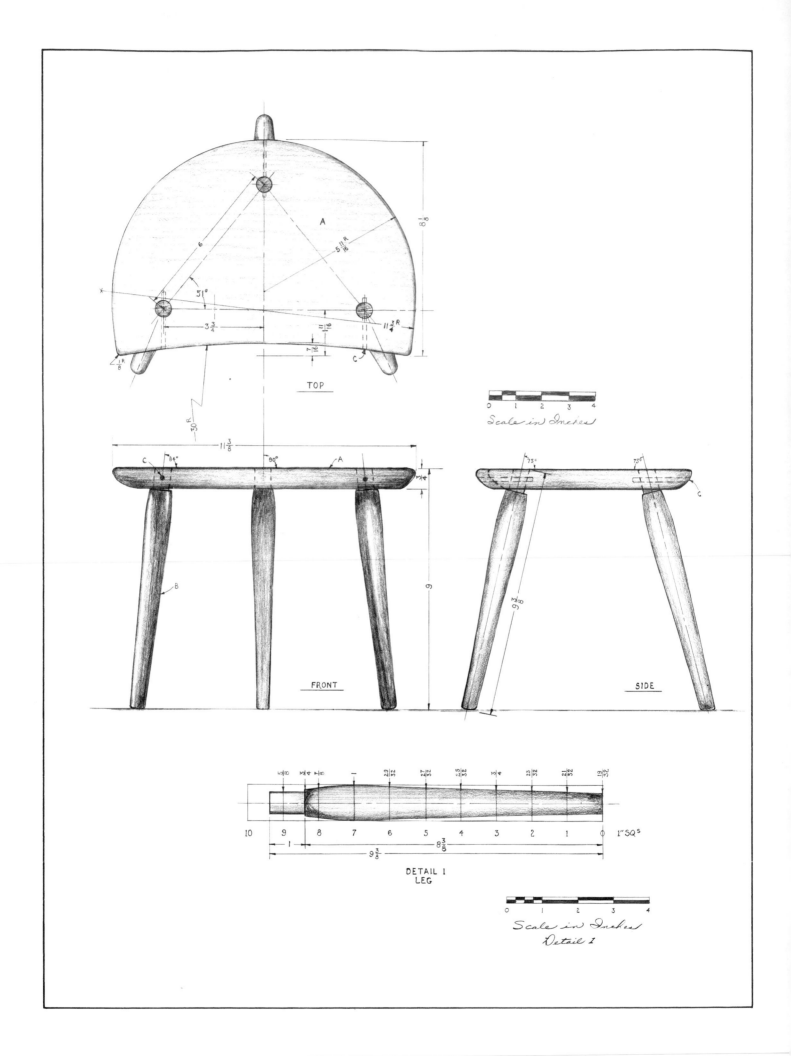

TOP

0 1 2 3 4
Scale in Inches

FRONT

SIDE

DETAIL 1
LEG

0 1 2 3 4
Scale in Inches
Detail 1

10. The community origin of this three-leg milking stool is unknown; however, the form of the partly circular seat and the legs suggests it was made in an eastern community during the first half of the nineteenth century. A through dowel on the end of each leg is pinned to the plank seat to prevent its fall-ing out. Efforts to identify the initials *H. B. to E. D.* which are on the underside of the seat were unsuccessful. Collection of the Western Reserve Historical Society, Cleveland, Ohio. Photograph by Elroy Sanford.

H. 9, W. 11-3/8, D. 9-5/8.

Letter	No.	Name	Material	T	W	L
A	1	seat	walnut	3/4	8-1/8	11-3/8
B	3	legs	walnut	1 dia		9-3/8
C	3	pins	walnut	1/8 dia		2-1/4

11. The shape of the seat on this milking stool is similar to that of the stool illustrated in figure 10, however, the legs are less graceful and appear to have been shaped by hand. The stool is made of pine and is in original yellow wash paint. The letters *F. S.* and the date 1851 are stenciled in blue-green paint on the underside of the plank seat and were most likely applied at the time of manufacture. Efforts to identify the Believer who used this milking stool have been unsuccessful. Hancock has been credited with its origin, but this has not been substantiated. Private collection.

H. 11, W. 15, D. 13.

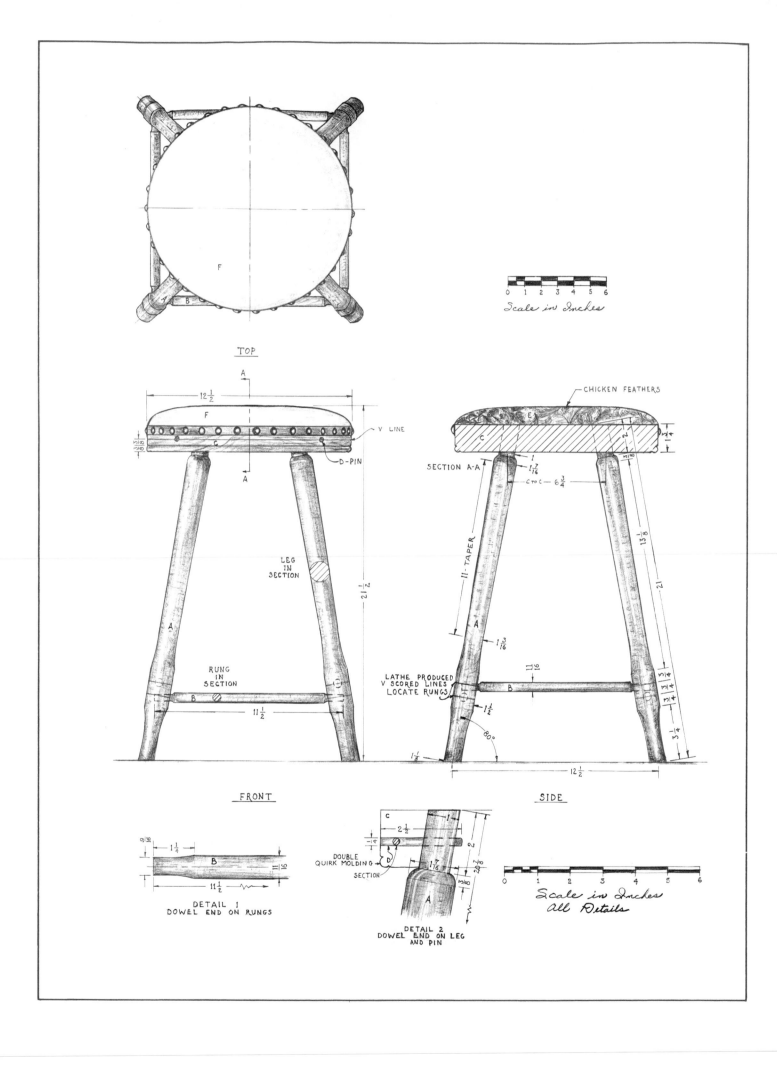

TOP

Scale in Inches

12 1/2

F

V LINE

D-PIN

LEG
IN
SECTION

21 1/2

RUNG
IN
SECTION

11 1/2

FRONT

CHICKEN FEATHERS

E

C

SECTION A-A

1
1 7/16

C TO C — 6 3/4

11 – TAPER

13 1/8

A

1 3/16

11/16

LATHE PRODUCED
V SCORED LINES
LOCATE RUNGS

B

1 1/2

80°

1 1/4

12 1/2

2

21

3/4
3/4
3/4

3 3/4

SIDE

9/16

1 1/4

B

11/16

11 1/2

DETAIL 1
DOWEL END ON RUNGS

C

2 1/2

1/4

DOUBLE
QUIRK MOLDING

D

SECTION

1

1 7/16

A

2

20 7/8

DETAIL 2
DOWEL END ON LEG
AND PIN

Scale in Inches
All Details

12. Three different woods were used in making this shop stool. The top is pine, the legs are maple, and the rungs are oak, all stained a medium brown. The lathe-turned top has a V-scored line at its edge which was used to locate holes for pins that lock the doweled legs to the top. The legs taper downward, then curve outward and enlarge, for added strength, where the straight rungs join. Below this point of intersection the legs curve inward and the taper continues to the floor. A replacement leather seat cover holds a padding of chicken feathers. The edge of the leather is finished nicely with a darker strip, nailed in place with round-head brass tacks, all duplicating as nearly as possible the original upholstery. The stool was made during the second half of the nineteenth century in Enfield, Connecticut. Author's collection.

H. 21-1/2, W. 13-5/8, Dia. of top, 12-1/2.

Letter	No.	Name	Material	T	W	L
A	4	legs	maple	1-1/2 dia		21
B	4	rungs	oak	11/16 dia		11-1/2
C	1	top	pine	1-3/4	12-1/2 dia	
D	4	pins	maple	1/4 dia		2-1/2
E		padding	chicken feathers			
F		cover	leather			
Hardware						
		upholsterers' tacks #3				
		roundhead furniture nails	brass			1/2

13. The turnings on the legs of this shop stool are slightly different from those on the one shown in figure 12 and appear to be less graceful. The stool has a plank seat of walnut, maple legs, and ash rungs, all of which have developed a natural brown patina. A single scored line on each leg was used to locate the center of the rung holes. The lathe-turned legs were produced one at a time and made slight variation in form inevitable and acceptable. At some time the seat was probably equipped with a tie or slip cushion. The stool was made at Hancock about 1840. Collection of the Shaker Museum, Old Chatham, N. Y.

H. 18, W. 14, Dia. of top, 11.

14. These sewing steps of walnut are stained red mahogany and were made in the New Lebanon community about 1860. The piece has simple lines and equally simple joinery. The steps and the quarter-round cleats are nailed to the sides. Collection of Shaker Community, Inc., Hancock, Mass.

H. 7-3/8, W. 10-3/8, D. 9-3/4.

15. A paper label pasted on the underside of these pine sewing steps reads: "Ednah E. Fitts, Canterbury, N. H." Eldress Ednah was born in 1846 and died in 1924 and it is safe to assume that the steps were used by her. The steps are unusual because a storage compartment located under the hinged upper step has been incorporated in the unit. The bottom of the storage area and lower step is one piece and is dadoed into the sides. The back is let into the sides and joined with glue and nails. It is finished with a coat of orange-red varnish-stain. The Stokes Collection.

H. 11-1/8, W. 14-3/4, D. 10-7/16.

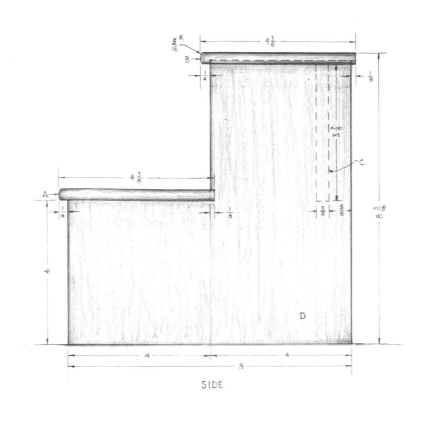

SIDE

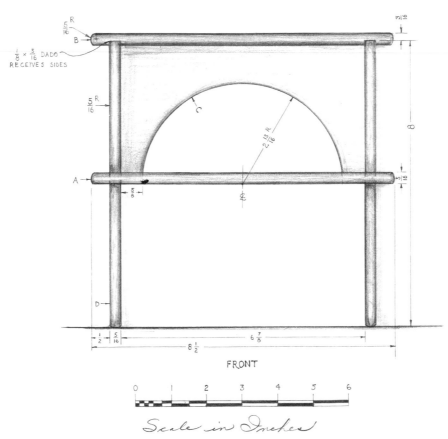

FRONT

Scale in Inches

0 1 2 3 4 5 6

16. Made of walnut, these sewing steps from the New Lebanon community served as a footrest. The upper step elevated the knee so that reading or sewing materials could be brought closer to the user's eyes. The beautifully arced cross brace was grooved 1/8-inch into the sides for added strength. With the exception of the back edges, all other edges are nicely rounded, including the lower ends of the sides. This may have been done to facilitate sliding the steps about and also to prevent splintering. The upper step is dadoed to receive the sides. The lower step was not also dadoed, but simply nailed, which is inconsistent construction and unexplainable. Though the sewing steps are small, their quality of craftsmanship and details are well above average. Collection of the Philadelphia Museum of Art. Photograph by A. J. Wyatt.

H. 8-3/16, W. 8-1/2, D. 8-3/16.

Letter	No.	Name	Material	T	W	L
A	1	lower footrest	walnut	5/16	4-3/8	8-1/2
B	1	upper footrest	walnut	5/16	4-3/8	8-1/2
C	1	cross brace	walnut	3/8	3-7/8	7-1/8
D	2	legs	walnut	5/16	8	8

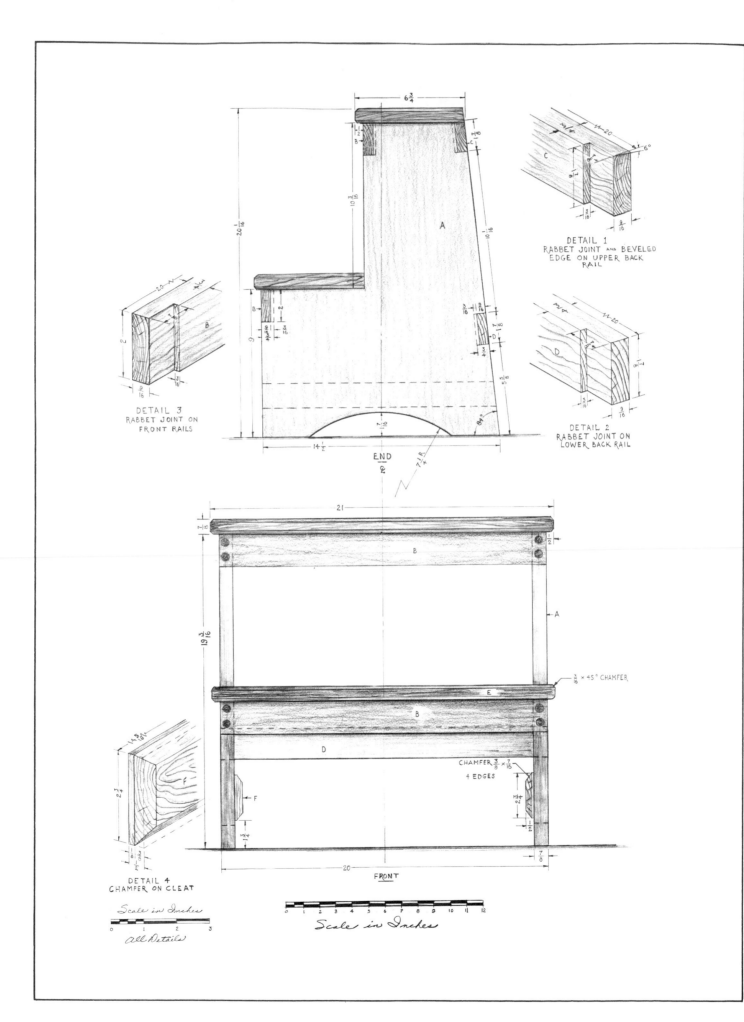

DETAIL 1
RABBET JOINT and BEVELED
EDGE ON UPPER BACK
RAIL

DETAIL 3
RABBET JOINT ON
FRONT RAILS

DETAIL 2
RABBET JOINT ON
LOWER BACK RAIL

A

END
½

DETAIL 4
CHAMFER ON CLEAT

CHAMFER 3/8 × 7/16
4 EDGES

3/16 × 45° CHAMFER

FRONT

Scale in Inches
All Details

Scale in Inches

17. Step-stools were designed to make the contents in tall chests and cupboards more accessible and were referred to as two, three, or four "steppers." This unusually sturdy "two stepper" from New Lebanon was made early in the third quarter of the nineteenth century. It is pine painted red-brown. The choice of material and its plain form suggest the piece was designed to be used in a shop rather than in an office or dwelling. It is sensibly designed, generously wide and deep with a comfortable step height. The rear edges of the sides are angled toward the front, putting the top step nearer the front and the user's weight nearer the center of gravity, thus contributing greater stability. The cleats and rails are assembled to the sides with countersunk wood screws, the heads of which are hidden with putty. Finishing nails, their heads set below the surface, were used to fasten the steps to the sides. Private collection.

H. 20-1/16, W. 21, D. 15.

Letter	No.	Name	Material	T	W	L
A	2	legs	pine	7/8	14-1/2	19-3/16
B	2	front rails	pine	3/4	2	20
C	1	back upper rail	pine	3/4	1-7/8	20
D	1	back lower rail	pine	3/4	1-7/8	20
E	2	steps	pine	7/8	6-3/4	21
F	2	cleats	pine	1/2	2-3/4	14-5/16
Hardware	16	wood screws		FH 1-1/2-8		
	10	wood screws		FH 1-8		

18. The steadying rod on this pine, stained walnut, two-step stool helped one maintain one's balance. The stool was made in Canterbury during the fourth quarter of the nineteenth century. The generous use of curves on the sides conveys a feel of "busyness," a result of the Victorian influence that set in during the fourth quarter of the nineteenth century in several New England Shaker communities. Collection of Mrs. Julius Zieget.

H. to upper step, 14-3/8, H. to tip of steadying rod, 30, W. 16, D. 12-1/2.

19. This three-step stool from Hancock was made during the second half of the nineteenth century. It has butternut risers and steps, and pine sides, cleats, and cross brace. The cross brace has a half-lap joint which was nailed in place. The brace appears to lack the same level of craftsmanship evident in the rest of the stool and may have been added later by the Shakers as a strengthening device. The arc cutouts on the sides which form feet, the double quirk-bead molding on the lower front edge of the risers, and the quarter-round molding on the ends and front edges of the steps are all pleasingly mild, decorative contributions. The molding on the top step faces upward. This molding style was popular in the Hancock and New Lebanon communities and was used on the tops of chests of drawers (fig. 16) and dining tables (fig. 30). The "three stepper" has developed a warm brown patina which has been protected over the years by a light coat of varnish. Collection of the American Museum in Britain, Bath, England. Photograph by Derek Balmer.

H. 25-1/4, W. 17-1/2, D. 13-3/4.

Tables

Tables were made in all the societies and some date from the earliest days of communal organization. They were made for Believers' use and except for a few rare cases were never made for sale. Like all furniture, they were considered community property and therefore were part of a member's "joint inheritance."

To facilitate the societies' numerous occupations and industries, Shaker turners and joiners produced tables in a variety of styles and sizes. Kitchens and dining rooms, canneries and dairies, sewing, tailoring, and retiring-rooms, weave, herb, printing, and nurse-shops all required special types.

Shaker sisters spent a great deal of time mending clothes, darning socks, and making new garments for members. Numerous tables, many of which are very attractive, were designed to serve these occupations. Although they exhibit considerable variation in form, each has either a rack of drawers or a gallery added to the top to hold sewing items.

Many tables with square, tapered legs were made and used in a variety of ways. These tables usually had rectangular tops, some had rims and one or more drawers. The worldly equivalents of these tables are Hepplewhite forms, a style of furniture that is part of the Federal period, dating from approximately 1788 to 1825.

Tables fabricated with turned legs are another style that was produced in quantity. Usually these tables were more attractive than those with square, tapered legs. However, turned legs—even those as plain in form as the Shaker style—probably took slightly longer to produce. The tops of these tables range in length from two to more than twelve feet and are usually fitted with up to three drawers. This table form also has a worldly counterpart in the Sheraton designs which were also popular during the Federal period.

Drop-leaf tables were being made in all the communities by the first quarter of the nineteenth century. Their utility and space-saving features were attractive to the Shakers. They ranged from two to ten feet or more in length; the shorter served many functions and the longer were used as utility tables in kitchens and as worktables in the sisters' shops. In some examples the tops are one board wide with exceptionally narrow leaves. The bases usually contain a drawer at each end.

X-trestle tables, also referred to as saw-buck tables, were being made in colonial America more than a hundred years before Mother Ann and her little group arrived in New York harbor. Though not widely produced within the society, a few were made and used in dwellings and shops.

Trestle tables also were made during the early years of the society. They solved the problem of serving meals to all the members of a family at one time. These tables also ranged from short to long; some examples are as long as twenty feet. The short tables were used by the ministry who had the exclusive privilege of eating together, separate from the rest of the membership. The problem of passing dishes along a dining table was eliminated by setting tables in one or

3

2

more "squares" of four persons each. Each square shared dishes of food set on "tableboards" and, above the tables, condiments were readily available from hanging shelves. Trestle legs were either rectangular or straight cylinders with beading at each end. The earliest feet were only slightly arced in a long curve. The longitudinal medial stretcher held the trestles and was usually set directly under the top.

1. Similar in form to the table in figure 6 and also from South Union but made slightly later is this sewing table of cherry. The table has square, splayed legs with unique turned ends (for a similar example, see fig. 8), an underslung drawer with a pullout work surface below, and a unique lift-up spool-implement rack. When elevated the rack is held in place with a wooden catch. The scalloped corners on the front edges of the top and the cyma curve on the ends of the rims are a mild aberration from Shaker rules of plainness. Collection of South Union, Ky.

H. 27-1/2, W. 25-7/8, D. 21-1/2.

2. The additions of a rim on the edge of the top and of a rack with a three-section till and drawer transform what is essentially a small rectangular table into a sewing facility. The table was made in New Lebanon early in the nineteenth century and at one time was used by Sister Amelia Calver (1844–1929). It has legs, stretchers, and drawer pulls of maple, drawer interiors of pine, and remaining parts of black birch. Most becoming to the table are the step-turned legs, a leg style rarely found on Shaker furniture. The upper section of the turned portion of the leg is straight but, interestingly, the lower part is tapered downward to the floor. The upper surfaces of the stretchers are flattened, indicating they may have supported a shelf. The sides and back of the small drawer are narrower in width than the drawer front. This was found necessary, for in order to install the drawer it had to be tilted above the drawer stops. The table is finished in a red wash paint. Collection of the Metropolitan

Museum of Art, Purchase, 1966, Friends of the American Wing Fund. Photograph courtesy of the museum.

H. 30-3/4, W. 24, D. 18-1/2.

3. Museum records show this sewing table was made for Sister Angeline Perryman (1815–1909) of the South Union community. Sister Angeline was a caretaker of girls in the childrens' order. The table dates from about 1860 and is made of cherry with a maple gallery. The legs are tenoned into the feet and half-lapped to the side aprons. In form the shoe feet are somewhat similar to those found on some eastern towel racks. A footrest, dadoed into the front legs and fastened with wood screws, ties the front legs together. A lock on the underslung drawer could be used to secure its contents. The gallery is constructed from both mill work and lathe turnings and has a till, spoolrack, and finials on the corner posts made from drawer pulls of walnut. Collection of the Kentucky Library and Museum, Western Kentucky University, Bowling Green, Ky.

H. 29-1/2, W. 23, D. 16.

4. From New Lebanon, this rectangular rimmed-top, three-drawer sewing table dates from the first half of the nineteenth century and is of mixed woods. The frame is cherry, the top and drawer fronts are butternut, and the interior components are pine. All the drawers are dovetailed and those at the ends are the same size. Collection of Shaker Community, Inc., Hancock, Mass.

H. 25, W. 29-3/16, D. 18-1/4.

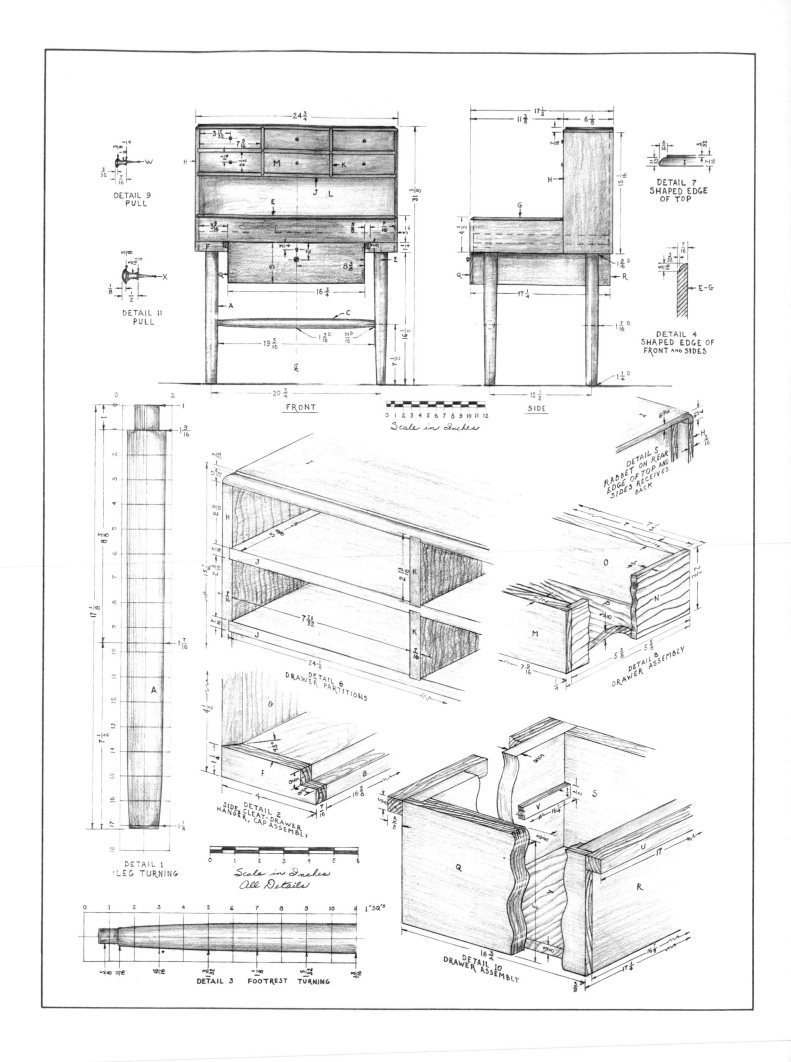

DETAIL 9
PULL

DETAIL 11
PULL

FRONT

Scale in Inches

SIDE

DETAIL 7
SHAPED EDGE
OF TOP

DETAIL 4
SHAPED EDGE OF
FRONT AND SIDES

DETAIL 5
RABBET ON REAR
EDGE OF TOP AND
SIDES RECEIVES
BACK

DETAIL 1
LEG TURNING

DETAIL 6
DRAWER PARTITIONS

DETAIL 8
DRAWER ASSEMBLY

DETAIL 2
SIDE CLEAT-DRAWER
HANGER, CAP ASSEMBLY

Scale in Inches
All Details

DETAIL 3   FOOTREST   TURNING

DETAIL 10
DRAWER ASSEMBLY

5. This seven-drawer sewing table from Harvard dates from the first half of the nineteenth century and is pine with maple legs and stretcher; all are painted red. Four turned legs held together with two cross cleats and a single stretcher constitute the table frame. Prior to assembly, the cleats were rabbeted to support the large underslung drawer. The top is fastened to the cleats with exposed but countersunk flathead wood screws driven through the top. Front and side table rims were applied after their upper edges were molded. To hide the end grain, caps were fastened to the exposed cleat ends. The rims and caps were secured with nails. The rack for the six small drawers was constructed with dado joints and installed as a separate unit. The back is let into rabbet joints cut into the top and sides. Most atypical are the rabbet joints on the drawer fronts instead of the customary dovetailed joints. A commercially made lock and brass pulls were used on the drawers. Collection of Fruitlands Museums, Harvard, Mass.

H. 31-5/8, W. 24-3/4, D. 17-1/2.

Letter	No.	Name	Material	T	W	L
A	4	legs	maple	1-9/16 dia		17-1/8
B	2	cleat-drawer-hangers	pine	1-1/4	3-9/16	16-5/8
C	1	footrest stretcher	maple	1-3/16 dia		20-13/16
D	1	top	pine	1-1/8	16-5/8	23-7/8
E	1	front	pine	7/16	3-1/4	24-3/4
F	2	cleat-drawer-hanger caps	pine	7/16	1-1/4	4
G	2	horizontal sides	pine	7/16	4-1/2	11-3/8
H	2	vertical sides	pine	7/16	6-1/8	15-1/16
I	1	top	pine	7/16	6-1/8	24-3/4
J	2	drawer supports	pine	7/16	5-5/8	24-1/8
K	4	drawer divisions	pine	7/16	2-13/16	5-5/8
L	1	back	pine	1/2	15-5/16	24-3/8
Small drawers						
M	6	fronts	pine	1/2	2-1/2	7-9/16
N	12	sides	pine	1/4	2-1/2	5-3/8
O	6	backs	pine	1/2	2-1/2	7
P	6	bottoms	pine	3/8	4-5/8	7
Large drawer						
Q	1	front	pine	5/8	5	16-3/4
R	2	sides	pine	5/8	5	16-7/8
S	1	back	pine	5/8	5	15-1/2
T	1	bottom	pine	3/8	16-1/4	15-1/2
U	2	runners	pine	5/8 sq		17
V	2	supports for missing sliding tray	pine	1/4	1/2	16-1/4
Hardware						
W	6	pulls	brass	3/8 dia		3/4
X	1	pull	brass	5/8 dia		1

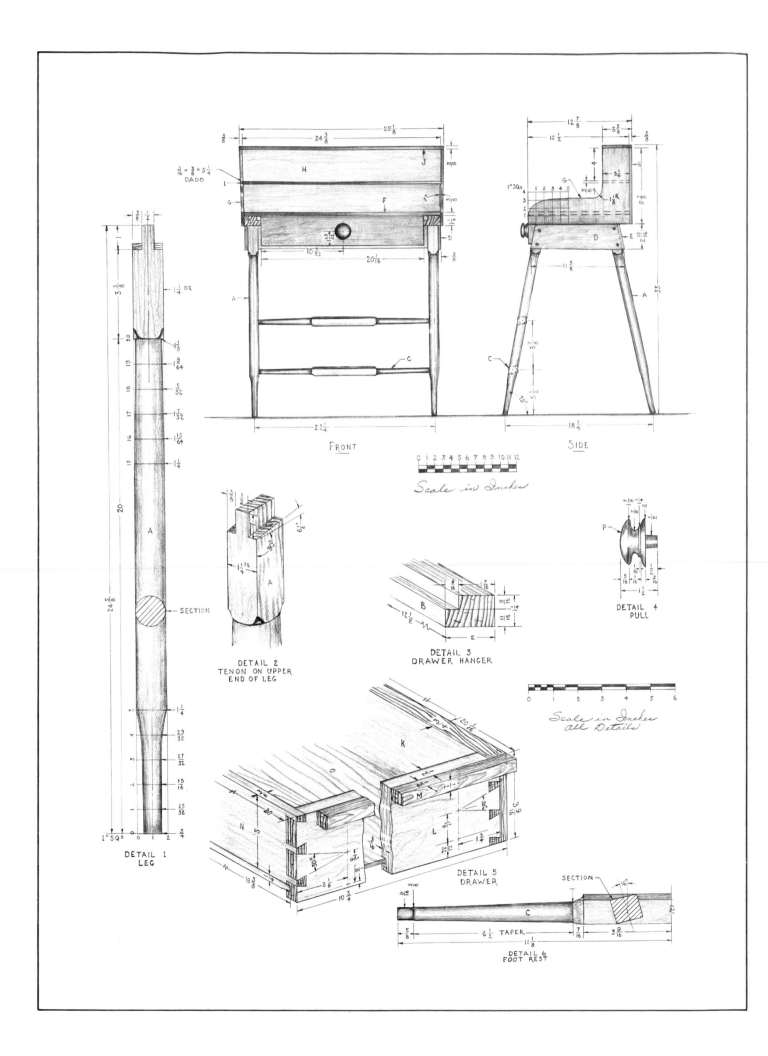

FRONT

SIDE

Scale in Inches

DETAIL 1
LEG

DETAIL 2
TENON ON UPPER
END OF LEG

DETAIL 3
DRAWER HANGER

DETAIL 4
PULL

DETAIL 5
DRAWER

DETAIL 6
FOOT REST

Scale in Inches
All Details

DADO

SECTION

SECTION

6. This sewing table was made in the first half of the nineteenth century at the South Union community. It has two footrests, a single underslung drawer, an applied rack with a shelf for holding sewing paraphernalia, and, except for the poplar drawer bottom and back, is made of cherry. The slight outward sloping of the sides of the rack, whether by design or accident, is not an isolated example, for side splashboards on washstands were at times so constructed (see Stands, fig. 22). The footrests are the same shape as the stair spindles in the Centre family sisters' laundry and they may be left over from the stairs. If so, the unknown brother who made this table is to be complimented for his imagination in incorporating them in the table. The piece is stained light cherry-red and finished in clear varnish. Collection of Shaker Museum, South Union, Ky.

H. 33, W. 25-1/8, D. 19.

Letter	No.	Name	Material	T	W	L
A	4	legs	cherry	1-1/4 sq		24-5/8
B	2	cleat-drawer-hangers	cherry	1-1/4	2	12-1/2
C	2	footrest	cherry	1	1-1/8	22-1/4
D	2	side aprons	cherry	3/8	2-15/16	11-5/8
E	1	back apron	cherry	3/8	3-1/8	23-1/4
F	1	top	cherry	3/8	12-1/2	24
G	2	sides	cherry	3/8	12-1/2	9-3/8
H	1	back	cherry	3/8	9-3/8	25-1/8
I	1	shelf	cherry	3/8	3-1/4	24-1/2
J	1	top shelf	cherry	3/8	3-5/8	25-1/8
Drawer						
K	1	front	cherry	3/4	3-9/16	20-1/16
L	2	sides	cherry	1/2	3-9/16	10-3/4
M	2	runners	cherry	1/2 sq		11
N	1	back	poplar	3/8	3	20
O	1	bottom	poplar	1/4	10-3/8	19-3/8
P	1	pull	cherry	2 dia		1-1/2
Hardware	20	wood screws		FH 1-7		

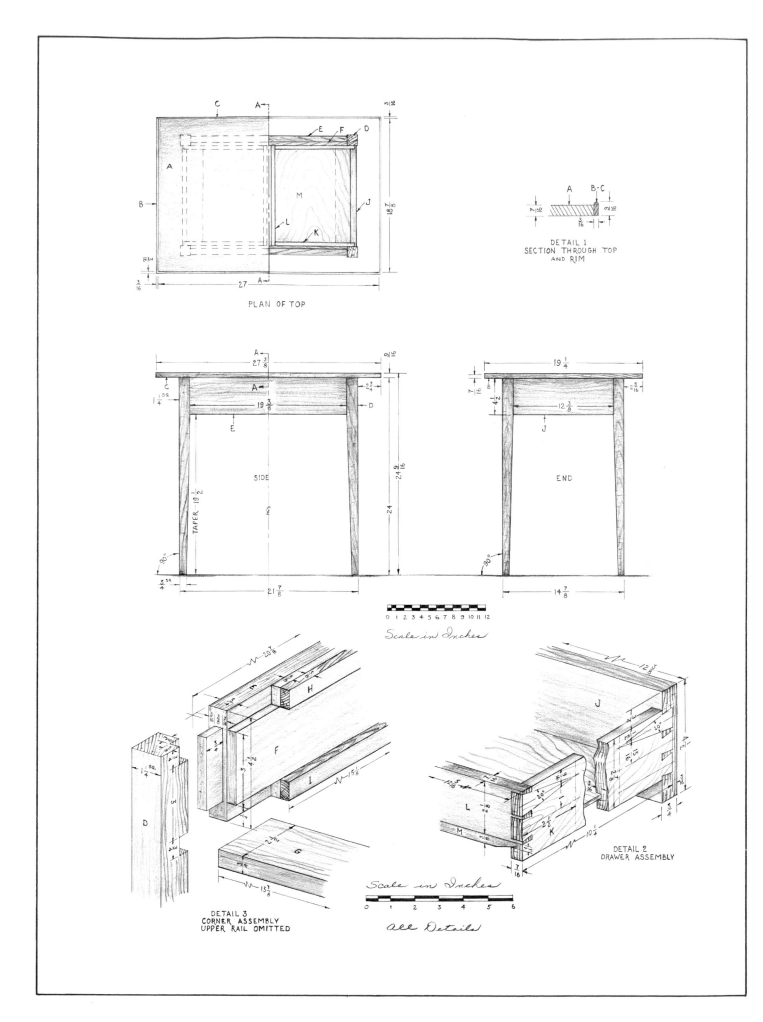

PLAN OF TOP

DETAIL 1
SECTION THROUGH TOP
AND RIM

SIDE

END

Scale in Inches

DETAIL 3
CORNER ASSEMBLY
UPPER RAIL OMITTED

DETAIL 2
DRAWER ASSEMBLY

Scale in Inches

All Details

7. An interesting feature of this two-drawer rimmed-top sewing table is the absence of pulls on the drawer fronts. They are pulled out by the lower projecting edge of the front, a design concept much used in contemporary furniture. The table was made in the first half of the nineteenth century at Hancock and is cherry with secondary woods of poplar and pine. Aprons and rails are assembled to the square, tapered legs with mortise-and-tenon joints, and the drawers are constructed in the traditional manner. Collection of Shaker Community, Inc., Hancock, Mass.

H. 24-9/16, W. 27-3/8, D. 19-1/4.

Letter	No.	Name	Material	T	W	L
A	1	top	poplar	7/16	18-7/8	27
B	2	short rims	cherry	3/16	9/16	19-1/4
C	2	long rims	cherry	3/16	9/16	27-3/8
D	4	legs	cherry	1-1/4 sq		24
E	2	side aprons	cherry	3/4	4-1/2	20-7/8
F	2	filler pieces	cherry	3/8	4-1/2	19-3/8
G	4	rails	cherry	3/4	2-1/2	13-7/8
H	2	kick rails	cherry	3/8	3/4	15-1/8
I	2	drawer runners	cherry	3/8	3/4	15-1/8
Drawer						
J	2	fronts	cherry	3/4	4-1/2	12-3/8
K	4	sides	pine	7/16	2-7/8	10-1/4
L	2	backs	pine	7/16	2-1/8	12-5/16
M	2	bottoms	pine	3/8	9-7/8	11-3/4

8. This small single-drawer rectangular table was made in the first half of the nineteenth century in an unidentified eastern community. The table is made of cherry and has interior parts of pine. The finish is original and appears to be shellac. The drawer front sets flush with the legs and is assembled with the ubiquitous dovetails and let-in bottom. The square, tapered legs have small delicate turnings at the floor line and the top has two decorative diamond-shaped curly maple inlays. Other examples of inlay work on Shaker furniture are very rare. Collection of Mrs. Edward Deming Andrews.

H. 22-15/16, W. 24-1/2, D. 14-7/8.

9. Made in the first half of the nineteenth century, this small two-drawer cherry table from Canterbury has square, tapered legs, thumb molding on the drawer fronts, rounded edges on the top, and cyma-scrolled corner brackets. Two side cleats hold the top to the base. This is a simple and direct method for fastening tops to bases and was often employed by Shaker cabinet-makers. Collection of Greenfield Village and the Henry Ford Museum, Dearborn, Mich. Photograph courtesy of the museum.

H. 25-3/4, W. 23-3/4, D. 16-1/8.

10. Also from Canterbury and dating from the same period as the table in figure 9 is this small two-drawer rectangular table of pine. The square, tapered legs are mortised to receive tenons cut on the ends of the rails and aprons and are pinned for greater joint security. Most unusual is the curve at the point where the square part of the leg begins to taper; this is a form often used on contemporary furniture. The drawers have a thumb molding on their front edges. The reason why only the front edge of the top has this same molding is unknown, but it may have been done at a later date, possibly to remove scarring along the edge. The table is stained a yellow wash that is protected with shellac. Collection of Philadelphia Museum of Art, Photograph by A. J. Wyatt.

H. 30-3/8, W. 28-3/4, D. 19-1/2.

11. This rectangular two-drawer lift-top table of pine painted an orange-red wash was made in the second half of the nineteenth century at New Lebanon. The piece is a paradox of the Shaker cabinetmaker's art because unsightly wood screws hold four unattractive flat-board tapered legs to a beautifully made dovetailed case. Dowel ends at the bottom of the legs are separate pieces glued into corresponding holes; they were probably added as an afterthought, when it became necessary to increase the knee room below the front apron. The hinged top, which gives the seated user greater access to the contents of the two long drawers, may also be a modification of the original plan. The right drawer is partitioned across the width and the left has a partitioned till. The drawer pulls are cherry. Collection of Darrow School, New Lebanon, N. Y.

H. 29, W. 33, D. 21-1/4.

12. The community origin of this mid-nine-teenth-century worktable is unknown. The base is cherry stained red and the top is well-scrubbed maple. The table has square, tapered legs, a single drawer, and a top which is fastened to the base with wood screws let into three cross cleats. Collection of Greenfield Village and the Henry Ford Museum, Dearborn, Mich. Photograph courtesy of the museum.

H. 29-1/4, W. 68-3/4, D. 33-5/8.

13. A good example of Shaker improvisation is this worktable from New Lebanon which actually is two small table bases joined by a removable shelf and a one-board top. One base contains a single drawer and the shelf rests on four small wooden brackets nailed to the inside surfaces of the legs. Tongue-and-groove, bread-board ends kept the top from warping. The table is pine painted red and was used in the canning industry at New Lebanon. It dates from the first half of the nineteenth century. Collection of Mrs. Edward Deming Andrews. Photograph courtesy of the Smithsonian Institution.

H. 25, W. 55, D. 20.

14. This three-drawer side table from Canterbury was made in the first half of the nineteenth century and is of mixed woods. It has bird's-eye maple legs, curly maple aprons, drawer fronts, and top, and interior parts of pine. The square-to-round area of the legs has a small transitional collar. Drawer rails and side aprons are off-set (set back) from the surface of the legs, and are tenoned to the legs and secured with pins. The graduated drawers are fabricated with dovetails and have their original pulls. The natural brown patina of the wood is protected with varnish. Collection of the Shaker Museum, Old Chatham, N. Y.

H. 25-5/8, W. 33-7/8, D. 19-1/4.

15. Also from Canterbury is this single-drawer side table in figured maple with interior parts of pine. The table dates from the second quarter of the nineteenth century. The natural patina of the wood is protected with a thin coat of shellac. A small turned collar between the square and round portion of the legs serves a physical and visual transitional function. The tenoned sides and drawer rails are pinned to leg mortises and the top is fastened to the base with wood screws let into pocket holes. The single, scored line on each leg indicates the point of major diameter. The quarter-round, molded-lip drawer is traditionally constructed and has its original apple wood pull. Collction of Philadelphia Museum of Art. Photgraph by A. J. Wyatt.

H. 27-1/2, W. 36-1/8, D. 21-3/16.

16. The abrupt square-to-round turning on the legs of this single-drawer side table is a leg style that was used often on furniture made in the western communities (see figs. 18 and 23). The table is from Pleasant Hill and is signed and dated "L. Gettys Jan. 1861." Brother Leander was born in 1832 and left the society in 1865. While a Shaker, he worked as a joiner. Mortise-and-tenon joints hold the rails and aprons to the legs; wood screws let into pocket holes hold the top to the base. The drawer front sets flush with the legs. All parts of the table are cherry except the drawer sides, back, and bottom, which are poplar. The table has its original clear varnish finish. Collection of Shakertown at Pleasant Hill, Inc., Harrodsburg, Ky.

H. 27-5/8, W. 31-1/2, D. 27-1/2.

Letter	No.	Name	Material	T	W	L
A	1	top	cherry	1	27-1/2	31-1/2
B	4	legs	cherry	2-1/16 sq		26-5/8
C	1	rail	cherry	1-1/4	2-1/16	22-7/8
D	2	side aprons	cherry	1-1/8	5-3/8	20-1/8
E	1	back apron	cherry	1-1/8	5-3/8	22-7/8
F	2	drawer guides	cherry	13/16	1-1/2	18-1/8
G	2	drawer runners	cherry	5/8	1-1/4	18-15/16
Drawer						
H	1	front	cherry	1-1/8	4-1/8	20-3/4
I	2	sides	poplar	5/8	4-1/8	20-1/2
J	1	back	poplar	9/16	3-3/8	20-5/8
K	1	bottom	poplar	9/16	20	20-1/8
L	1	pull	cherry	1-1/2 dia		2-1/8

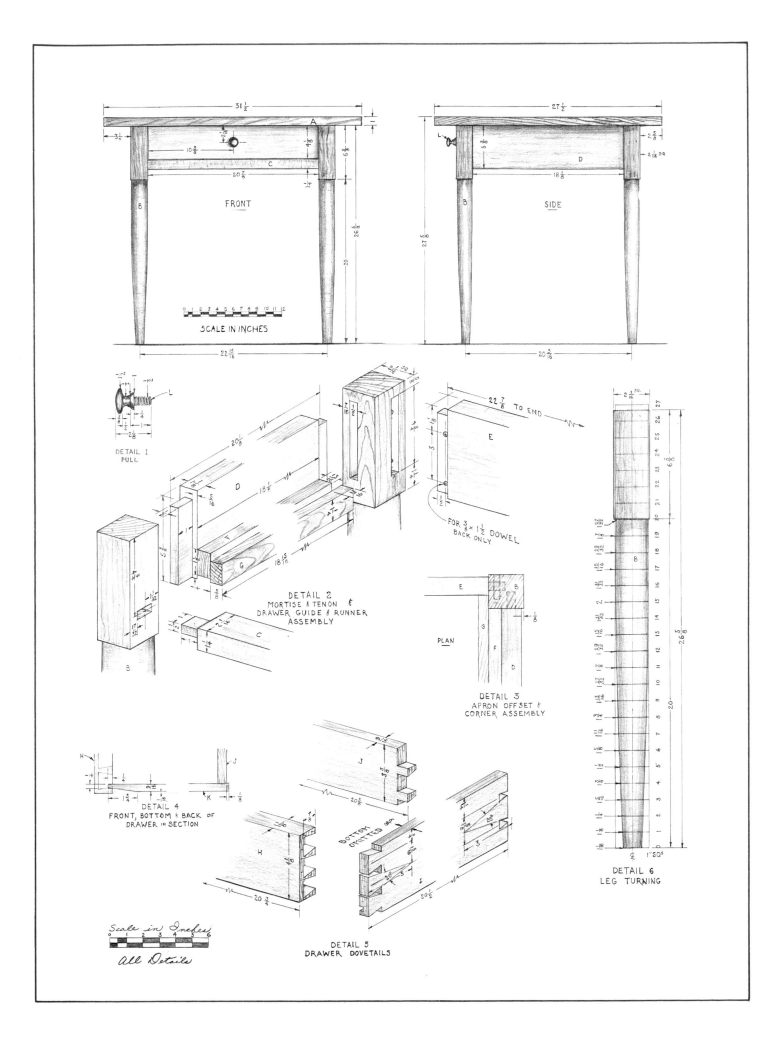

FRONT

SCALE IN INCHES

SIDE

DETAIL 1
PULL

DETAIL 2
MORTISE & TENON &
DRAWER GUIDE & RUNNER
ASSEMBLY

FOR $\frac{3}{8} \times 1\frac{1}{2}$ DOWEL
BACK ONLY

PLAN

DETAIL 3
APRON OFFSET &
CORNER ASSEMBLY

DETAIL 4
FRONT, BOTTOM & BACK OF
DRAWER IN SECTION

BOTTOM OMITTED

DETAIL 5
DRAWER DOVETAILS

DETAIL 6
LEG TURNING

Scale in Inches

All Details

17

18

19

17. Another table from Canterbury made during the first half of the nineteenth century is this side table of birch with pine interior. The base is fabricated with pinned mortise-and-tenon joints and the top is fastened with wood screws let into pocket holes. The conventionally built drawer has a thumb molding on the front. The generous overhang of the top gives the table a delightful cantilever feel and also increases the working surface. The ring turning at the lower end of the legs is a decorative form associated with American Sheraton furniture. Private collection. Photograph by Bill Finney.

H. 25-3/4, W. 33, D. 20-3/4.

18. This worktable was made in the Union Village community during the first half of the nineteenth century. It has a three-board-wide top, turned legs, and a single drawer. The wood is cherry that has been varnished, and the interior parts are pine. The three turned decorative beads below the square part of the legs are similar to those on the Pleasant Hill two-unit cupboard (fig. 20). The Federal style drawer pulls, replacements for turned wood pulls, are inappropriate for the piece. Collection of the Otterbein Home, Lebanon, Ohio.

H. 33-3/4, W. 72-3/4, D. 35-1/4.

19. Community origin of this communal dining table is unknown, but it is similar to those made at New Lebanon during the second quarter of the nineteenth century. It has mildly ornate, turned legs of cherry, and deep aprons made of the same wood. They are joined together with conventional pinned mortise-and-tenon joints. The top is pine with maple bread-board ends and is fastened to the base with wood screws let into pocket holes. The overhang of the top is almost four inches on the sides and thirteen on the ends. Not shown in the photograph are the table's two drawers. Collection of New York State Historical Association, Cooperstown, N. Y. Photograph courtesy of the Association.

H. 26-7/8, W. 134, D. 31.

20. The size of this single-drawer table suggests it may have been used as a worktable in one of the New Lebanon shops or stores. It dates from the second quarter of the nineteenth century and has legs and aprons of cherry and a pine top. Cleats are nailed to the ends of the top and have helped to keep the top flat. The drawer has a molded lip front and is assembled in the traditional manner. Mortise-and-tenon joints, triple pinned, hold the aprons to the mildly ornate turned legs; wood screws, their heads plugged, hold the top to the table base. The cantilevered overhang of the top at the ends is eighteen inches. The Stokes Collection.

H. 27-3/8, W. 72-1/2, D. 27-1/16.

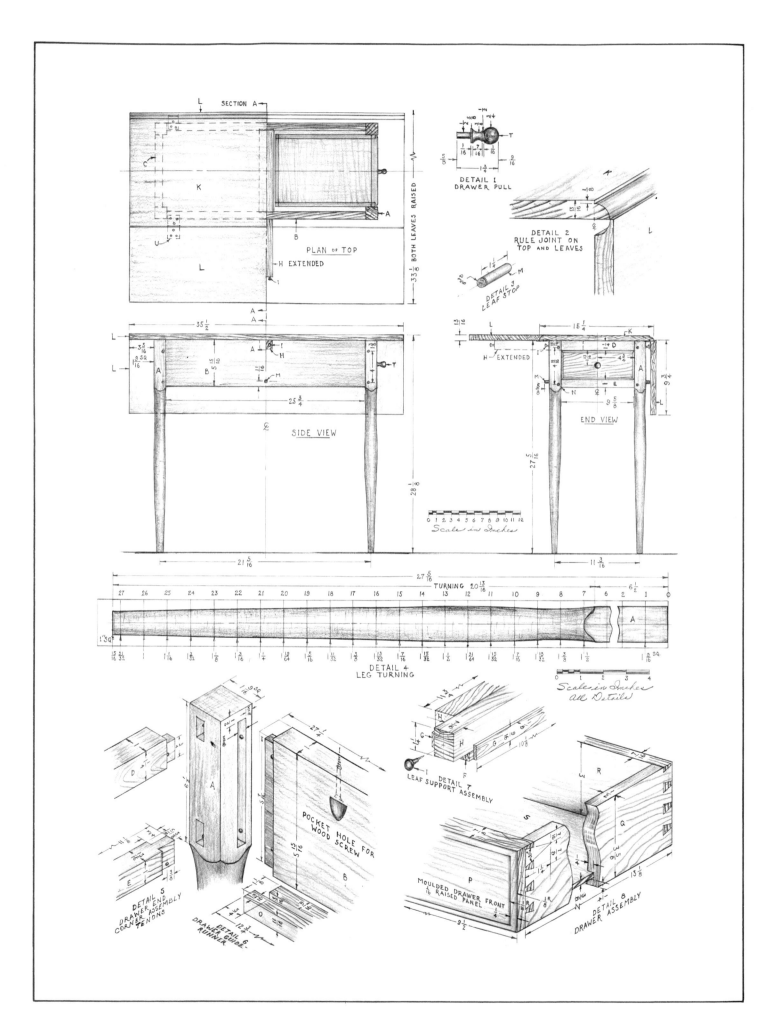

SECTION A

L

PLAN OF TOP

H EXTENDED

C

K

U

B

A

33 1/8 BOTH LEAVES RAISED

DETAIL 1
DRAWER PULL

T

DETAIL 2
RULE JOINT ON
TOP AND LEAVES

K

L

DETAIL 3
LEAF STOP

M

SIDE VIEW

35 1/2

25 3/4

28 1/8

21 5/16

L

A

B 5 15/16

H

M

T

END VIEW

15 1/4

D

H EXTENDED

M

N

E

9 5/8

9 3/4

27 5/16

11 3/16

0 1 2 3 4 5 6 7 8 9 10 11 12
Scale in Inches

TURNING 20 13/16

27 5/16

6 1/2

27 26 25 24 23 22 21 20 19 18 17 16 15 14 13 12 11 10 9 8 7 6 2 1 0

A

1" SQ

1" SQ

DETAIL 4
LEG TURNING

0 1 2 3 4
Scale in Inches
All Details

DETAIL 5
DRAWER END
CORNER ASSEMBLY
TENONS

D

A

E

POCKET HOLE FOR
WOOD SCREW

27 1/4

5 15/16

B

DETAIL 6
DRAWER GUIDE-
RUNNER

DETAIL 7
LEAF SUPPORT ASSEMBLY

H

G

H

G

F

I

MOULDED DRAWER FRONT
RAISED PANEL

P

S

R

Q

9 1/2

13 1/8

DETAIL 8
DRAWER ASSEMBLY

21. From Hancock, this drop-leaf table is of cherry and dates from the first quarter of the nineteenth century. The wood has, through natural aging, developed a lovely, walnut-like, dark brown color. The legs lack a transitional turned collar between the upper, square section and the lower, turned-leg portion, and hence change gradually from square to round. The side aprons and drawer rail have tenons pinned to mortises in the legs. The single drawer has its original turned apple wood pull. The drawer has a raised, molded front, the edges of which are set flush with the drawer rails. The table top and leaves have hinged rule joints and, when raised, are supported by sliding pullout supports. The center portion of the top is fixed to the base with wood screws let into apron pocket holes. Collection of Dr. and Mrs. Thomas Kane.

H. 28-1/8, W. 35-1/2, D. 15-1/4,
D. with leaves up, 33-1/8.

Letter	No.	Name	Material	T	W	L
A	4	legs	cherry	1-9/16 sq		27-5/16
B	2	side aprons	cherry	1	5-15/16	27-1/4
C	1	end apron	cherry	1	5-15/16	11-1/8
D	1	upper end rail	cherry	1	1-1/4	11-1/8
E	1	lower end rail	cherry	13/16	1	11-1/8
F	1	leaf support shelf	oak	3/8	1-3/4	11-1/8
G	2	leaf support keepers	oak	1/8	9/16	10-1/8
H	2	leaf supports	cherry	7/8	1-3/16	11-3/4
I	2	leaf support pulls	brass	3/8 dia		1
J	2	leaf support stops	oak	1/8 dia		1/2
K	1	top	cherry	13/16	15-1/4	35-1/2
L	2	leaves	cherry	13/16	9-3/4	35-1/2
M	2	leaf stops	cherry	3/8 dia		1-1/4
N	16	dowel pins	cherry	1/4 dia		1-1/4
O	2	drawer runners	oak	1	1-1/8	12-3/4
Drawer						
P	1	front	cherry	7/8	3-5/8	9-1/2
Q	2	sides	pine	1/2	3-5/8	13-1/8
R	1	back	pine	7/16	3	9-1/2
S	1	bottom	pine	3/8	12-15/16	9
T	1	pull	apple	3/4 dia		1-3/4
Hardware						
U	4	drop-leaf hinges	steel		1-1/2	1-3/8–1-3/4
V	10	wood screws	steel	FH 1-1/4-8		

22. Also from Hancock and made about the same time as the table in figure 21 is this small drop-leaf table of maple with cherry top. The plain, rod-shaped legs have a transitional collar that visually ties the square and round parts of the leg together. The beaded aprons have tenons double pinned to mortises in the legs. When raised, the drop-leaves are supported with pivoting brackets. A natural warm brown patina appears to be the table's only finish. Collection of the Shaker Museum, Old Chatham, N. Y.

H. 26-3/4, W. 23-3/4, D. 13-3/4,
D. with leaves up, 31-1/16.

23. From the Pleasant Hill community, this two-drawer single-drop-leaf table of cherry dates from the third quarter of the nineteenth century. The turnings on the legs were made without a transitional collar. The table is both physically and visually heavy; the top is a full inch thick and the aprons are nearly as thick. Collection of the Shaker Museum, Old Chatham, N. Y.

H. 29, W. 33-1/8, D. 15-3/4, D. with leaves up, 25-1/8.

24. One of the most beautiful pieces of Shaker furniture is this small X-trestle table from New Lebanon. The table dates from the first half of the nineteenth century and has a rimmed top, an underslung drawer, and a turned stretcher that joins the tapered legs. The legs, stretcher, and cleat drawer hangers are butternut, the drawer pull is cherry, and the remaining parts are pine. The drawer is assembled with dovetails and the molded rim is mitered at the corners and nailed to the top. Collection of Shaker Community, Inc., Hancock, Mass.

H. 22-3/4, W. 22-7/8, D. 15-3/4.

25. More functional than attractive is this X-trestle side or serving table from the Upper Canaan family. The table dates from the first half of the nineteenth century and is made of pine which has acquired an attractive natural brown patina. The legs taper in width, have stopped chamfers on their edges, and are assembled with pinned cross-lap joints. Their upper ends have tenons that fit into mortises cut into the cross cleats. Flat-head wood screws fasten the cleats to the top. Collection of John S. Roberts.

H. 29, W. 34-5/8, D. 19-1/2.

26. This large X-trestle table has a pine top with a chestnut base and was made during the first half of the nineteenth century in the Enfield, Connecticut, society. It was used for ironing and is similar to tables made in other communities that were used in varied domestic and shop occupations. In a Shaker community, where cleanliness and neatness prevailed, laundering and ironing were important domestic occupations. Each family had within its cluster of buildings one set aside for such purposes. The X-style legs of this table are assembled with double-pinned half-lap joints. Tenons on the upper ends fasten to mortises cut into the cross cleats. They also are double pinned. End tenons on the horizontal cross brace are joined to mortises in the legs and are secured with single pins. The tongue-and-groove joints on the bread-board ends on the top are held with wood screws. Wood screws also hold the top to the cross cleats. Collection of Mr. and Mrs. David V. Andrews. Photograph courtesy of the Smithsonian Institution.

H. 27, W. 57, D. 34.

27. The function of this exceptionally low ministry dining table was probably changed from dining to sewing or shop use when three underslung drawers (of which only the runners are now present) were added. The table was made in Enfield, Connecticut, and dates from the first quarter of the nineteenth century. All parts are maple except the stretcher, which is chestnut. Double-pinned mortise-and-tenon joints hold the feet and cross cleats to the legs and draw-bolts hold the legs to the stretcher. Most unusual are the flat surfaces of the lathe-turned legs, which were produced after the legs were turned, by cutting away two rather large slabs of wood parallel to each other. This was done probably to improve their form by lightening their look and eliminating the overhang at the sides of the feet. Nail-applied end cleats have kept the four-board top from warping excessively. The top is fastened to the cross cleats with wood screws.

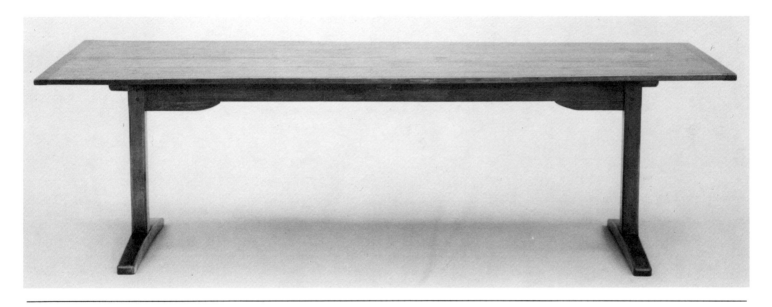

Collection of the Metropolitan Museum of Art, Purchase, 1966, Friends of the American Wing Fund. Photograph courtesy of the museum.

H. 24-1/8, W. 50, D. 27.

28. This classic communal dining table from Hancock was made in the first quarter of the nineteenth century. The feet, legs, and cross cleats are maple; all other parts are pine. Double-pinned mortise-and-tenon joints hold the feet and cleats to the legs. Tenons on the ends of the stretcher penetrate the legs and are also double pinned. The top has bread-board ends and is fastened to the base with flat-head wood screws driven through the cross cleats into the underside of the top. Two braces were nailed to the underside of the stretcher and were probably installed at a later date to increase the stability of the piece. For no reason other than mild human error, the right brace is one inch shorter than its companion. The legs have 3/8-inch cor-

ner chamfers and all edges of the table have been rounded through years of service. What appears to be a varnish finish protects a light honey-colored, maple-pine patina. Collection of Metropolitan Museum of Art, Purchase, 1966, Friends of the American Wing Fund. Photograph courtesy of the museum.

H. 28-1/2, W. 96-1/2, D. 31-1/4.

29. Unusually small for a trestle table is this example from the Harvard community dating from the first half of the nineteenth century. It is made of mixed woods that have developed an attractive brown patina which is protected with clear varnish. The table is cherry with interior parts of pine. The purpose of the table is difficult to determine. Its low height, the absence of a rim around the top, and its questionable strength (the stretcher has undergone repairs) tend to rule out sewing or heavy shop use. The single drawer suggests it might have been used as a side or serving table. Using maple rather than cherry for the drawer front further suggests the drawer may not have been incorporated in the original design. Through-tenons at the lower ends of the legs impart internal strength to the short grain at the upper part of the feet. The style of leg and foot is similar to that in figures 30 and 31. A combination edge-lap and mortise-and-tenon joint holds the stretcher to the cross braces and to the legs. The joint is held together with a flat-head wood screw driven through the stretcher and cross brace and into the leg end. Flat-head wood screws driven from the underedge of the stretcher and cross braces hold the top to the base. The high placement of the all-too-narrow stretcher has necessitated repairing this part of the table. Collection of Fruitlands Museums, Harvard, Mass.

H. 27-1/8, W. 28-7/8, D. 17-1/2.

Letter	No.	Name	Material	T	W	L
A	2	legs	cherry	7/8	3-5/8	20-7/8
B	2	feet	cherry	7/8	7-1/2	16-1/8
C	2	cross braces	cherry	7/8	1-5/8	16-1/2
D	1	stretcher	cherry	1	1-5/8	28-3/4
E	1	top	cherry	1/2	17-1/2	28-7/8
F	2	drawer runners	cherry	1/4	3/8	7
Drawer						
G	1	front	maple	11/32	2-5/16	21-3/4
H	2	sides	pine	11/32	2-3/16	7-1/8
I	1	back	pine	11/32	1-3/4	21-3/4
J	1	bottom	pine	5/32	7	21-3/8
Hardware						
	4	wood screws		FH 1/2-8		
	2	wood screws		FH 1-3/4-7		
	4	wood screws		FH 1-8		

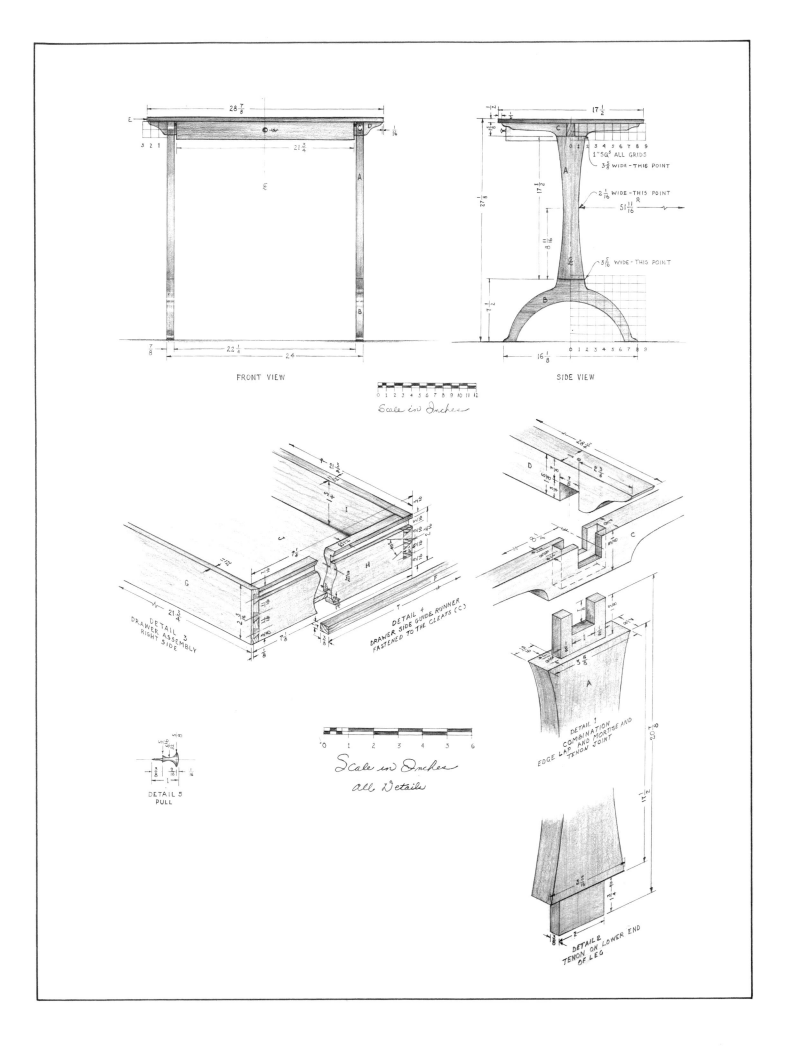

FRONT VIEW

SIDE VIEW

Scale in Inches

DETAIL 3
DRAWER ASSEMBLY
RIGHT SIDE

DETAIL 4
DRAWER SIDE GUIDE RUNNER
FASTENED TO THE CLEATS (C)

DETAIL 5
PULL

Scale in Inches
All Details

DETAIL 1
COMBINATION
EDGE LAP AND MORTISE AND
TENON JOINT

DETAIL 2
TENON ON LOWER END
OF LEG

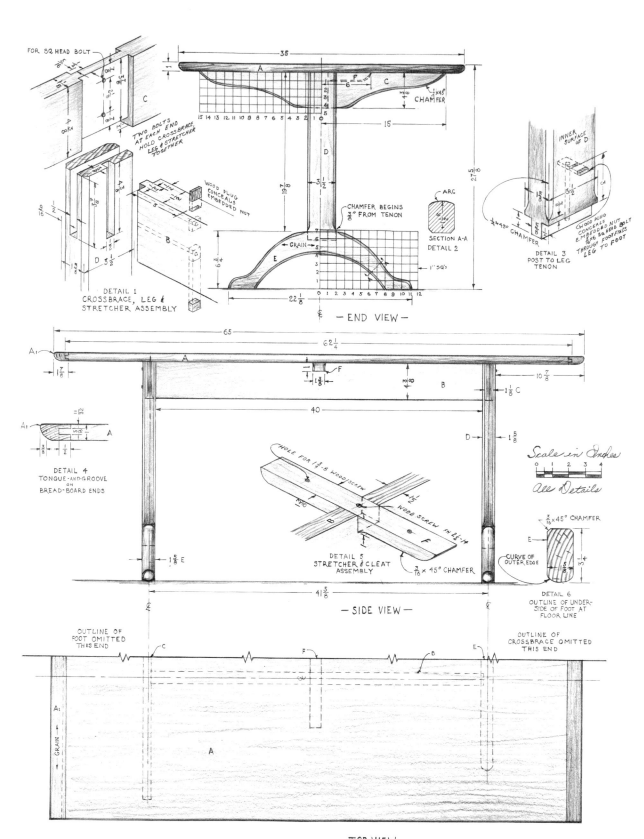

FOR SQ HEAD BOLT

TWO BOLTS AT EACH END HOLD CROSSBRACE LEG & STRETCHER TOGETHER

C

WOOD PLUG CONCEALS EMBEDDED NUT

B

D

DETAIL 1
CROSSBRACE, LEG & STRETCHER ASSEMBLY

35

A

F

C

CHAMFER

15

D

19⅞

3½

CHAMFER BEGINS ¾" FROM TENON

GRAIN

E

22⅛

27⅝

ARC

SECTION A-A
DETAIL 2

1" SQ's

— END VIEW —

INNER SURFACE OF D

WOOD PLUG CONCEALS EMBEDDED NUT FOR SQ HEAD BOLT THROUGH FOOT FIXES LEG TO FOOT

CHAMFER

DETAIL 3
POST TO LEG
TENON

65

62¼

A₁

A

F

B

C

10⅞

1⅛

40

D

1⅝

Scale in Inches
0 1 2 3 4
All Details

DETAIL 4
TONGUE-AND-GROOVE ON BREAD-BOARD ENDS

HOLE FOR 1⅜·8 WOOD SCREW

WOOD SCREW FH 2½·14

DETAIL 5
STRETCHER & CLEAT ASSEMBLY

3/16 × 45° CHAMFER

1⅝ E

41⅝

— SIDE VIEW —

3/16 × 45° CHAMFER

E

CURVE OF OUTER EDGE

DETAIL 6
OUTLINE OF UNDER-SIDE OF FOOT AT FLOOR LINE

OUTLINE OF FOOT OMITTED THIS END

C

F

B

E

OUTLINE OF CROSSBRACE OMITTED THIS END

A₁

GRAIN

A

— TOP VIEW —

0 1 2 3 4 5 6 7 8 9 10 11 12

Scale in Inches

30. The origin of this ministry dining table is uncertain, but it is very similar to tables made during the first half of the nineteenth century in the Hancock community. It is made of cherry painted a red wash. The table is unique in that it was designed to be easily taken apart for storing or transporting to other communities where it could be used as a prototype for copying. The feet are joined to the legs with draw-bolts through mortise-and-tenon joints and the cross cleats are assembled to the legs with bridle-joints. The legs are fastened to the stretcher with draw-bolts through a very shallow mortise-and-tenon joint. Wood screws through the cross cleats hold the top in place. The two-board top has tongue-and-groove bread-board ends which are held with wood screws. The molded edges on the underside of the top, the curved profile on the cross braces and its chamfered edges, and the chamfered edges on the legs that flow into the molded upper edges on the feet all make this piece exceptionally beautiful and an outstanding example of classic Shaker cabinetwork. Private collection.

H. 27-5/8, W. 65, D. 35.

Letter	No.	Name	Material	T	W	L
A	1	top	cherry	1	35	62-1/4
A1	2	bread-board ends	cherry	1	1-7/8	35
B	1	stretcher	cherry	1-1/2	4-3/8	40-3/4
C	2	cross braces	cherry	1-1/8	4-3/8	30
D	2	legs	cherry	1-5/8	3-1/2	20-7/8
E	2	feet	cherry	1-5/8	6-3/4	22-1/8
F	1	cleat	cherry	1	1-3/8	12
Hardware	6	square-head bolts		3/8 × 6		
	6	square-head nuts		3/8		
	6	flat washers		3/8		
	1	wood screw		FH 2-1/2-14		
	2	wood screws		FH 1-3/4-8		
	4	wood screws		FH 1-1/2-10		
	4	wood screws		FH 2-1/2-10		

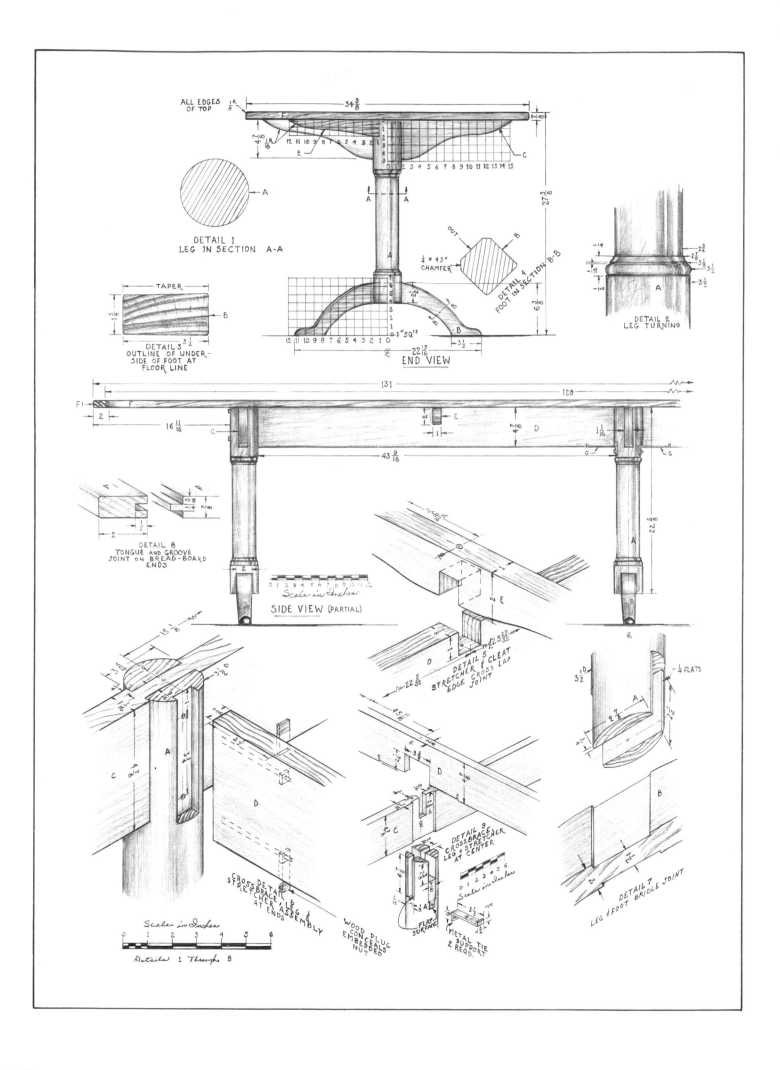

ALL EDGES OF TOP

DETAIL 1
LEG IN SECTION A-A

TAPER

DETAIL 3
OUTLINE OF UNDER-
SIDE OF FOOT AT
FLOOR LINE

OUT
IN
¼ × 45°
CHAMFER

DETAIL 4
FOOT IN SECTION B-B

END VIEW

DETAIL 2
LEG TURNING

SIDE VIEW (PARTIAL)

Scale in Inches

DETAIL 8
TONGUE AND GROOVE
JOINT ON BREAD-BOARD
ENDS

DETAIL 5
STRETCHER & CLEAT
EDGE CROSS LAP
JOINT

DETAIL 6
CROSSBRACE, LEG &
STRETCHER ASSEMBLY
AT ENDS

DETAIL 9
CROSSBRACE,
LEG & STRETCHER
AT CENTER

Scale in Inches

WOOD PLUG
CONCEALS
EMBEDDED
NUT

FLAT
SURFACE

METAL TIE
SUPPORT
2 REQD.

DETAIL 7
LEG & FOOT BRIDLE JOINT

Scale in Inches

Details 1 Through 8

31. The origin of this communal dining table is unknown, but it is very similar to those produced in the New Lebanon and Hancock societies. It was made in the first half of the nineteenth century and is cherry with a clear-varnish finish. The table is approximately eleven feet long, has three moderately ornate turned legs and high-arced, tapered feet. Bridle joints permanently fastened with glue hold the feet and cleats to the legs. The stretchers are held to the legs with draw-bolts. A bridle-edge lap joint and metal ties support and hold the center leg in place. Bolts and wood screws make it possible to disassemble the table for storage or transportation. Collection of Fruitlands Museums, Harvard, Mass.

H. 27-3/8, W. 131, D. 34-5/8.

Letter	No.	Name	Material	T	W	L
A	3	legs	cherry	3-1/2 dia		22-5/8
B	3	feet	cherry	2	6-3/8	22-13/16
C	3	cross braces	cherry	1-1/16	4-7/8	30-1/4
D	1	stretcher	cherry	7/8	4-7/8	91-3/8
E	2	cleats	cherry	1	2	23-7/8
F	1	top	cherry	7/8	34-5/8	128
F1	2	bread-board ends	cherry	7/8	2	34-5/8
G	2	tie supports	iron	1/8	3/4	5
Hardware	4	hexagon-head bolts		5/16 × 6		
	4	square nuts		5/16		
	4	flat washers		5/16		
	10	wood screws		FH 1-1/2-10		
	6	wood screws		FH 2-1/2-14		
	4	wood screws		FH 1-3/4-12		
	1	square-head bolt		1/4 × 3-1/2		
	1	square-head nut		1/4		

32

33

32. From Union Village, this communal dining table is made of walnut and dates from the second half of the nineteenth century. The table differs from eastern prototypes in that its components are heavier, the stretcher is set a good deal lower on the legs, and the top has rounded corners. Tenons on the ends of the legs join to mortises on the feet and cross cleats to make a firm, permanent joint. The stretcher is fastened to the legs with double-pinned through-tenons and the top is fastened with wood screws through the cleats. Collection of Warren County Historical Society Museum, Lebanon, Ohio.

H. 29-1/2, W. 87-1/2, D. 37-1/8.

33. The top of this dining table is fabricated from twelve boards run crosswise. This method is somewhat unconventional—and the results are not too attractive—but it does solve the problem of making a long table from short-length boards. The table has a walnut top and an ash base and was made sometime during the first half of the nineteenth century in the South Union community. Pinned mortise-and-tenon joints hold the trestle parts; wood screws through three heavy longitudinal cleats hold the top to the base. Collection of Shaker Museum, South Union, Ky.

H. 28-7/8, W. 93-1/2, D. 37-1/2.

34. This children's ironing table was made in the first half of the nineteenth century in the New Lebanon community. The table rests on two movable, three-legged stands or horses. The case is pine and has dovetailed drawers with cherry pulls. The stands are pine with maple legs. Holders (hot pads) were kept in the underslung shallow drawer. Six girls could iron at this table and receive instructions.

In a Shaker community boys and girls were given formal schooling in basic subjects; boys went to school in the winter months and girls attended classes during the summer. Boys were taught the "arts and mystery" of a trade or trades by a master craftsman and Shaker sisters instructed girls in appropriate domestic occupations. Each caretaker sister and her charges were expected to take their turns at the family laundry. Private collection.

H. 27-3/4, W. 105-1/8, D. 22-1/2.

Appendix

Frequency of Wood Species Used in All Parts of Shaker Furniture.

Eastern Communities

Species	Frequency
cherry	1
maple—hard	1
pine	1
birch	2
butternut	2
chestnut	2
poplar	2
walnut	2
ash	3
basswood	3
beech	3
elm	3
hickory	3
oak—red	3
oak—white	3
apple	4
hemlock	4
mahogany	4
pear	4
rosewood	4
spruce	4

Western Communities

Species	Frequency
cherry	1
maple—hard	1
pine	1
walnut	1
ash	2
maple—soft	2
poplar	2
butternut	3
hickory	4

This tabulation is based on examination of approximately fifteen hundred pieces of furniture in public and private collections. *Frequency:* 1, often; 2, occasionally; 3, seldom; 4, rarely.

Museums and Public Collections

Delaware
The Henry Francis du Pont Winterthur Museum, Winterthur

District of Columbia
Smithsonian Institution

Kentucky
Kentucky Library and Museum, Western Kentucky University, Bowling Green
Shakertown at Pleasant Hill, Inc., Harrodsburg*
Shaker Museum at South Union*

Maine
Shaker Museum, Sabbathday Lake Shaker Community*

Massachusetts
Boston Museum of Fine Arts
Fruitlands Museums, Harvard*
Shaker Community, Inc., Hancock*

Michigan
Greenfield Village and the Henry Ford Museum, Dearborn

New Hampshire
Shaker Village, Inc., Canterbury*

New York
Albany Institute of History and Art
Metropolitan Museum of Art, New York
New York State Historical Association, Cooperstown
Shaker Museum, Old Chatham*

Ohio
Dunham Tavern Museum, Cleveland
Golden Lamb Inn, Lebanon
Kettering-Moraine Museum, Kettering
Shaker Historical Society Museum, Cleveland*
Warren County Historical Society Museum, Lebanon
Western Reserve Historical Society, Cleveland

Pennsylvania
Philadelphia Museum of Art

Vermont
Shelburne Museum, Shelburne

Wisconsin
Milwaukee Art Center

England
The American Museum in Britain, Bath

*Museums devoted exclusively to Shaker artifacts.

Shaker Communities

	Founded	Disbanded
Alfred, Me.	1793	1931
Canterbury, N. H.	1792	still active
Enfield, Conn.	1790	1917
Enfield, N. H.	1793	1918–23
Groveland, N. Y. (also known as Sonyea)	1836	1892
Hancock, Mass.	1790	1960
Harvard, Mass.	1791	1919
Mount Lebanon, N. Y. (New Lebanon until 1861)	1787	1947
North Union, Ohio	1822	1889
Pleasant Hill, Ky.	1806	1910
Sabbathday Lake, Me.	1794	still active
Shirley, Mass.	1793	1908
South Union, Ky.	1807	1922
Tyringham, Mass.	1792	1875
Union Village, Ohio	1805	1910
Watervliet, N. Y.	1787	1938
Watervliet, Ohio	1806	1910
Whitewater, Ohio	1824-25	1907

Short-lived communities

	Founded	Disbanded
Gorham, Me.	1804	1819
Savoy, Mass.	1817	1825
Sodus Bay, N. Y. (moved to Groveland)	1826	1836
West Union (Busro), Ind. (abandoned during Indian troubles 1812-14)	1810	1827
White Oak, Ga.	1898	1902
Narcoossee, Fla.	1896	ca. 1911

From Mary Richmond's *Shaker Literature, A Bibliography.* Published by Shaker Community, Inc., Hancock, Massachusetts, and distributed by the University Press of New England, Hanover, New Hampshire, 1977. Reprinted by permission of Shaker Community, Inc.

Glossary

annual ring: one of the concentric rings of wood which mark annual growth; when viewed in cross section, it is made up of a light band (early wood) and a darker band (late wood).

apron: the horizontal member immediately below a table top that extends between and joins the legs.

auger: a hole-making hand tool for wood having a bit and T-handle which are rotated under pressure.

bevel: the edge or end of a board that is cut to any angle other than ninety degrees to the surface.

bird's-eye: a grain occurring in maple resulting in a knotlike arrangement of wood fibers resembling birds' eyes.

boring machine: a hole-making machine for wood having a bit which is rotated and applied under pressure to the work.

bracket feet: case piece leg supports under the body running two ways at the corners.

bread-board: the name given to end cleats fastened to the ends of table tops, desk lids, or lids on wood-boxes to restrain warping. Their grain direction is ninety degrees to that of the top and they are nailed, doweled, or screwed in place.

bridle: a joint commonly used on trestle tables; the stretcher passes through the inner trestle. This joint is also used in joining cross cleats to legs.

cabinetmaker: a craftsman who works in wood producing and assembling furniture components. Also called a joiner.

cabriole leg: curved leg with outcurve knee and incurved ankle.

cane: a slender, jointed woodlike flexible stem used as upholstery material for chair seats.

carpenter: a craftsman who works in wood preparing and assembling components for buildings.

chamfer: the third flat surface formed by sawing or planing at an angle along the corner of a board.

circular saw: a machine designed to hold and rotate a circular disc (or blade) of steel having saw-teeth around its outer edge; also called a tablesaw.

cleat: a strip of wood fastened across one or more boards to hold them together and restrain warping.

clinch: the process of securing a nail or similar fastener by bending down or flattening the protruding end that has been driven through two (or more) pieces of wood.

counterbore: a hole slightly larger in diameter than the head of a screw or bolt. It is made at the top of the shank hole to allow the head to be sunk below the surface.

countersink: the process of making the upper part of a screw hole concave so that a flat-head screw will set flush or slightly below the surface.

cove: a concave shape used on surfaces, edges, or moldings.

cross-lap: one type of joint in a large group of lap joints. The broad surfaces of two pieces of wood are joined by removing half their thickness where they cross so that their surfaces are flush.

crown molding: a type of molding used at the top of case pieces such as cupboards. The molding ends and front are fastened to each other at an angle to the cupboard top.

curly: a name for maple wood having a grain that appears curly or ringletlike.

cyma: an S-shaped molding having a partly concave and partly convex curve.

dado: a slot cut across the grain of wood; when cut with the grain it is referred to as a groove or plough.

decal: a gold-colored decalcomania picturing a rocking chair surrounded by the words "Shakers' Trade Mark, Mt. Lebanon, N. Y." It was applied to chairs, foot benches, and stools made in the chair factory.

dovetail: a fan-shaped tenon that forms a tight, interlocking joint when fitted into a corresponding mortise. It was widely used on boxes, chests, cupboards, drawers, and other boxlike structures. It may be shouldered, as in drawer fronts, or open, as in drawer backs.

dowel: a round wooden pin which is fitted to corresponding holes bored in adjacent pieces and used to align and strengthen wood joints.

draw-bolt: a method of joining two members. (An example is the attaching of a horizontal rail or stretcher to a leg; a nut embedded in the horizontal piece is engaged by a bolt through the leg.) This mechanical joint may be disassembled.

draw-bore: a pinned mortise-and-tenon joint in which the hole through the tenon is bored out of alignment with the hole bored through the mortise. Its location is such that when the pin is driven in place it exerts pressure on the tenon and forces it inward against the mortise edges.

drawer guides: strips of wood installed on the inside of furniture along each side to prevent drawers from binding. Guides are used in conjunction with runners.

drawer runners: strips of wood installed on the inside of furniture at each side to support drawers. Runners are usually used in conjunction with guides.

dry joint: a joint in which the members are assembled without glue thereby allowing for expansion and contraction. Used in assembling a solid panel within a frame or when applying bread-board ends to a top.

edge-cross-lap: a method of joining two boards at their edges made by removing part of the width of each piece.

end-cross-lap: a method of joining two boards at their ends made by removing part of the thickness of each piece.

finial: a small, lathe-turned, somewhat ornamental form used on the upper ends of legs and posts of chairs.

fret saw: a hand tool, later machine designed to hold a long, thin, fine-tooth blade; used to make small intricate cuts in thin materials, especially in wood.

gain: a recess cut in a piece of wood into which a hinge leaf is fitted.

graining: the art of imitating wood grain using paints on uninteresting or inexpensive woods to simulate the color and grain of more attractive costly woods.

inlay: the process of setting pieces of wood of contrasting colors into a surface, usually at the same level, to form a design.

jig and fixture: a jig takes no specific form but is a device used to guide a tool to make parts; a fixture is a device also without a fixed pattern, used to hold material as it is being formed.

jointer: a machine designed to plane the surfaces and edges of boards.

key: a wooden, wedge-shaped pin installed in the projecting end of a tenon as in a mortise-and-tenon joint.

lag screw: a heavy wood screw having a square bolt head.

leg: pertaining to chairs—the front upright members that hold the side and front rungs; pertaining to tables—they hold the aprons and stretchers.

marriage: a term used to describe a piece of furniture made up of major parts not original to the piece.

miter: a joint formed by two members usually cut at an evenly divided angle.

mortise: a recess, usually rectangular in shape, cut into a piece of wood to receive a joining piece (the tenon).

ogee: a molding or form having an S-shaped profile.

panel: a thin board, usually rectangularly shaped, set in a frame, as in a door or chest side. It has either a flat surface or beveled edges. If beveled, they are referred to as being raised or fielded.

patina: a surface condition of old furniture in which, through aging, waxing, polishing, wear, and dirt, the wood develops a soft, warm, mellow look.

pedestal: a single support for table tops. Pedestal tables have feet instead of legs.

peen: the process of securing a nail or similar fastener by rounding over the protruding end that has been driven through two (or more) pieces of wood.

penny: a term used to indicate nail size, as in "a 4 penny nail"; abbreviated "d."

planer: a machine used to true the surfaces of rough lumber and reduce its thickness. Also called thickness planer or surfacer.

plinth: the ends and sides of a cabinet or chest that form a raised, enclosed base at the floor line.

pocket hole: an early method of fastening table tops to aprons by means of wood screws let into recesses cut into upper, inside surfaces of the aprons. Holes for the screw shank are bored at the end of the pocket.

posts: pertaining to chairs, the rear upright members that hold the back slats.

quarter round: a molded edge treatment used on drawer fronts, table and cupboard tops, and bottoms of boxes and chests.

quarter sawn: a method of sawing a log into boards in which the greatest number of annual rings are exposed on the broad surfaces. The dimensional stability of lumber produced in this manner is greatly increased.

quirk bead: a molded edge treatment of case pieces consisting of a quarter round terminating in a small, shallow groove. On a double quirk bead each end of the quarter round has a groove.

rabbet: an L-shaped or shouldered cut made along the end, edges, or face of a board that allows another to fit into it to form a joint.

rail: the horizontal member of a frame holding a panel, as in a door or case piece, into which the vertical members (stiles) are fitted.

rattan: a palmlike climbing plant used as upholstery material for chair seats.

riser: the vertical part of a step.

rule joint: a hinged joint used on drop-leaf tables in which a cove molding on the leaf slips over a quarter round (thumb molding) on the table.

rush: a marsh plant, grasslike in nature, used as upholstery for chair seats.

scarf: a joint made by cutting the ends of boards on a taper and joining them together with wooden pegs or copper nails. This joint is used in making the sides of oval boxes.

sconce: a wall rack or shelf designed to support a candle in a holder.

scribe line: a scored or incised line made with a knife, awl, or lathe skew-chisel. Usually used to locate points where furniture components are joined.

shoe foot: that part of a trestle-table leg which rests on the floor; so named because of its similarity to a shoe.

skew chisel: a wood-turning tool whose cutting edge is on an angle to the edges and sides of the blade.

skirt: a cross member, frequently valanced, found on case pieces at the lower end of the body.

slat: one or more horizontal members of a chair back; also called a ladder.

snake foot: that portion of a Queen Anne cabriole leg which rests on the floor, so named because of its similarity to a snake's head.

spear-point chisel: a wood turning tool whose cutting edges are on a thirty-degree angle to the edges and sides of the blade.

spindle: a lathe-turned, slender, vertical member of a chair or settee back.

splayed: a term used to identify chairs or table legs which angle outward in two directions from the seat or top.

spline: a thin, reinforcing piece of wood glued into grooves cut in adjacent edges of a joint, especially a miter joint; also referred to as a slip-feather joint.

splint: inner bark of a tree, usually ash or hickory that is stripped from the tree and split into widths suitable for weaving chair seats.

stile: the vertical member of a frame holding a panel, as in a door or case piece, into which the horizontal members (rails) are fitted.

stretcher: the horizontal piece of wood used to tie and reinforce table and bench legs.

tenon: a rectangularly shaped projection which conforms in size and shape and fits into a recess (the mortise) which is cut into an adjoining piece.

thumb molding: a molding used on table and chest tops, so called because its form suggests the end of a thumb.

tiger-stripe: a name for maple wood having a grain that appears ripplelike as the fur of certain animals.

till: in table-desks, a small compartment for pens and pencils. In six-board lidded chests, a small box with a lid.

tilt-top table: a table having a tripod base with a circular or square top, hinged to tilt to the perpendicular to use less space.

tongue-and-groove: a joint made by fitting a tonguelike projection on the edge of a board into a matching groove on another board.

trestle: a table support consisting of a cross cleat, vertical legs, standards, and arced feet.

tripod table: a table with a pedestal supported with three legs.

try square: a woodworking tool consisting of a ruled metal straight-edge blade set at right angles to a wooden straight handle; used for measuring, marking, and testing square work.

turner: a craftsman who works in wood producing in a lathe turned parts for furniture such as legs, rungs, drawer pulls, and pegs for rails.

turning saw: a hand saw designed to cut curve forms. It consists of a narrow saw blade held under tension in a wood frame.

varnish-stain: a varnish with pigments added so that both varnish and stain are applied at the same time.

veneer: a thin layer of fine wood glued to a secondary wood to present a more attractive grain and color.

wood screw: a tapered, round metal rod having a point on one end and a slotted head on the other, and a continuous spiral thread.